UNI-WISSEN

Michael K. Legutke
Andreas Müller-Hartmann
Marita Schocker-v. Ditfurth

Teaching English in the Primary School

Klett Lerntraining

Bibliografische Information der Deutschen Nationalbibliothek
Die Deutsche Nationalbibliothek verzeichnet diese Publikation in der Deutschen Nationalbibliografie; detaillierte bibliografische Daten sind im Internet über http://dnb.dnb.de abrufbar.

3. Auflage 2017

Dieses Werk folgt der reformierten Rechtschreibung und Zeichensetzung. Ausnahmen bilden Texte, bei denen künstlerische, philologische oder lizenzrechtliche oder andere Gründe einer Änderung entgegenstehen.

www.klett-lerntraining.de
Umschlaggestaltung: Sabine Kaufmann, Stuttgart
Satz: Kassler Grafik-Design, Leipzig
Druck: medienhaus Plump GmbH, Rheinbreitbach
Printed in Germany
ISBN 978-3-12-939023-8

Table of Contents

1 Why have we written this book and who have we written it for

Our motives to write a book about the teaching of English in the primary school are manifold.

Primary EFL: an approach with a specific focus on young learners' needs

To begin with, there is the generally accepted view that teaching young learners requires an approach that is tuned to their particular learning needs. General methodologies on the teaching of English (MÜLLER-HARTMANN & SCHOCKER-V. DITFURTH 2004) do not provide the pedagogical content knowledge needed to do justice to this particular group of learners even though, of course, there are insights that overlap and are valid for both secondary and primary education.

Primary EFL: a European development

Meanwhile, all countries across Europe have introduced foreign languages – mostly English – as a mandatory subject in primary education. There is an enormous demand for the basic knowledge that is needed to qualify teachers appropriately to teach groups of young learners with particular learning needs all across Europe (see ENEVER 2005). We have therefore included the European perspective in our publication by discussing European developments in education policy and by referring to relevant research. But at the same time we *focus* on the particular conditions under which English as a Foreign Language (EFL) is organized in the educational context of German state primary classrooms (→ ch. 1).

A research-based perspective on teaching young learners

Wherever available, we have based our arguments on available research, which has been particularly lively and expanding in the last few years (→ ch. 2). LYNNE CAMERON's *Teaching Languages to Young Learners* which appeared in 2001 (Cambridge University Press) has been a seminal and comprehensive publication in English to explicitly summarize relevant research for children learning a foreign language. It has been quite a while since then, and, therefore, her book does not include relevant research that has been published in the last couple of years. While CAMERON's book is an important study, it is also of limited value for our specific teaching-learning context, because of a diversity of definitions that say what a 'young learner' actually is. While CAMERON (2001) writes her book for learners between five and twelve years of age and ELLIS (2004), referring to the international EFL context, says that 'young learners' *"cover children and teenagers from kindergarten to school leaving age, representing a range of developmental differences and cognitive stages"* (ELLIS in ELLIS & MORROW 2004: 1), we refer to children from the time they start primary education (in grade 1 or 3) until they transfer to secondary school, which is either after four or six years of primary schooling, depending on the state government's education policy. To discuss the special needs of 'very young learners' at pre-school level we have included a separate chapter in our book (→ ch. 14).

Organising content: discussing principles based on examples

As regards the way we have organized content within the chapters, we have tried to proceed inductively, that is, by illustrating and discussing principles on the basis of primary specific materials, tasks or teaching experiences from primary classrooms. We would like to have included more examples of how principles may be put to practice – which we could not do, given the limited space that an introduction to such a varied field of knowledge provides. We therefore refer to relevant readings and materials that may be used to supplement the topics we have covered.

Target groups

The book may be used to prepare pre-service students, students in their internship and teachers in service for the specific competences they need to cope with in this particular teaching-learning situation. We hope the book will contribute to a lively discussion as to what counts as appropriate professional qualification in competence-based teacher education (Hallet 2006).

A methodology in English

We have decided to publish our book in English for various reasons. Not only do we believe that there is a potential readership interested in the subject-matter all over Europe (see above). We also believe that teachers and beginning teachers should be able to discuss issues to do with the teaching of English in English so that they are prepared to join the professional discourse and may share and profit from participating in it. Furthermore, teachers should have a chance to contribute to the knowledge-base from their experiences and questions in their particular contexts. This knowledge-base is constantly expanding and finds expression in a multitude of professional circles and forums on the teaching of English to young learners.

2 What is our experience with primary EFL?

What qualifies us to write a book on primary EFL

All three of us have had experience in the teaching of primary EFL in primary classrooms in Hessen and Baden-Württemberg. We have also supervised primary EFL students of our universities during their teaching practice internships at local primary schools and offered seminars on the teaching of English at primary level across Europe. We have developed an online MA course that qualifies students to teach English organized in blended learning format, "E-LINGO – Didaktik des frühen Fremdsprachenlernens" (www.e-lingo.de). The course involves a classroom research component. Marita has co-authored a course for primary EFL called *Magicland* (Langenscheidt/Longman). She is also co-editing a journal on primary EFL, *Grundschulmagazin Englisch* (Oldenbourg-Cornelsen Verlag), Michael is a member of the BIG advisory group, and has been responsible for several small scale research projects in the state of Hesse.

3 How have we structured our book?

Primary EFL: our 'house in the world' metaphor

We thought it would be best to structure the comprehensive relevant knowledge for the teaching of primary EFL by providing readers with an illustration. We have chosen the image of a house (= the primary school) with stairs at its foundation, leading into the house (= explaining why the teaching English at the primary level is relevant and what we know from research about how foreign languages are learned at this level →❶, ❷). The primary school is part of the world in which we live. This world influences us in many ways and tells us, why and how foreign languages are learned as well: our house has windows and doors that open up to this world from which our learners come from and from which they bring certain needs, motives, attitudes and competences. We also prepare them for the world to cope with the multiple demands that global discourse requires. We have therefore placed the purpose of teaching EFL, intercultural communicative competence (ICC), in the roof of our house (→ ❽). ICC is developed by way of tasks which we have placed at the center of your book (→❸, → ❹). We have dealt with them in two separate chapters which focus on the features of good learning tasks as a work plan and on how teachers and peers may support successful task completion in the process of doing them. All of the other areas connected to the teaching and learning of foreign languages at this level contribute to this knowledge. We have therefore grouped them around our big task window.

4 Some words of thank you

Finally, we would like to thank a few people who have supported us in writing this book in many ways.

Many thanks to Günter Gerngross, who has consented to include results of his work he has done in collaboration with Marita on the quality of course books (→ ch. 11) in our book. Günter and Marita have co-authored a module for the M.A. course "E-LINGO – Didaktik des frühen Fremdsprachenlernens" on this topic. Much of our chapter on the quality of course books is based on this module.

We owe special thanks to Otfried Börner for giving us critical feedback from an experienced practitioner's point of view. Many thanks go to Christina Bailey, who made sure through her professional editing that we did not deviate from standard language use. It was a pleasure for us to cooperate with Jonas Thiel who designed the figure for our introductory chapter. Finally we would like to thank Sebastian Schmidt, Vera Biedenkopf, Nadine Kalbfleisch, and Annika Schäfer for their meticulous work on the bibliography and the resources of chapter 15.

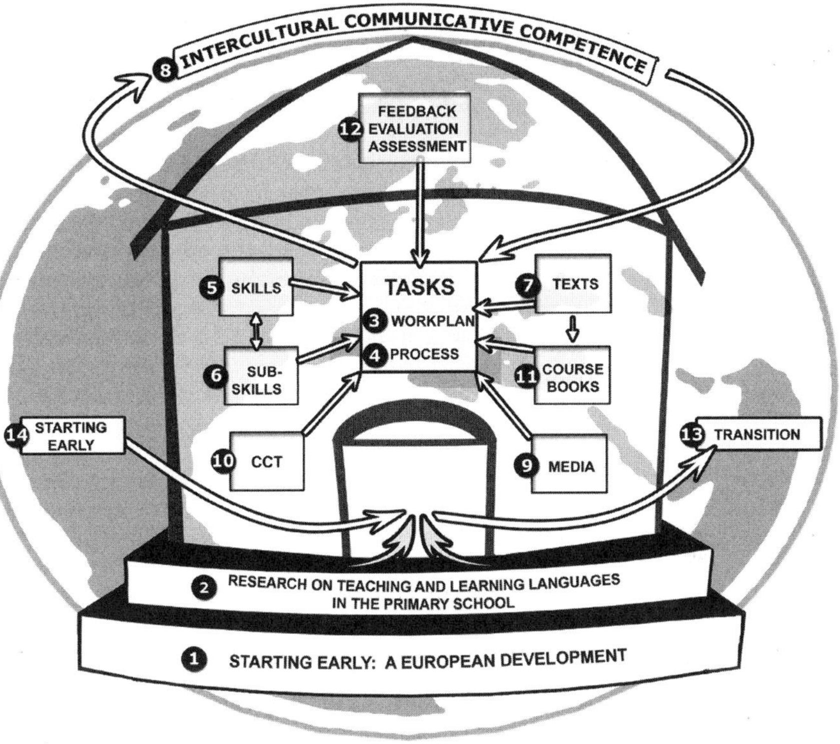

The structure of our book

1 The classroom as a focus of interest

Teaching and learning in a classroom: a complex process

Teaching and learning a foreign language is a complex process: it is situated in a classroom where many factors influence what children can learn. SCRIVENER (1994: 202), for example, has developed an observation task to make student teachers aware of the many factors that help students learn a foreign language. He mentions *the room* (i.e. seating, sight-lines, space, light, equipment), *the activities* (i.e. kinds of activities used, nature of student involvement, balance of students and teacher doing things), *the teacher* (i.e. his or her personal qualities, rapport, the atmosphere generated by him or her), and *the learners* (i.e. their motivation, their active involvement). It is therefore very difficult to make general statements about this environment which has had characteristics such as uncertainty, complexity, uniqueness, instability, and value conflict attributed to it (SCHÖN 1983). We therefore need to be aware of the fact that no two classrooms are alike and that what works in one classroom may not necessarily work in another.

Features of the primary EFL classroom

Heterogeneity: a constituent feature of primary EFL classrooms

As CAMERON (2001: 1) says, some differences between adult and secondary classrooms are immediately obvious: *"[C]hildren are more often enthusiastic and lively as learners. They want to please the teacher [...]. They will have a go at an activity even when they don't quite understand why or how. However, they also lose interest more quickly and are less able to keep themselves motivated on tasks they find difficult. Children [...] do not have the same access as older learners to meta-language that teachers can use to explain about grammar or discourse. Children often seem less embarrassed than adults at talking in a new language, and their lack of inhibition seems to help them get a more native-like accent."* Research by EDELENBOS ET AL (2006: 67ff.) confirms this. They show clearly that the benefit of introducing a modern language at the primary school level lies in the positive attitudes and motivation which children develop and sustain. CAMERON concludes her list of primary-specific learner characteristics with a cautious note, saying that generalizations may hide the diversity of the children. *Heterogeneity* is *the* constituent feature of primary classrooms: there may be children who are more outgoing than others, and others who prefer to be silent. You find a multitude of individual learners and learning styles as a result of their different personalities, cultural backgrounds, and preferences as well as their social, intellectual, or linguistic development (see also LIGHTBOWN & SPADA, 1999; → ch. 3). Therefore your choice of topics, materials, activities and teaching strategies depends very much on who your learners are. This is why we will introduce you to the idea of *classroom action research or practitioner research* in the next paragraph, which aims at helping teachers develop the quality of their teaching and their students' learning in their particular learning-teaching contexts.

Developing the quality of learning in classrooms

Classroom action or practitioner research: a tool for developing the quality of classroom teaching and learning

Results of findings of empirical studies that have looked into how languages are learned at the primary level (→ ch. 2) can never be directly *transferred* to improve teaching in a particular classroom, because there are no general solutions for complex practical situations such as the teaching and learning of a foreign language in a classroom. These situations demand specific solutions that may be best developed and tested within a particular classroom by the teacher and his or her learners who are *the* constituent factors that determine the quality of learning. Furthermore, a simple *transfer* of research-based ideas is impossible for yet another reason: *"If we ask what we know with certainty about language learning, the answer is likely to be disappointingly small [...] We are talking here of a complex and inaccessible psychological phenomenon, and can only hope for a concept which has plausibility, not a fact which has certainty"* (Prabhu 1989, chs. 1 & 3). We therefore subscribe to an approach to professional development that enables teachers to find out – in collaboration with their learners and their colleagues – if an idea, an activity or an experience that has been reported from elsewhere – has the potential to improve the quality of learning in their particular classrooms. This is best done by doing classroom-based action research projects (see Burns 2005; Dörnyei 2007, ch. 8; Legutke & Schocker-v. Ditfurth in press 2008). There is not enough space to make you familiar with the concrete proceedings of this approach here. In general terms, it is *"a process in which teachers examine their own educational practice systematically and carefully, using a range of data collection and analysis techniques"* (Karen Johnson, TESOL 2008). We believe that you need to be aware that the quality of learning in any classroom is shaped by the participants' perceptions and understandings and their definition of the social situation. But let us first turn our attention to what influences primary EFL learning on a 'macro level', that is anything ranging from European language policy, institutional affordances or constraints or teacher qualification programs.

2 Starting early: A European trend

Policies and rationales: the Europeanization of starting early

One of the most remarkable changes in European education in recent years has been the universal spread of early language learning programs throughout Europe since the 1990s (see Christ 2003; Edelenbos et al 2006: 13; Enever 2005: 179). This trend appears to have been linked in part to the opening of borders across Europe and the enormous increase in economic and cultural exchanges as by-products of globalization. According to Edelenbos' et al study (2006: 19–20), which is based on data from 30 countries, most of which was retrieved in 2003/2004, the situation in Europe is as follows:

"[A]pproximately 50% of primary pupils learn at least one foreign language [...], a second foreign language in primary education is compulsory in four countries (Luxembourg, Estonia, Sweden and Iceland). [... M]ost

member states expected that all pupils would have to learn at least one foreign language. All learners in that year were obliged to start in primary school, with the exceptions of Belgium (the Flemish speaking community outside Brussels), the United Kingdom and Bulgaria. Two foreign languages are compulsory in four EU states (Estonia, Luxemburg, Sweden and Iceland). [… As regards the choice of language], the data […] clearly show the dominance of English as a foreign language in primary education."

Policies and rationales: the Europeanization of starting early

Variability: a key feature of primary EFL

The teaching of English within primary schools is globally increasing but: *"Variability is a key characteristic of the practice of ELL. Many of the problems associated with ELL are related to provision factors, such as class-size, amount of continuing professional development, support for teachers, availability […] of appropriate materials, amount of time made available and teachers' L2 proficiency"* (Edelenbos et al 2006: 22). This means that in the classroom there are important differences in the quality of language learning due to differences in the frequency and duration of language classes, in the funding of the programs, in the consistency of teacher education programs, and in quality assessment. *"Contextual factors of implementation at school level will finally be what defines the value of a policy"* (Enever 2005: 180). In Germany, the federal education system has resulted in a variety of different state government programs on the basis of different theoretical assumptions and curricula (see Sekretariat der Ständigen Konferenz der Kultusminster 2005).

Criticism: introducing foreign languages in primary schools

It has been criticized that as a result of the hasty introduction of foreign languages in primary schools in some German states, insights from empirical studies have only been considered in part, if at all (see Edelenbos et al 2006: 147 ff.; Schmelter 2007: 86; Brusch 2000a for a survey of different approaches to teaching languages at primary level). This is also what Rück (2004: 22) assumes when he says that views on early language learning are often dominated by *"vorwissenschaftliche Ansichten etwa zur 'optimalen Phase des Grundschulalters', zur 'Imitationsfähigkeit von Primarschülern' oder zum 'spielerischen Lernen'"*. It has also been criticized that the time of exposure provided by schools (in most states two lessons a week) is not enough to achieve satisfactory results (Sauer 2000).

3 Starting early: Reasons why

Younger does not necessarily equal better

Languages: a prerequisite for social and cultural participation in diverse contexts

The commonly shared *reasons* why early start programs have been implemented during the last years are therefore interesting. These reasons differ considerably from those given when languages were first introduced at primary level in the 1970s. These earlier attempts were based on the assumption that "younger is better." In other words, that an early start is more likely to ensure competency in a foreign language because a young child is endowed with certain language learning abilities that will allow him or her to become a more proficient user of the language. But there is a lack of empirical support for the "younger is better" hypothesis (see Singelton, 1989 and Roos 2007: 14–22). There are many additional factors which need to be considered, such as the quality of resources, the quality of teaching, the time of exposure, as well as issues of motivation or cognitive development. But to this day, education policy uses the factor 'age' to argue for the introduction of foreign languages at primary level: *"Die Länder begründen die Aufnahme des Fremdsprachenlernens in den Grundschulunterricht im Wesentlichen mit der veränderten Lebenswirklichkeit und den für den Spracherwerb günstigen Lernvoraussetzungen der Kinder dieses Alters"* (Sekretariat der Ständigen Konferenz der Kultusminster 2005: 2). Lightbown and Spada (1999: 164-5) qualify this assumption as just another *"popular idea about language learning"* for which research evidence is lacking. *"[R]esearch doesn't show any particular age when there's a sudden change in attainment across the board – either for phonology or grammar. And there is also evidence of [a minority] of learners achieving native-like proficiency well after any purported critical age."* (McMorrow 2008, quoting from Moyers 1998, n.p.) This is why Moyers (2003) concludes that attainment in second language learning is 'multiply determined'. Young learners' particular qualities may be useful for learning and should be recognized, but they still do not justify a simple equation.

Foreign language learning is a basic human right

Languages: a prerequisite for social and cultural participation in diverse contexts

This argument is related to no less than an individual's quality of life: Languages are a prerequisite for participation in social and cultural life, they are, as Lewis says, a *"personal asset [...], an important tool of self-definition, a powerful creator of identity"* (Lewis 1993: 50). One could say language is a condition of inclusion in processes of mobility and change. It is the declared European goal to create a trilingual community with English as the lingua franca that Europeans may use when they communicate with each other. *"The ability to understand and communicate in other languages is a basic skill for all European citizens"* (Commission of the European Communities 2003). The chances of creating a Europe of multilingual citizens will be greatly improved if citizens have access to language learning at primary school or before. Monolingual speakers do not have the chance to participate in cultural discourses which are already multilingual. Between one half and two-thirds of the world's population is bilingual to some degree, and a significant number are multilingual or as you can also say, polyglots. Diversity of languages and of cultures is increasingly being seen as a good and beautiful thing in and of itself. Each language has its own way of seeing the world and is the product of its own particular history. All languages have their individual character and values, and all are equally adequate as modes of expression for the people who use them. English is the lingua franca and learning it helps people connect.

FLL: contributes to positive attitudes and cognitive development

Foreign language learning supports the development of further competences
The potential to encourage a positive attitude applies to learners from all cultures, whether native or non-native, and should be used as early as possible. This is why the COUNCIL OF EUROPE *"is concerned to improve the quality of communication among Europeans of different languages and cultural backgrounds. This is because better communication leads to freer mobility and more direct contact, which in turn leads to better understanding and closer co-operation [... which] contributes to the promotion of democratic citizenship"* (CEF 2001, xi-xii). There is also evidence that an early start in foreign language learning enhances wider cognitive development, intellectual flexibility, and is believed to support literacy development in the L1 (MARSCHOLLEK 2002, 2003).

European education policy: English plus one or more additional languages

Finally, early start FLL opens the curricular space needed to introduce at least a second and in many cases also a third FL before graduation from high school. This is in keeping with the recommendations of the action plan of the COMMISSION OF THE EUROPEAN COMMUNITY (2003). It calls for learning *"the mother tongue and two other languages"*. Early start foreign language learning provides the stepping stone for language awareness and is the gateway to other languages. It is the beginning of life-long learning. The arguments that back early start programs are powerful. It therefore does not come as a surprise that foreign languages are considered to be part of a child's basic literacy education claiming the status of a core subject. BRUSCH (2000 b: 34) has rightly allocated English the rank of a *"vierte Kulturtechnik"* with the same status as reading, writing, and mathematics. There has been a controversial discussion on the role of English as a foreign language as compared to the role of other foreign languages in education which we will not present in detail here; the controversy being that the dominance of English might prevent the development of multilingual citizens. It has therefore been argued that receptive multilingualism is an alternative option to using English as lingua franca (see for example FINKENSTAEDT & SCHRÖDER 1992; MEISSNER & LEGUTKE 2007). We do not subscribe to this view but argue for English as lingua franca while at the same time supporting the learning of other languages. In Germany, this view is mirrored in the curricula of all the federal states, as all early start FLL is outcome and proficiency based. There are standards which define the competences learners have a right to achieve. States and communities are legally required to provide the contexts and means to show that this right is being provided. Whichever first foreign language is chosen, schools and authorities need to make sure that the first foreign language opens the gate to learning other languages. This development is revolutionary and has far reaching implications for the teaching of foreign languages at secondary schools (→ ch. 13).

4 Purposes and principles for teaching primary EFL

Developing intercultural communicative competences

Developing intercultural communicative competences: no common standards provided

The ambitious purposes European education policy links with early start programs require learners to develop intercultural communicative competences (→ ch. 8). And yet, the *Kultusministerkonferenz* is not planning to develop standards for competences for English at primary level as they have done for English at secondary level (information by DR. HELMUT KAUFMANN, *Sekretariat der Ständigen Konferenz der Kultusminister der Länder in der Bundesrepublik Deutschland, Referat IV A*, January 2008). This may be because the conditions under which primary EFL teaching is organized across state governments vary tremendously across schools. There are individual state government curricula that define what learners *can do* with English at the end of their primary education (you will find all of the *Bildungspläne* on www.bildungsserver.de, 02.03.2008), but there is no common competence profile for all state governments on which secondary schools could reliably build (see discussion in BEHR & KIEREPKA 2004; SCHLÜTER 2003; MINDT & SCHLÜTER 2003; SCHOCKER-V. DITFURTH 2004a). A group of experts on primary EFL, the so-called 'BIG Circle' (an acronym for *Beratungs-, Informations- und Gesprächskreis* for foreign language teaching at primary level), have tried to develop *minimal standards* for what learners can achieve, based on a minimum total of 120 lessons at the end of grade four (see: PROJEKTE DER STIFTUNG LERNEN, www.praktisches-lernen.de, 11.03.2008). According to them, minimal standards for primary students comprise a number of fundamental intercultural communicative competences, including listening, speaking, reading and writing, language mediation, intercultural competences, methodological competences and competences in the sub-skills of pronunciation / intonation, vocabulary, and grammar (see BIG 2005: 9–11 for a detailed list; → ch. 5).

Principles for teaching primary EFL

General primary specific pedagogy and foreign language related pedagogy

Principles for teaching English at the primary level are based on two knowledge sources: what we know about primary specific pedagogy in general and what we know about the teaching of foreign languages at this level in particular. When talking about *primary specific pedagogy* we refer to principles such as learner-orientation, action orientation, process- and product-orientation, holistic and cross-curricular learning (see BIG 2005: 8; CAMERON 2001, ch. 1). This aspect will be discussed in detail in chapter 2, whereas our focus here is on presenting the principles of primary specific foreign language pedagogy. They include the following which are illustrated by references of classroom examples.

Principles of primary specific foreign language pedagogy

- Learners *experience what they can do* with the foreign language in *authentic* and challenging communicative situations that motivate them to get involved (for a detailed discussion see SCHOCKER-V. DITFURTH 2004b; RÜSCHOFF 2003; for classroom ideas see CLAUS 2003; ESSER 2004; → ch. 3).

- Learners experience language in the context of *topics* that are interesting, relevant and meaningful to them (see for example OVERLACK 2004).
- Topics are, whenever possible, offered in *cross-curricular projects* to support sustainability (see RYMARCZYK 2005; WASZAK 2005).
- Learners experience language within activities that provide *a holistic, multi-sensory, whole-person, and action-oriented access to learning* (see for example HAHN & BÄCHLE 2003; GERNGROSS 2004a; LIEBENHOFF 2004; WASCHK 2004).
- Learners experience *ample exposure to English* in lessons in which *the language of communication is mostly English* (see BUTZKAMM 2005; SCHMID-SCHÖNBEIN 2006c).
- Learners are exposed to examples of *authentic language* using *authentic materials* in predominantly oral communicative situations (SCHOCKER-v. DITFURTH 2004b).
- Learners are encouraged *to communicate personal meanings* with a focus on getting their message across rather than using formally correct language; errors are seen as a natural process in a learner's language development ('interlanguage') (see GROSS 2007; HUTZ & KOLB 2007; → ch. 4).
- Learning a foreign language is *a multilingual process* that integrates learners' existing resources (languages, cultures) when learning one or more new foreign languages (see SAUER 2006).
- Learning a foreign language is *both an individual and a social process* which needs continuous *support*, appreciative *feedback* on what has been learned, and a method of *diagnosing and documenting competences*; learners are involved in this process from the start (DIEHR & FRISCH 2006; SCHMID-SCHÖNBEIN 2004, 2007).
- Primary EFL classrooms are most *heterogeneous*; it is therefore important to *acknowledge individual learner differences* by offering learning environments that respect their personalities, preferences and competence levels (see BÖTTGER 2006a, 2006b; BECKER 2007; HOFFER 2007; OTHMER 2007; TYDECKS 2007).

5 Implementation of primary EFL: Issues and challenges

Foreign language learning as an integrative school subject

Use the potential of linguistically and culturally diverse children

Learners in Germany, like in most other European counties, draw from a culturally and linguistically diverse population. For quite a number of children, the first encounters with a foreign language in primary school (in most German states in grade 3) happen against the background of German being a second or sometimes even a third language for them. A lot of teachers have found ways of appreciating this diversity by encouraging pupils to be proud of their heritage and the linguistic and cultural wealth they have, and make this an integral task of their classroom work. For example, teachers ask learners to share their language biographies, as the following examples show (see KRUMM & JENKINS 2001):

German is my mother tongue. We learn English in school. I know only one word in Hebrew, which is Shalom [peace]; we learned that in RE (that is: Religious Education). *My dad speaks Steirisch [an Austrian dialect]. I often hear people speak Viennese [the dialect spoken in Vienna]. I go to a Japanese martial arts class, Jiu Jitsu, which means soft art. I was in Italy and spoke to an ice-cream vendor.* (Samuel)

Slovak is my mother tongue, but I also speak Croatian, because my Dad speaks that language. When I first came to Austria, I learned English and German pretty well. I also learn Spanish in school. But I think the most important language is English. I can also speak a little bit of Czech, because I have a friend who is from the Czech Republic. (Katarina)

These heritage languages must be preserved and their further development be fostered. A school's foreign language program in a specific language (for example English) must find ways to benefit from the fact that many children are linguistically and culturally diverse. Work in related subject areas should supplement the foreign language work and should not, as often seems to be the case, be separated into compartmentalized and disconnected subject areas (see example in Rymarczyk 2005 and → ch. 10).

Foreign language learning as a continuum

Recognize competence in transition from primary to secondary EFL

Although most German states have a well-articulated curriculum and assessment framework in place which build coherently from one grade level to the next, this does by no means guarantee that language learning is actually experienced as a continuum. In particular the transition from primary to secondary education is a major challenge (→ ch. 13). The holistic, highly experiential and action-oriented approaches which have emerged in the primary school are still quite alien to many secondary school teachers who feel the pressure to change, i.e. rethink and redesign their established classroom routines. Too many tend to react to early start programs by rejecting them. Instead of building on what children can already do with the language and thus appreciating their (understandably limited) competences, they downgrade the work done in the primary school, perceiving it as childish, superficial and disappointing – producing quite a negative impact on the children. Enacting successful primary EFL programs requires much more than developing curricula and propagating standards. It needs to affect teachers' attitudes, their willingness to learn and no less than their professional ideas of themselves.

Foreign language learning and life-long learning

Recognize competence development as a life-long process

It takes a considerable amount of time to learn a second language under the general conditions of schooling, and it takes a lot of energy to maintain one's language skills and continue to develop them outside of school. While it is easy to advocate life-long learning, it is a huge challenge to make it happen. In the last decade considerable attention has been given to the question of how best to meet this challenge. One instrument that is widely discussed and piloted all over Europe is the *European Language Portfolio* (www.coe.int/portfolio, 04.05.2008). It allows the individual to document their intercultural experiences and the development of language competence in a way which is comprehensible in all the member states. Portfolios allow their owners to demonstrate what they *can do* in different languages, including their heritage languages. It therefore has an important *reporting and demonstrating function*. It also has a very important *pedagogical function*, in that it helps learners to document their processes and products of foreign language learning. Learners plan and evaluate learning paths and recognize and use learning opportunities. In this way the portfolio contributes to lifelong learning as the prerequisites are established for being able to seek independently for learning opportunities in the immediate environment and making learning outside and beyond the school successful (→ ch. 13).

Teaching competences and teacher education

Primary EFL teachers need a profound professional education

As in all areas of education, well-trained teaching professionals are the prerequisite to excellence in education. Although national and regional governments strongly advocate the implementation of early start programs and although a number of publications have discussed the varied competences qualified primary EFL teachers need (see BIG 2007), governments are reluctant to fund adequate teacher education programs, both at pre- and in-service level. When FLL was made mandatory in Hessen's elementary schools, about 20% of the teachers had been professionally trained to do the job – a situation that is symptomatic for most German and European states. This is why additional programs at pre- and in-service teacher education level need to be developed to make up for this deficit (SCHOCKER-v. DITFURTH 2003a; GERNGROSS 2004b).

English as a global language

The multilingual citizen as a prerequisite for global and local participation

Surveys of European early start foreign language policy demonstrate very clearly the increase in primary school FL programs. At the same time, they demonstrate the global increase in the teaching of English, because the vast majority of these programs have opted for English as the first FL. Even in German border regions with Poland or France where it would make sense to teach the language of your immediate neighbors, parents pressure the authorities to offer English instead. Why, one could ask, should students bother with learning languages other than English? Wouldn't it make much more sense if the notion of the multilingual citizen was dropped in favor of the much more realistic goal of the global speaker of English? A recent document of the Scottish Executive entitled "Citizens of a Multilingual World. Rationale. Why are languages important?" (2005) argues strongly for language education in Scotland that is based on the concept of the multilingual citizen. The paper argues that if young Scots leave school in a state of entrenched monolingualism, knowing only English, they will not experience the equality with their much more mobile peers elsewhere in Europe. It is important to note that 'mobility' goes beyond the physical change of places, including intellectual flexibility, and is coupled with the notion of participation and inclusion. 'Mobility' is only possible if people have developed the capability of establishing relationships and participation in local cultures, and these local cultures tend to be linguistically diverse. All over Europe we see a growing awareness of local identities providing the necessary security of a sense of belonging. Those Europeans who have only English as a means of communication are fundamentally disadvantaged because they are excluded from local discourse and all its potential for social, cultural and economic participation. Monolingual speakers of English become marginalized in a multilingual world. To avoid such new forms of cultural and linguistic impoverishment, foreign language education is presented as a must: it is one of the foundations of citizenship in greater society and in the pursuit of happiness for all human beings.

1 On the difficulty of researching language learning

1 Coping with a complex process

Language learning: a complex process, determined by a multitude of interacting factors

The question we deal with in this chapter seems to be straightforward: What do we know about how children (in contrast to adolescents, for example) learn foreign languages that may help us know what we can do in the primary classroom to stimulate and to support language learning? Simple though the question may be, the answer is anything but straightforward. This is because learning a foreign language is an extremely *complex process* in which learning depends on a multitude of factors which interact in many ways. This complexity makes language learning difficult to research, which is presumably one of the reasons why researchers tend to *isolate individual factors* that they think affect successful language learning, thereby aiming to understand at least an aspect of this complex process. Before we discuss results, we will introduce you to different research approaches so that you will understand in what way they may be relevant to inform teaching.

2 Different types of research

Academic LAQ research and practitioner classroom-based research

In the attempt to understand FL learning we may broadly distinguish between two perspectives: academic (psycho-linguistic) language acquisition (LAQ) research and practitioner research, that is, research conducted by teachers and associated partners in their classrooms. Both use tasks (best translated as *Lernaufgaben*) as a tool to identify the task features that are likely to support learning. However, they differ in their focus of interest: "*Psycho-linguistically oriented studies seek universal items in TBLT [task-based language teaching] by reducing complexity and therefore have the tendency to treat learners as information processing units and tasks as something that takes place in a vacuum. [... But] I need to accept my learners as historically situated active agents. What I am interested in is not the acquisition of linguistic forms through task-based lessons in general terms, but the development of one particular class under the condition of task-based lessons. Tasks are seen as a 'resource for participation'* (Zuengler & Miller, 2006: 36) *rather than input for language learning*" (Schart 2008: 43). Until recently, LAQ researchers have investigated the mental processes of individual learners in their attempt to produce and understand language under laboratory conditions. But language learning in a classroom is determined by complex factors that you need to consider to get valid results, such as the atmosphere created by the participants in a classroom which may support (or hinder) language development in many ways. In other words: learning in a classroom is fundamentally social learning. The limited LAQ perspective is gradually changing. Eckerth, for example, a LAQ researcher, concluded at the 2008 TESOL conference: "*Tasks are carried out by individuals with different dispositions in different settings. What individual learners do when confronted by task X is likely to be codetermined by a host of other variables. In other words, tasks, patterns of interaction, cognitive processes, and learning outcomes may not be directly related. We may therefore conclude that a generic understanding of task-based interaction and learning should be complemented by an inquiry into local settings, curricular purposes, and individual dispositions"* (ECKERTH 2008). Done in this way, both research perspectives contribute to our understanding of the learning processes in the foreign language classroom.

3 On the relative value of research

On the limitations of research to clarify teaching practice

We could say that all research *contributes* to our knowledge of how languages are learned. But none of the theories or reports captures the complexity of the many interacting factors that will determine successful language learning in a particular classroom (→ ch. 1). It is therefore inappropriate that you may read about researchers who just investigate the effect of *one* factor or who collect data to support *one theory* on language acquisition, but nonetheless claim that their study is 'research-based' and therefore can be generalized as a valid interpretation of learning in any classroom. The most comprehensive European survey on early language-learning across Europe therefore appropriately presents its results with a cautious note which is in line with our concerns: *"Only limited evidence is available as to the precise nature and eventual outcomes of different models of the languages education curricula that are actually being implemented, and as such great difficulty in making judgments as to effectiveness and improvement; [... there is] very little strong evidence on how children's internalized language development actually takes place. [...] Given that many important questions about the role of particular contextual factors remain unanswered [...] , it is necessary to warn against over-reliance on one particular formula for offering a foreign language in pre-primary education"* (EDELENBOS ET AL 2006: 147 & 27).
They conclude: *"None of the research which has been surveyed should be considered as demonstrating universal proofs which lead directly to particular desirable practices"* (ibid. 147).

4 The research we refer to

A survey of different types of research

This chapter presents results from primary EFL research to help us understand the nature of foreign language learning in this particular context. They are of three kinds:

1 Reviews of European studies on the teaching and learning of modern languages with young children
  Two of the most comprehensive European studies we will refer to are the research reviews done by BLONDIN ET AL (1998) and its recent update in a comprehensive follow-up report by EDELENBOS ET AL (2006). The latter presents three perspectives: that of research, of 'good practice', and of the underlying pedagogical principles.

2 Studies that have been conducted in connection with introducing or piloting primary EFL programs in Germany
We refer to findings of studies from Baden-Württemberg (Werlen et al 2006), Hessen (Legutke & Lortz 2002a), Hamburg (Börner 2006 & 2008; Bos & Pietsch 2004 & 2005 [KESS] → results see ch. 5), Nordrhein-Westfalen (Groot-Wilken & Thürmann 2007; Groot-Wilken, Engel & Thürmann 2007), and Saarland (Franceschini 2002).

3 Studies that are interested in psycho-linguistic language acquisition processes
We will refer to studies conducted by Kessler (2006), Peltzer-Karpf (2003), Pienemann (1999, 2006) and Roos (2007).

We will proceed as follows: we will first make you aware of some basic insights into language learning by asking you to reflect on data taken from two primary classrooms (2). This will be followed by a summary of what the empirical studies in primary classrooms that we have listed above tell us about language learning (3). We will then give you a survey on the different approaches which have been developed over time to understand language learning and say in what way they have contributed to the knowledge about teaching (4). We will conclude this chapter by listing the issues (5).

2 Tuning in: Making you aware of the complexity of classroom language learning

Let us begin to explore this chapter's question by looking at what foreign language learners do when they *want* to communicate something in a language that is more or less 'foreign' to them. Read the following classroom data examples: What do they tell us about language learning? Try to delineate some first basic principles about how children learn a foreign language.

Analyzing classroom data to understand learning

▶ Example 1: Learning English as a Second Language
David Nunan (2000) tells the following story about one of his ESL learners: *"Luis was one of the most gifted and charming students I have ever had – a joy to have in class and always ready to help weaker learners. Although concerned to get it right, he wasn't afraid to make mistakes. One day, we were practicing possessions (Is this your pencil? Is that her bag?). The lesson went well, and I was feeling pleased with myself as I left the classroom. On this particular day I was driving my brother's rather fancy car instead of riding the beaten-up bicycle that was my usual mode of transportation. As I drove through the school gates, I saw Louis and stopped to give him a ride. Most surprised to see me driving a fancy car, he got in and said, "Teacher car?" Again, I ended up in a state of depression, as my instruction appeared to be making the learners worse, not better"* (Nunan 2000: 1).

▶ Example 2: Learning English in a primary classroom in Baden-Württemberg
Here is an example of the language a 4th grade learner produced when she was trying to retell a story that the class had previously read (a simplified version of ROALD DAHL's *The Magic Finger* 2001): "*Mr. Gregg loved go hunting. On weekend he goed to the woods and looked birds and shoot animals. The little girl hate it. She do magic. She maked a plan [...]*"

How children learn a foreign language: Some basic principles

First insights into language learning from interpreting classroom data

(a) Learners do not necessarily learn what teachers teach. There is an asymmetrical relationship between teaching and learning. But if children *want to* communicate something that is *personally relevant and meaningful* to them (see example 1: expressing surprise at the teacher's unusual mode of transportation), they use whatever resources they have and *actively construct meaning* to get their message across (here: "*Teacher car?*": a simplification strategy that focuses on the content of the message only: *teacher car?*).
(b) Learning a language is *not primarily motivated by wanting to master a particular form correctly* (see example 1: possessive pronouns) *but to communicate personal meanings*. Young learners' processing capacities may not be developed in a way to allow them to focus on content *and* form at the same time when they communicate. This takes time.
(c) There is no simple *transfer* of classroom learning to *using* the foreign language in real life. But learners may be *motivated* and *involved* by tasks that support this transfer (→ ch. 3).
(d) *Errors* that learners make when they try to communicate, act as *a window on to their developing internal grammars*, that is, teachers get an idea about the rules they continuously generate about how the foreign language works (see example 2: an emergent understanding of how the simple past tense is formed). This process corresponds with what we know about 1st language acquisition (see for example HUTZ & KOLB 2007).

3 What empirical studies in primary classrooms tell us about language learning

1 A summary of findings

Some surprising findings

(a) Young learners tend to be extremely motivated to learn a foreign language (FRANCESCHINI 2002: 13; GROOT-WILKEN & THÜRMANN 2007: 33; WERLEN ET AL 2006: 52). There is "*continuing evidence that generally pupils' attitudes and motivation are strongly positive*" (EDELENBOS ET AL 2006: 11). They enjoy *experimenting with language* and are not afraid to use whatever resources they have available to make themselves understood. "*Die Kinder setzen [...] ihre gesamten Ressourcen ein, um das Unbekannte zu erschließen. In der Sprachlernsituation [...] versichern sich Kinder ihrer Lernschritte durch verschiedene Strategien, wie zum Beispiel: Rückgriff auf die Muttersprache, explizites Nachfragen, [...] Vergewisserung, ausdrückliche Bewusstmachung, Sprachmischung [...]"* (WERLEN ET AL 2006: 47). This is why WERLEN concludes that the results of her longitudinal study are best summarized in one sentence: *"Kinder lernen die Zielsprache in der Interaktion durch die Interaktion für die Interaktion"* (ibid, 45). WERLEN's results have been confirmed by recent studies in Northrhine-Westfalia on the competences that learners develop after two years of English in grades 3 and 4 (GROOT-WILKEN & THÜRMANN 2007: 33).

(b) In primary classrooms peer-learning plays an important role (WERLEN ET AL 2006: 55). This observation has been confirmed by other studies: *"Verstehen und Äußern im Klassenraum sind nicht nur primär individuelle Vorgänge, die im Kopf eines Schülers ablaufen, sondern zugleich auch an die Interaktion mit anderen gebunden und durch Kooperation ermöglicht"* (LEGUTKE & LORTZ 2002b: 98-99).

(c) Young learners seem to transfer the strategies they know from the acquisition of their first language to learning a foreign language: *"Aktive Prozesse des Mustererkennens, der Regelfindung, der kognitiven Orientierung und der sozial-emotionalen Entwicklung"* are some of the processes PELTZER-KARPF has identified (2003: 444). This is why she concludes that beginning to learn a foreign language very much follows the processes of learning a first language (PELTZER-KARPF 2003: 447). For a survey of first language acquisition research see LIGHTBOWN and SPADA (1999, ch. 1).

(d) Young learners are able to build up a capacity to reflect on learning strategies. *"An important principle might be that early language-learning should provide possibilities to develop language awareness and meta-cognitive skills"* (EDELENBOS ET AL 2006: 80). *"Children at all levels (from kindergarten onwards) benefit from being encouraged to reflect on their learning. This includes reflecting on how they might learn from and support each other, as well as on how they might learn from their teacher or others, or how they might learn things for themselves. It is worthwhile for teachers to help their pupils document, share, evaluate, supplement and refine how they learn not only in respect of languages but also in respect of their other learning at school. In this sense, a Portfolio approach has much to offer, provided teachers create time and explain the purpose to the children"* (EDELENBOS ET AL 2006: 149). There is also empirical evidence on *the important role of the teacher* – to help children progress and *"to provide feedback which may be positive (encouragement) or may be corrective, to help them further refine their underlying language system"* (EDELENBOS ET AL 2006: 9).

(e) Young learners benefit from reading and writing at an early stage, rather than concentrating solely on listening and speaking (EDELENBOS ET AL 2006: 80) (→ ch. 5).

To initiate and support this demanding language learning process it takes well qualified teachers (→ ch. 4).

2 Primary LAQ studies

On the relevance of primary specific LAQ research

The last few years have seen a growing number of studies in Germany that claim to explain foreign language acquisition for children (KESSLER 2006; PIENEMANN 1999, 2006). These studies try to predict in which order learners are able to process a grammatical structure of a foreign language in their language acquisition development. According to PIENEMANN in his *learnability* and *processability theory*, language acquisition is based on certain procedural skills that have to be internally developed so that processing a language becomes possible. He says that the acquisition of these skills follows a fixed sequence that is universally valid for all language learners – no matter what language and content they may be exposed to. His theory is based on Chomsky's idea of generative grammar, a type of an inborn internal grammar which is said to produce (= to generate) grammatical sentences according to a set of universal rules. This theory has recently been empirically tested in primary classrooms by ROOS (2007). ROOS' classroom-based study has been motivated by the concern to confirm PIENEMANN's hypotheses. This is why valuable classroom observation data has been selected into *a priory* categories: observations of language growth were categorized to the PIENEMANN's assumed phases of acquisition that were defined *prior* to the actual empirical study to test Pienemann's hypotheses. This way new insights and interpretations of classroom data which *might* have emerged during the process of the research have therefore only been considered as a kind of by-product when reflecting on the study (see below). This kind of LAQ research usually excludes many of the relevant factors that contribute to successful language learning. With DÖRNYEI (2007: 36) we believe that it is a positive development that in applied linguistics there is *"a growing recognition that almost every aspect of language acquisition and use is determined or significantly shaped by social, cultural, and situational factors"* (DÖRNYEI 2007: 36).
In addition, this type of LAQ research captures only a limited number of grammatical categories, and the selection of these categories disregards structures that have been identified by corpus data from English children (see criticism in MINDT, forthcoming). Therefore, a learnability and processability theory of LAQ based on a grammatical progression may provide criteria for the selection and gradation of words and structures to inform course book designers on the appropriate input for primary learners. It may inform the *planning phase* of a language learning curriculum. But it does not provide answers for appropriate pedagogy. Teachers need research that supports them in understanding and developing their teaching.

3 Current practice and insights into language learning

Don't waste the potential of your learners to experiment with language

There is evidence that, to this day, there is a strong emphasis on the correct and repetitive reproduction of prefabricated language patterns in our primary classrooms. This has been confirmed by different longitudinal primary EFL classroom studies in Germany. Three examples:

Wie die Unterrichtsbeobachtung gezeigt hat […], wurde in den untersuchten Klassen ein methodisch-didaktischer Ansatz verfolgt, der den Lernern nur wenig Gelegenheit zur kreativ-produktiven Verwendung des Englischen bot. Vielmehr erfolgte der Umgang mit der Fremdsprache in Musterdialogen, die auf der Basis vorgegebener Redemittel eingeübt und gesprochen wurden (Roos 2007: 181f.).

Der Austausch als Interaktion mit ‚echten' fremdsprachlichen Kommunikationen ist ein unverzichtbarer Faktor für den institutionalen Spracherwerb und müsste dringend verstärkt, im Curriculum integriert und als didaktisches Prinzip ausgebaut werden (Werlen et al 2006: 45).

Damit sich weitere Erfolge für das Sprechen […] einstellen können, müssen die Kinder im Unterricht mehr Sprechgelegenheiten haben, um erkundend und experimentierend mit den Elementen der neuen Sprache umgehen zu können (Groot-Wilken & Thürmann 2007: 33).

We must be careful not to waste the creative potential of learners but create opportunities so that they can experiment with language in meaningful communication scenarios (→ chs. 3 and 4).

4 Different approaches to researching language learning: From behaviorism to psycho-linguistic LAQ studies to classroom research

Developments in research approach to understand language learning

The following section demonstrates how prevailing assumptions about language acquisition have informed research interests and how these interests have developed over time. It also demonstrates how these assumptions have informed teaching approaches in classrooms.

1 Focus on L1 – L2 interferences: Language learning as habit formation (Lado 1964)

Up to the 1960s it was assumed that most of the difficulties learners of a foreign language have to struggle with results from interferences from their first language. This is what comparison of the linguistic systems of the first and a new language by way of *contrastive analysis* demonstrated – an assumption which was supported by behaviorists who believed that language learning is habit formation. What learners would therefore need is correct input followed by intensive imitation of this input so that gradually new language habits would be formed. Therefore, practicing, memorizing and immediate correction of errors (to avoid the development of incorrect habits) were the primary processes teachers had to support to form new language habits in classrooms.

2 Focus on interlanguage: Language learning as mental construction of internal grammars (Selinker 1972, Corder 1981)

Analysis of the learner's language (error analysis) demonstrates that many of the errors learners make are not the result of wrong transfer of first language habits but evidence of developing linguistic rules that each child constructs when generating language. A learner who says I **goed home or there are three *childrens* (see more examples in Hutz & Kolb 2007: 6) demonstrates that she has internalized a concept of how past tense and plural are formed – she just has not yet realized that this rule is not universally valid. This implies a change of perspective away from selecting appropriate input to a focus on the learning process. Analysis of learners' language performance (in Selinker's term: *interlanguage*) demonstrated that language acquisition may probably be described most appropriately as a process of creative construction.

3 Focus on individual language acquisition processes: Psycho-linguistic research (Ellis 2003)

In the last two decades, second language acquisition (LAQ) researchers have used different *tasks* to elicit samples of language use from learners to understand learning (Ellis 2003). Examples of learner language document how learners re-structure their *interlanguages* over time and how the quality of learner language depends on the *task features* (for example, if it requires information-exchange, if the information gap is one way or two way, if the outcome is closed or open). Much of this research has been dominated by a *psycho-linguistic research paradigm*, that is, research that studies the mental processes of people when producing and understanding language (for an evaluation of the relevance of this type of research see the introduction to this chapter).

4 Focus on the social context: Language development as social development (Vygotsky 1978, Long 1985, Swain 1985)

Trying to understand language learning by looking at what a child can do alone is one perspective to take. But to perceive the language acquisition process *merely* as an internal mental process of re-structuring grammars misses an important point: Language development is social development, that is, it takes place in a social context, in an environment where other people play an important role (Vygotsky 1978). *"Any learning outcome is the result of a fairly unpredictable interaction between the learner, the task, and the task situation. [...] Any language learning task will be reinterpreted by a learner in his or her own terms"* (BREEN 1987: 24). This is why social interactionist research identifies how the social context influences language learning and what other people can do to support language development. For *interactionists* (LONG 1985, SWAIN 1985) this is best done through meaningful interaction in conversations where mutual understanding is attempted in a constant process of negotiating meaning. They have identified various interactional modification strategies that help learners acquire a language through tasks that offer them a chance to try out new forms and expressions.

5 The issues

1 Research needs to be classroom-based and focus on the needs and understanding of teachers and learners

We need more classroom-based research that integrates learners' perspectives

'Research' means *"trying to find answers to questions ... to learn more about the world around us"* (DÖRNYEI 2007: 15). But it would be wrong to rely on conclusions from experts only, because *"no two language learning/use situations are exactly the same, and therefore the guidelines that we can find in the literature rarely provide the exact answers to one's specific questions"* (ibid: 16). It is a teacher's basic concern how they may improve the quality of learning in their respective classroom. From research into teacher development we know that improvement of classroom learning works best if it focuses *"on the activity of teaching itself; it should center on the teacher who does it, the contexts in which it is done, and the pedagogy by which it is done"* (FREEMAN & JOHNSON 1998: 397). This claim has recently been confirmed in connection with studies on the implementation of task-based language learning in Belgium: *"It is not so much the educational training enjoyed by teachers or the academic wisdom they are offered in in-service training or in educational journals, but what they have done and do in the classroom itself, and the meaning that they attach to these experiences, that constitute the backbone of what they think and believe about education"* (VAN DEN BRANDEN 2006: 222). Therefore, *"until classroom-based studies become a mainstream for research ..., the pedagogical use of language learning tasks will never be properly researched, and we will have to make do with whatever researchers feel motivated to explore"* (SAMUDA & BYGATE 2008: 190–191).

Two encouraging examples of classroom-based studies that look at what we can learn from what primary school children say about how they learn are KOLB's study on the use of portfolios in the primary classroom (KOLB 2007) and DE LEEUW's study on how primary children describe which learning strategies they use (DE LEEUW 1997).

2 The quality and quantity of exposure matters: On the central role of the teacher to support learning

We need to take a learner- and a learning-centred perspective on classrooms

The time-frame that has been institutionally provided to learn foreign languages at primary school usually is two lessons a week. This is why talking of a 'language bath' teachers have to offer their learners seems inappropriate, given the limited time of exposure – unless it describes the limited but nonetheless refreshing diving into the foreign language environment to do meaningful things with the new language. A teacher needs to be absolutely confident in using the target language and s/he needs to be an expert in knowing how to initiate and to support this process to be able to comfortably experiment with the foreign language in spontaneous interaction and to flexibly react to unpredictable learners' contributions (→ chs. 3 & 4). But what could be the central perspective to guide teachers in their classrooms? CAMERON's distinction between a learner- and a learning-centered perspective on teaching seems to be useful here (CAMERON 2001). In a learner-centered approach, a teacher sees the child in the center of what determines her teaching in the classroom, for example when the activities she chooses for her learners are tuned to the needs of what children like doing (i.e. playing games or singing songs). There is nothing wrong with this attitude but there is a danger: *"I have seen too many classrooms where learners are enjoying themselves on intellectually undemanding tasks but failing to learn as much as they might. The time available in busy school timetables for language teaching is too short to waste on activities that are fun but do not maximize learning"* (CAMERON 2001: 2). This is why we also subscribe to a learning-centered approach on teaching, that is, to look at what a teacher does, to support the child in what it may not yet be able to do without teacher support and *"to move the child towards increasingly demanding challenges, so that no learning potential is wasted"* (CAMERON 2001: 2). It is generally a positive development that most primary EFL classrooms work with a course book. But there may be a danger of 'doing the course book' in the sense of 'ticking off the activities' and neglecting to respond flexibly to the learning process and to learners' needs (→ ch. 12).

1 Principles of TBLL

A definition of tasks: focus on meaning vs. focus on form

After having looked at how children learn languages and how LAQ has tried to make sense of language development, we will now focus on what teachers can do to facilitate language learning in the English foreign language (EFL) classroom. When people communicate, they interpret each other's utterances and collaborate to help each other understand, making or negotiating meaning in the process. This is why the communicative approach to language teaching focuses on the meaning potential of language and on the social contexts in which language is used (→ ch. 2). The task-based approach to language learning and teaching (TBLL) developed from this idea and strove to provide teachers with a tool to organize interaction in the target language by selecting and sequencing activities in the social context of the language classroom. PRABHU (1987) was one of the first to develop and experiment with a task-based syllabus in the Bangalore project in India where children worked on problems in Math, Geography, and other subjects using English in a clearly meaning-focussed way (see also → ch. 10). You might say that the task-based approach to syllabus and curriculum design organizes *"activities in which language is used for carrying out meaningful tasks to promote learning"* (RICHARDS & RODGERS 2001: 161). A language learning task is, then, *"a piece of classroom work that involves learners in comprehending, manipulating, producing, or interacting in the target language while their attention is focused on mobilizing their grammatical knowledge in order to express meaning, and in which the intention is to convey meaning rather than to manipulate form"* (NUNAN 2004: 4, see also EDELENBOS ET AL 2006: 71). Consequently, a *task* differs from an *exercise* whose focus it is to produce a correct linguistic form (a grammatical structure or words), but not to communicate meaning. In exercises, language is practiced for its own sake, for example, by putting the right verb form in a gap-text (see DE LEEUW & LEGUTKE 1997: 106). What do these principal considerations mean for the teaching and learning in the primary classroom?

Real-world tasks vs. pedagogic tasks

When children are asked to find out about each other's pets by asking questions (e.g. *How old is your dog? How many guinea pigs do you have? What color is your rabbit?*), they are practicing a linguistic form (the structure of questions) but at the same time they are communicating meaning as they really want to find out about each others' pets. This example is a typical 'real-world task' for children (COUNCIL OF EUROPE 2001: 157), as it *"requires learners to approximate, in class, the sorts of [behaviors] required of them in the world beyond the classroom"* (NUNAN 1989: 40). This is why TBLL tries to provide *authentic learning activities* that allow learners to use real language for real purposes. But Nunan had adult learners in mind whose goal it was to use the language they had learned to make telephone calls, write e-mails, or book hotel rooms, etc. But these are not the needs primary school children have. This is why we have to ask ourselves what the concept of *authenticity of language use* means for young learners in the primary classroom. Age-appropriate activities that relate to the socio-cultural experiences and interests of young learners would be activities such as playing games, identifying the differences between two pictures or making sense of a story. We call these problem-solving or discovery-oriented activities 'pedagogic tasks' since they structure learners' social interaction in the way they would do outside the classroom (see also SCHOCKER-v. DITFURTH 2004b).

The relevance of tasks for teachers

While research on TBLL in the primary language classroom is rather scarce (see PINTER 2007), the study by EDELENBOS ET AL (2006: 132) has shown that when primary school teachers plan their teaching, tasks are central. When asked which didactic concepts they consider important, they rated task-orientation on a scale of 1–5 as 3,57. Only two out of four didactic concepts scored higher. They are: topics that *"should be personalized (3,67)"* and language learning which *"happens in meaningful contexts and thematic areas (4,86)"*. Both are principles that are fundamentally related to TBLL. Having presented the main characteristics of TBLL, we will now show you how to design tasks and how to work with them in the classroom.

2 Characteristics of tasks

The main task criteria

As CAMERON (2001: 31) points out, tasks *"can be defined as classroom activities [...but] not all activities that take place in a classroom will qualify as 'tasks'"*. Here is a list of criteria that characterize good tasks for young learners according to Cameron's concept of learner- and learning-centeredness (2001: 31; for an explanation see → ch. 2).

Criteria for classroom tasks
- Have coherence and unity for learners (topic, activity and/or outcome)
- Have meaning and purpose for learners
- Have clear language learning goals
- Have a beginning and an end
- Involve the learners actively

Tasks also take into account learners' limited foreign language skills. But they still encourage learners to deal with intellectually challenging tasks, focussing on the active, playful, and creative participation of the learners. At the same time they consider learners' experiences and promote their confidence and willingness to take risks. For example, to experiment with language without being afraid to make mistakes. Tasks try to develop learners' autonomy and responsibility by allowing them to take part in developing or selecting tasks, for example teachers can offer learners a number of topics to choose from. Tasks integrate the different language skills (→ ch. 5) and also support the use of non-linguistic skills, such as miming characters in a role play, drawing pictures, cutting out animals, or making things. Regular feedback in discussions about the quality of pupils' work in the follow-up phase (see below) can contribute to social learning, boost vocabulary development, and signal the importance of the outcome of the learning process (→ ch. 12).

3 Designing tasks

1 Alternative: Dimensions of using tasks in the classroom – an example

Analyzing story tasks – *The Very Hungry Caterpillar*

While these characteristics constitute the basis for a first approach to designing successful tasks, we need to be more explicit as to what teachers can do to deal with the different dimensions that influence language teaching in the classroom in which tasks are at the center of learning (→ graph: Our house of language learning, p. 11). To do so, we will look at a typical storytelling situation in a primary school classroom. The teacher has decided to choose the storybook *The Very Hungry Caterpillar* by Eric Carle (1974), an authentic story which is suitable for her first-year learners (→ ch. 9). It is her purpose that learners are going to eventually be able to retell the story. This target task will be made up of a number of different steps or sub-tasks. To begin with, the learners will sit in a semi-circle around the teacher and listen to her telling the story. Before she begins, she elicits what learners already know (e.g. the different kinds of fruit, the days of the week and numbers) and makes them familiar with new words by, for example, bringing some fruits to the classroom. The children will listen to the story once, and then all join in and try to reconstruct the story sequence by using real pieces of fruit or flash cards with pictures of the different kinds of fruit.

2 Nunan's framework for choosing tasks

However, the target task also involves a lot more. Nunan (2004: 40-73) has provided a framework that helps teachers become aware of the different dimensions/factors that are relevant when choosing a task. They are listed in the graph below.

A framework for analyzing communicative tasks (Nunan 2004: 41)

(a) Goals

Every task has one or more language learning goals, as does our task example. While the learners might already know the numbers one to five, they now have to learn the days of the week, different kinds of fruit, the adjectives big and small (to compare the caterpillar's size at the beginning of the story to its size at the end), and, depending on their level of proficiency, other items of fruit or food. They will also encounter the plural form as well as certain language chunks, such as *"he ate (through) one, two, three (...)"* or *"he was (still) hungry"*. Another goal is to talk about things the learners themselves eat when they are hungry, as well as to ask questions about which food items they like/don't like and like best/like least. Yet another goal is to give learners an opportunity to produce more discourse by encouraging them to retell and/or to act parts of the story.

Language learning goals

(b) Input

Each task requires some input for learners to work on. In our example this input is a story with certain features. It includes words, such as apple, pear, plum, strawberry, orange, the days of the week, and caterpillar and butterfly. The language is organized in repetitive sentence structures or language chunks, such as *"on Monday"*, *"on Tuesday"* etc, *"he ate through (...)"* and *"but he was still hungry"*. In terms of structural items, prepositions play a role (*"a little egg lay on a leaf"* or *"he ate through (...)"*), as well as a form of negation (*"he wasn't hungry any more"*). Since a story is a discourse event in itself, the learners are also confronted with extensive discourse (beginning of the story, development of the plot, climax, and end), yet another aspect of language input (→ ch. 7).

Words, structures, and discourse as input

(c) Activities

We use the term 'activity' following NUNAN, who sees an activity as something *"which is in some way derived from the input and which sets out what the learners are to do in relation to the input"* (NUNAN 1989: 10). This is why after the learners have encountered new language material and repeated the language items and chunks to become familiar with the pronunciation, they listen to the story and try to understand it. The second time the teacher tells the story, they can participate by filling in the gaps with one-word items and by producing the language chunk *"But he was still hungry"* in chorus form. The teacher could then ask the children to retell or act out individual scenes of the story as yet another activity that focuses on more extensive discourse production. Such an activity could also include moving around the room (from pears to plums to strawberries etc) to illustrate the caterpillar's progress through the different stages of growth.

Activities for language production

(d) Setting

The following three aspects NUNAN mentions, i.e. the setting, the learn-

Social forms in the classroom

er and teacher roles, all have a large influence on the task dimensions listed above. Setting means the concrete arrangements in the classroom as well as the different forms of social interaction between teacher and learners. Our primary classroom might have a storybook corner which is why learners may already be familiar with the book the teacher has chosen to use. To create a good storytelling atmosphere the teacher has asked the children to form a semi-circle or storytelling circle to make them curious for what is to come. While the social interaction of the first storytelling phase is determined by the teacher talking to the whole class, this changes in the following phases when the learners participate in chorus or when they act out scenes of the story in small groups. There are different ways in which the group can interact. Apart from teacher-centered teaching, teacher-learner interaction and communication and group work, there is also pair work which can be an especially productive form of classroom organization, since learners will be involved in both speaking and listening activities.

Teacher and learner roles

(e) Teacher and learner roles

While the teacher is responsible for the presentation of the input, it is through the set-up of the task that s/he allows her or his learners to take on increasing responsibilities for the learning process, slowly turning them into more autonomous learners. In terms of developing communicative competence, the teacher consequently reduces teacher talking time while increasing learner talking time. In our example, the teacher slowly integrates the learners into the storytelling process. First s/he gets them to fill in single words, at the same time encouraging them to pick up and say the repetitive structures in the story's plot (*"But he was still hungry"*). Gradually the teacher takes on the role of facilitator, who hands over the activities to the learners themselves by asking them to tell and/or perform scenes of the story. Learners could also evaluate the outcome of a task or discuss ideas on the strategies they used to do the task (see De Leeuw 1997).

3 Task types

Stir and settle activities

With young learners it is important to consider which kind of involvement a task triggers. For example, does a task stir up or calm down your learners? A TPR activity in which your learners jump up and down when they follow the commands in the game of *"Simon says"* might be a helpful strategy to get them going in the morning, but it might also lead to commotion or restlessness at other points during the day. Thinking about the sequence of activities, a varied balance of stir and settle activities is necessary to keep learners engaged and motivated, as well as providing opportunities for physical action and quiet anchors for individual reflection where children have an opportunity to think about their learning. (see Halliwell 1992: 19–39, see pp. 22–27 for examples of stir and settle activities). Apart from this general differentiation of tasks, there are a number of different kinds of tasks the teacher can use. Willis (1996: 26–28, 149–54) lists six types of tasks (for different lists see Brewster & Ellis 2002: 57, 102-4; Legutke & Thomas 1991: 71–150, and Nunan 2004: 56–63):

Type of task	Example from *The Very Hungry Caterpillar*
Listing – a list learners put together or a mind map	Listing all the fruits or food items the learners already know before hearing the story.
Ordering and sorting – sequencing items according to some logical or chronological order; ranking items according to a hierarchy; categorizing or classifying items in groups	After having heard the story at least twice, learners can reconstruct the plot with the help of flash cards.
Comparing – finding similarities or differences, e.g. by comparing pictures	By comparing a picture of a small, thin caterpillar with one of a fat caterpillar, learners will be able to retell parts of the story in a simplified form: "How did the caterpillar get so big?" "He ate through … and …"
Problem solving – from short puzzles to real-life problems	Identifying healthy and unhealthy food items for some animal with a particular problem or preference
Sharing personal experiences – e.g. likes and dislikes	Learners share their likes and dislikes of different kinds of food.
Creative tasks – more complex tasks that could involve the task types above	Learners act out the story.

Task forms: one-way/ two-way, divergent/ convergent

According to LAQ research, tasks seem to produce more negotiation of meaning if there is an information exchange between partners and if it flows both ways (two-way instead of one-way tasks). If learners compare two pictures, trying to find similarities and differences (spot the difference task), they both contribute to the outcome of the task, listening to and producing the target language. The same is true when you compare tasks with closed outcomes (convergent task) with tasks that have an open outcome (divergent task). If learners have to find mistakes in two pictures, then a certain amount of language production can be expected since the description of the mistakes makes the use of certain structural forms and vocabulary items necessary. They might need prepositions to describe the place and order of items in the picture, and they might need a certain semantic field, such as objects in a classroom or in a room in a house. The way the task is set up, (for example as a kind of competition – "There are five mistakes hidden in the picture."), ensures that learners really try to find the mistakes, thus engaging intensively with the task (therefore: a convergent task). If, however, learners are asked to simply describe what they see in a picture, then this is a divergent task, since they might just name two or three items without making the effort of going into more detail. The teacher would then have to encourage them to find the rest, since the task itself is too open and unspecific to engage learners in more language production.

4 Working with tasks

1 From task-as-workplan to tasks-in-action

Negotiating tasks in the classroom

When the teacher is preparing the lesson, s/he develops a task-as-workplan (a lesson plan, for example). In the classroom this plan turns into tasks-in-action which often differs from the task-as-workplan because the learners will always interpret the tasks in relation to their own socio-cultural backgrounds and the specific setting of the classroom that they are working in (CAMERON 2001: 35). In the process, they might (re)create the task in a different form, actually performing the task in a way the teacher has not expected. For example, the teacher might have planned to focus on extensive language use by having learners retell a story. However, as the task progresses they realize that this is still much too complicated for her class and that it would therefore be better to first work with language chunks below the discourse level, e.g. simple sentences, before her learners will eventually be able to master the retelling of short scenes of the story. The real performance of the task-in-action will therefore demonstrate how useful the task is. If learners re-negotiate the task in the process, it is called 'negotiated curriculum' (see BREEN 1987: 25–26). Young learners, for example, might interpret a task as a fast-moving game where their goal is not extensive language production but winning the game, hence trying to complete the game as fast as possible, something the teacher might not have intended (PINTER 2006b: 626; see also PINTER 1999 for an example of how learners negotiate different kinds of tasks). Once learners are more able to participate in the actual setting up of tasks, such as in project work, it can lead to a genuine negotiation of tasks when, for example, learners choose the topic they want to work on or when they set their own agenda and timetable for a task (for example, when putting a story on stage, which scenes and props to use, or when doing station work). However, even with the most elementary TBLL, it is important for the teacher to realize how her/his tasks are being changed in action so they can make the necessary adjustments to enable learners to complete their tasks successfully. Consequently, careful monitoring of the learners' performance is vital (→ ch. 12).

2 Sequencing tasks

CAMERON's task sequence

There are different suggestions of how to sequence tasks in the task-as-workplan over shorter or longer periods of time. WILLIS (1996) suggests to use a task-cycle which combines the pre-task phase, the actual task cycle and the language focus. Since a metalinguistic discussion of language issues is only suitable for older learners (→ see ch. 6), we suggest to follow CAMERON's (2001: 32) concept of the three phases, which we call pre-task, target task, and follow-up.

(a) **Pre-task phase**

For young learners in particular, the pre-task cycle is always longer than the other parts. This "*preparation*" stage (CAMERON 2001: 32) prepares learners for the task(s) to come. The guiding principle should always be to build on existing knowledge and give learners the feeling that they know something already, thus developing their confidence and boosting their morale. Preparatory activities can therefore entail integrating the pre-teaching of language items in an activity that activates what learners already know about a topic. This way, making use of familiar vocabulary and unobtrusively slipping in new words appears as a natural and spontaneous process. Both "Guessing Games" and "Mystery Objects" (an activity where children are actually allowed to feel and touch items in a bag) easily stimulate young learners to use their imagination to the full. The motivation for children here is provided by "playing the game" and finding things out (the teacher only shows part of a picture, for example) which is much more fun than just showing them a flash card and asking them to repeat the word a couple of times.

(b) **Target task**

The target task consists of a set of shorter sub-tasks rather than one long task due to the limited concentration span of our very young learners. In our story the teacher prompts the different days of the week, i.e. "*On Monday he ate through one …*" – and a learner decides on a particular kind of fruit and says its name ("*apple*"). Then the class joins in as a chorus "*But he was still hungry.*" In this 'gap-filling sub-task' the learners have to find the correct piece of fruit to go with the respective day of the week. It also qualifies as an 'interactive dialogue task' because teacher and learners reconstruct the story together (→ ch. 7). This sub-task is at the centre of the larger target task of understanding, organizing, and eventually retelling a story. The target task has clearly defined language learning goals. It integrates the careful sequencing of tasks with exercises that allow learners to practice certain linguistic features. DE LEEUW and LEGUKTE (1997: 116) call such sequences "*Verstehensgeländer*" where the teacher "*systematisch, durch die Verknüpfung von Übungen und Aufgaben und ihre konkrete Inszenierung im Interaktiongeschehen die Voraussetzungen dafür schafft, dass die Kinder in der Lage sind, mit der Zielsprache … umzugehen*".

(c) **Follow-up**

According to CAMERON (2001: 32), "*the 'follow-up' stage builds on successful completion of the core, perhaps with a public performance of work done in the core […] Since one task can lead to another, the follow up of the first maybe, or lead into, the 'preparation' stage of the next.*" Oral production of a task could, for example, lead to writing based on keywords and pictures the teacher provides of a story (→ ch. 5).

Story-based, storyline and project approach to TBLL

Tasks can also be sequenced in terms of a narrative discourse. In the story-based approach tasks are designed around the telling of a story. Due to their narrative discourse, stories are decisive in language learning as research has shown (EDELENBOS ET AL 2006: 148; KUBANEK-GERMAN 1992; see also → ch. 7). Some textbooks, such as *Magicland* (HANCOCK, REED & SCHOCKER-V. DITFURTH 2003) or *Tell it Again!* (ELLIS & BREWSTER 2002) are completely organized on the basis of the story approach. In the story-line concept (see KOCHER 1999, BELL 2000), tasks provide a basic narrative structure, allowing the learners choices as to topic, continuation of story, developing materials, and creating dialogues. Here the teacher steps back and the learners are in the foreground doing the tasks. According to BELL (2000: 51), two major features of this approach are "*'starting from what the learner knows' through key questioning and communicating these ideas through 'visualization'*". All of these forms are longer tasks sequences, integrating a number of sub-task phases, thus pursuing a clear project-based approach (see PHILIPS 1999 for an overview and project suggestions, further examples are to be found in CLAUS 2003, DRESE 2000, and MARSCHOLLEK 2003). In projects, learners work on a topic for a longer period of time, which integrates all skills and which leads to a final product like the staging of a story or the presentation of the solutions and products of the story-line project.

3 Task demands and task support

Task challenges

NUNAN's framework allows the teacher to analyze important components of the task, but it does not yet constitute a tool for the teacher to judge the difficulties of a task and to design potential support measures the learners need to complete the task successfully. Here CAMERON's (2001: 27) concept of task demands and task support is helpful: "*A task that is going to help the learner learn more language is one that is demanding but not too demanding, that provides support but not too much support. The difference between demands and support creates the space for growth and produces opportunities for learning*". She differentiates between cognitive, language, interactional, metalinguistic, involvement, and physical demands which are met or scaffolded by specific support measures (CAMERON 2001: 22–25). Let us have a look at task demands and support in relation to CARLE's story:

Task demand (general)	Task demand – *The Very Hungry Caterpillar*	Task support – *The Very Hungry Caterpillar*
Cognitive: depends on the learners' concepts	Understanding the plot of the story, and the concept of the days of the week.	Knowledge of story concepts learners have heard in their L1 (→ ch. 9)
Language: understanding and producing words and discourse, correct stress and intonation of words, producing correct grammatical forms	Understanding and producing language items (fruits, days of the week), chunks ("But he was still hungry"), and grammatical aspects (prepositions, negation)	Repeating words, TPR activities, using visuals, realia, joining in the story (e.g. contextualizing words and grammar items), transferring word knowledge from the language/s learners are familiar with to decoding English words
Interactional: pair work, i.e. listening, explaining sth. to a partner, following teacher's instructions	Teacher-learner dialogue (→ filling in gaps), chorus, possibly doing short scenes in a group	Clearly delivered task instructions, familiar routines of working with one partner before working in a group, helpful partner(s)
Metalinguistic: talking about formal aspects of language, rare in the first years because language is taught inductively		This is not necessary here since structural concepts (prepositions) will be explained by showing/miming
Involvement: ease/difficulty learners have with task, length, link to child's interests, novelty, suspense	Possibly length of story-telling phase	Interest through the story of the growing caterpillar (suspense), and through the various food items it consumes (humour). Involvement by joining in the telling of the story
Physical: fine motor skills (e.g. using scissors), sitting still	Sitting still while listening, miming activities, cutting out caterpillars for further activities	Mixing settle (listening to story) and stir (joining in story telling, acting out) activities, drawing instead of cutting out

As Cameron (2001: 30–31) points out, tasks can help young learners to grow with the tasks' demands. Demands vary according to the specific activities the teacher chooses and the stage of learners' language proficiency (see also Pinter 2006a: 61). If any of the various demands are too high, the learners might not finish the task because it is too difficult. Or they might pretend to do the task without really having understood what is expected of them. On the other hand, if the tasks are too easy, learners will not learn enough since their language knowledge is not challenged and developed to a higher level. This is why Cameron differentiates between a learner-centered and a learning-centered approach (→ ch. 2). Task support or scaffolding the learners' language production are central to Vygotsky's concept of the zone of proximal development (→ ch. 2).

5 Beginning research on using tasks in the classroom

Research on task support

PINTER (2007) has pointed out repeatedly that we cannot generalize LAQ research to the primary classroom, but that we need to look very closely at the contextual factors that are involved (see also SCHOCKER-V. DITFURTH 2004b: 24 and → ch. 1). While there is hardly any primary classroom research in TBLL, some recent findings show the potential of qualitative research to better understand classroom processes. One line of research looks at improving task support for young learners. PINTER (2006a: 60), for example, relates that practicing new task types is central to successful task completion. *"Information gap tasks, discussion tasks, and other complex speaking tasks can hide various difficulties. It is important for teachers to explore these difficulties with their children and provide plenty of practice of new task types. In my own research (PINTER 2001) I found that even children at the age of ten needed a great deal of practice to be able to deal with the difficulties of two classic information gap tasks: 'Spot the differences' and 'follow the route on the map'"*.

Established routines in the classroom provide another major area of task support, such as the use of certain materials (e.g. hand puppet → ch. 9), moving into a semi-circle or circle, taking out the storybook, signaling to the children that it is story time and that they can relax and listen. Routines make tasks more manageable for the learners and for the teacher as well, since they provide a frame for the various activities for starting the lesson, repetitive activities such as the organization of certain games, or the change from one social form to another (see DE LEEUW & LEGUTKE 1997: 47-49). The children already know what to expect and this establishes a feeling of security, while keeping up the learners' motivation since they attach positive feelings to such routines as acting, singing or drawing. This framework allows the integration of new forms of activities that might be demanding for the learners by soothing away any feelings of insecurity or anxiety.

TBLL – a win win situation for learners and teachers

In her research on tasks PINTER (1999: 16) has shown that children use the strategy of *"'building patterns' whereby they repeat what they are comfortable with over and over again. They play safe and try to exploit a given phrase as much as possible"*. CAMERON (2001: 26) summarizes this by saying: *"When we think in terms of support, we try to use what the children can already do to help them master new skills and knowledge, or we try to match tasks to children's natural abilities and inclinations"*. While task planning time provides adult learners with task support, research in primary classrooms has shown that more planning time does not automatically lead to more language production. PHILIP, OLIVER and MACKEY (2006: 562) show that out of three different lengths of planning time allocated to learners in solving the same task, the longest planning time resulted in distraction of the learners. In her research on task repetition, another important aspect of task support, PINTER (2007: 191) found out that repeating the same kind of pair work task over a number of weeks helps learners appreciate each other's needs as communication partners in terms of listening to the partner's performance or helping each other in task completion (for further research on task support see → ch. 4).

Generally one can say that both learners and teachers profit from TBLL. The younger the children, the less familiar they are with independent groupwork and pairwork, and the more guidance is required from the teacher. The teacher monitors their task work in small groups, makes suggestions, helps with materials, helps dreamy pupils to concentrate on the task, and makes sure that their beginners' attempts do not end in frustration, but in a growing confidence in their language skills. And teachers will also feel much more comfortable with a task-based approach when designing their lessons from scratch and/or analyzing textbook activities to possibly re-write inappropriate tasks from the textbook in light of their specific context (→ ch. 11).

1 Introduction

What helps children learn? The teacher as *the* central factor

We have seen in chapter 1 that the classroom is an environment in which many factors affect the quality of learning. They range from seating arrangement and classroom equipment (BAILEY & SCHMID-SCHÖNBEIN 2005) to number and characteristics of the participants and which materials and tasks are available. Of all these factors, the teachers play a crucial role. They need to know how to choose or design motivating and challenging tasks as work plans that have the potential to stimulate learner involvement through their pre-course preparation. We have discussed this aspect in the previous chapter (→ ch. 3). But they also need to bring these activities to life *in the process of introducing and mediating these tasks* in the classroom: by creating an atmosphere in which learners are encouraged to get involved, by managing and sustaining the learning process through supportive teaching strategies while pupils are performing the task, and by evaluating the learning process and learner competences to draw conclusions for developments in the quality of learning in his or her classroom (→ ch. 12). Teachers' best plans may amount to nothing if they do not manage to involve their learners, and the potential of the most wonderful task can be spoiled by presenting it in a threatening or boring way. By the same token, a competent teacher may be able to bring even bad materials to life. Particularly in the primary EFL classroom the role of the teacher is central as learners tend to identify with their teacher *and* with the language and culture they represent and because in primary EFL the focus is on oral skills development which is why teachers are the central providers of input (KLIPPEL 2003: 53). In this chapter we will discuss *what a teacher can do* in the classroom so that *the learning potential of a task and the available teaching time is not wasted*. Our suggestions are based on research into primary EFL learning (where available) and on a multitude of successful teaching strategies that have been documented from experiences of teachers and teacher educators.

2 Focus on the teacher-student rapport

Aspects of the teacher's role: personality and attitude

In accordance with humanistic psychology we assume that classroom (language) learning is rooted in interpersonal relationships and is therefore 'facilitated' through 'attitudinal qualities' that exist in the personal relationship between the teacher and the students (ROGERS 1990 [1967]: 305). ROGERS mentions the following four attitudinal qualities:

- emphatic understanding of the students' process of education and learning from their perspective, to be able to 'experience the other side' and as a result to be able to base teaching on the reality of those who are being educated. This asks for cooperative and genuinely interested listening on the side of teachers but: *"Teachers are not famous for being good listeners"* (APPEL 1995: 46);

- valuing and respecting children, trusting the learner;
- realness of the teacher in his or her relationship with students and in the way they personalize content/knowledge and bring the task to life;
- all of which will result in a teacher's respect for a student's autonomy in that they hand over responsibility and enable students to make decisions about their own learning.

There is empirical evidence (from learning-to-teach-studies, for example) that without these learner-centered attitudinal qualities that find expression in the quality of classroom interaction, learners do not invest intensive mental energy in task performance and, as a result, 'deep-level learning' does not take place. BREEN (1987) contrasts a passive learner attitude, which he calls 'survival orientation,' with a learner's 'achievement orientation' which drives the learner to perform the task with maximum effort. Research into the implementation of TBLL in Belgium also emphasizes the central role of the teacher to support learning: "*Learners themselves decide to what extent they will actually engage with the task and perceive it as meaningful. [...] It is true that the effect of learning activities is, at least partly, dependent on the intensity with which the learner approaches them [...], one of the most prominent roles of the teacher is to try and get every single learner involved into actively engaging with the task that is presented*" (VAN DEN BRANDEN 2006: 177). These findings are further supported by studies that focus on a teacher's motivational practices and students' motivated behavior in language classes (DÖRNYEI 2001, 2007; GUILLOTEAUX & DÖRNYEI 2008). But what are some of the key aspects of a teacher's competence based on these basic attitudinal qualities we have outlined in our introduction?

Aspects of the teacher's role: creator of a relaxed positive learning environment

Tasks as work plans may help learners feel at ease by the demands they put on them (→ ch. 3). But this takes teachers who manage to create a relaxed positive learning environment. Research has shown that the more relaxed and comfortable students feel, the easier it is for them to acquire language. This is basically what KRASHEN's 'affective filter hypothesis' is all about: "*The 'affective filter' is an imaginary barrier which prevents learners from acquiring language from the available input. 'Affect' refers to such things as motives, needs, attitudes, and emotional states. A learner who is tense, angry, anxious, or bored may 'filter out' input, making it unavailable for acquisition. Thus, depending on the learner's state of mind or disposition, the filter limits what is noticed and what is acquired*" (LIGHTBOWN & SPADA 1999: 39).

Aspects of the teacher's role: provider for learners' security

STEVICK (1996) also believes that classrooms which expose students to negative evaluation by the teacher or by peers may promote anxiety, which, in turn, may affect achievement. He distinguishes between two kinds of learning, *defensive* and *receptive* learning. When learning is defensive, "*[w]hat the learner tries to do [...] is that [...] she tries to build a shell around herself. [...] The teacher is viewed as an adversary [...] against whom the learner may defend herself*" (STEVICK 1996: 196). In contrast to this, we can only promote *receptive* learning if we reduce threats to our students' egos. In a relaxed atmosphere they will lower their defense mechanisms, and only then can students turn their attention to learning activities. *"Most fundamental [...] is the need for security, and a fundamental component of security is predictability. [...] The second level [...] is social: 'Am I accepted as a member of a social group that I can depend on to support me?' [...] A third level of need [...] is the ability to do those things that will maintain and improve one's standing in the group"* (STEVICK 1996: 8–9). After these general remarks on the teacher's attitudes in the classroom, we will look at two aspects of *teacher competences* that are particularly relevant: the *teacher as mediator* and *the teacher as model.*

3 The teacher as mediator

What teachers and peers can do to support learners' mental development

For VYGOTSKY, language and the other people in a child's environment are important for his or her mental development. Therefore, mediation is a key concept. As a child's development and learning always takes place in a social context with other people (e.g. in a family or in a classroom), *"[t]hose people play important roles in helping children to learn, bringing objects and ideas to their attention, talking while playing [...] reading stories, asking questions. In a whole range of ways, adults mediate the world for children and make it accessible to them. The ability to learn through instruction and mediation is characteristic of human intelligence. With the help of adults, children can do and understand much more than they can on their own"* (CAMERON 2001: 6). Related to this idea is VYGOTSKY's concept of the 'zone of proximal development' (ZPD): *"Most of the psychological investigations concerned with school learning measured the level of mental development of the child by making him solve certain standardized problems. The problems he was able to solve by himself were supposed to indicate the level of his mental development at the particular time [...] We tried a different approach. Having found that the mental age of two children was, let us say eight, we gave each of them harder problems than he could manage on his own and provided slight assistance [...] We discovered that one child could, in cooperation, solve problems designed for twelve year olds, while the other could not go beyond problems intended for nine year olds. The discrepancy between a child's mental age [indicated by the static test] and the level he reaches in solving problems with assistance is the zone of his proximal development"* (VYGOTSKY 1986: 186–7). ZPD therefore describes *"the distance between the actual development level (of the learner) as determined by independent problem solving and the level potential development as determined through problem solving under adult guidance or in collaboration with more capable peers"* (VYGOTSKY 1978, 86). As VYGOTSKY says, it is important to acknowledge that it is not 'just' the teacher but also learners' peers that play an important role in providing this support. It is therefore the teacher's task to mobilize the potential of peer support.

What teachers can do to support learners' language development

If we look at the implications of this for language learning in the social context 'classroom', we need to look at what teachers can do to successfully *mediate the foreign language* for children so that they can actually learn more than they would if left on their own. Learners need to be *pushed* to *actively process* a new language item: the more they are *actively involved* in thinking about the meaning of a new word and the more they are allowed *to experiment with language*, the more likely they are to remember it – a hypothesis that CAMERON, following CRAIK and LOCKHART (1972), has described as *"deep processing"* (CAMERON 2001, 85). Task-based teaching offers this opportunity, but *"we need teachers who are able to cope in a professional way with a fair level of unpredictability of task performance and task processing"* (KUMARAVIDELU 2007: 22). Let us look at the strategies one of our trainee teachers used when trying to work with a story about ten little mice (for another example of a teacher's mediating strategies in a storytelling lesson see GERNGROSS 2001).

An example of how to support learners' developing interlanguages

HANCOCK, REED & SCHOCKER-V. DITFURTH (2004). *Magicland Class Book* 2, S. 6; Langenscheidt, München

The activity involved the activation and presentation of vocabulary for the rooms in the mice's house – *bedroom, living-room, kitchen, bathroom.* To do so, the trainee teacher had prepared a poster of the mice's house (set in the roots of a tree), that she put up on the board. The four rooms were covered up on the poster with four sheets of paper so that the children could only see the outline of the tree. First she introduced children to the activity and its setting: *Let's listen to a story about a family that lives in a house in the roots of a tree [...] Let's find out first what their house is like [...] What do you think? What rooms will we find?* By doing this, she activated language that the children had already encountered and possibly stored during their previous lessons [i.e. they knew the word *room* from the word *classroom* and they were familiar with some action words – verbs, such as *work, sleep, wash, eat* etc.]. Therefore, it was hardly surprising that the children actively tried to construct concepts for the new words they were asked to guess. They came up with *sleeproom* (teacher's feedback: *Good idea! But in English this room does not say what you do – sleep – but what there is in it – a bed – therefore we say bedroom*). Or they constructed and tried out similar forms for the other rooms, for example for *kitchen* they tried *eatroom* and for bathroom they created *washroom*. The learners were used to being activated in this way and were not afraid to get words wrong. In this way the teacher contributed to her students' developing interlanguages: She used whatever learners came up with, gave positive feedback on children's attempts to create new words and supported learning by providing the correct form and *by not abandoning the meaning-focused dialogue*. Findings from European studies on primary EFL point out how important it is to provide feedback to children which may be positive (encouragement) or may be corrective, to help them further refine their underlying language system (EDELENBOS et al 2006: 11). The knowledge and the skills teachers need to support learners' discourses may be categorized in the following aspects and techniques of *teacher talk* that overlap:

Strategies to support learners' discourses

(a) elicitation strategies to encourage learners' oral participation in English (SCHMID-SCHÖNBEIN 2005b);

(b) patient prompting strategies. Teachers must exercise patience, because it may take a lot of time until learners say what they want to say (the following example is from a 3rd grade primary school in Freiburg):
T: *Nashda, what's your favorite animal?*
N: *(no reaction)*
T: *A dog, a cat ... or even a crocodile, perhaps?*
N: *Was heißt Vogel?*
T: *(whispers in Nashda's ear: A bird!)*
N: *A bird!*

(c) scaffolding to support learners in interaction by building up the target language over several turns. Initially, learners may be unable to produce certain structures within a single utterance, but may build them up through mediated interaction with another speaker (SCHMID-SCHÖNBEIN 2005c; see example in → ch. 5, p. 56);

(d) scaffolding may involve supportive feedback to learner errors which are seen as a window to the developing interlanguages of learners (→ ch. 2; ASHEUER 2003; HUTZ & KOLB 2007; SCHMID-SCHÖNBEIN 2005a);

(e) giving feedback for praise and encouragement on what learners can already do with language rather than on what they cannot do yet (SCHMID-SCHÖNBEIN 2006c);

(f) building up language routines and rituals in the recurring situations of classroom management discourse as particularly young learners need railings, time and repeated exposure to acquire the new language (BAILEY & SCHMID-SCHÖNBEIN 2005; SCHMID-SCHÖNBEIN 2006c; SLATTERY & WILLIS 2001).

4 The teacher's language as model

The teacher as model for language use

The idea of teacher as model involves various aspects that range from the attitude they have and by what they implicitly communicate about the English language and culture to how they create a learning environment that is characterized by mutual respect and understanding. In this paragraph we focus on the teacher as model in terms of the way they use language in a classroom to support learning.

The teacher as model for implicit learning

There has been much discussion in language acquisition research about how much learning can be influenced by teaching. It has been observed that children reproduce the language types used by their teachers (CAMERON 2001: 16). These results correspond with our own experiences as primary teachers and teacher educators (→ see example of classroom discourse in ch. 5, p. 56). Consider the following examples that have been reported by GERNGROSS (personal communication). In a class of six-year-olds the teacher frequently said, "Let me check, please!" when the children had completed a task. After a while the children started to shout "Check, please!", whenever they wanted the teacher to come and see their work. In the same class of six-year-olds, which was, to say the least, very lively, the teacher often said "Relax!" whenever a child found it hard to concentrate and was busily involved in noisy off-task behavior. After hearing this for a while, the children began to use the word to calm one another down. It seems that taking over the language models used by their teachers is a strategy learners apply quite naturally during meaningful classroom discourse. We will discuss the consequences of this observation in our next paragraph.

The teacher as model to use English as the means of communication in the classroom

Teachers are a model in that they establish the English language as an authentic means of communication in their classroom as far as possible (PIEPHO 2000: 3). BUTZKAMM has argued for the occasional use of the language of schooling (in our context: German) if it supports learning and language awareness, if it helps to avoid misunderstanding, or if it makes learners feel more at ease in times of stress. He documents a number of convincing situations and strategies of how this may be done (BUTZKAMM 2005; BUTZKAMM & SCHMID-SCHÖNBEIN forthcoming 2008). The quality of exposure is as varied as primary EFL teachers are. Apart from many documented positive examples of language use there are others that found that English is not the language of communication in German primary classrooms: *"Das Prinzip der Einsprachigkeit [...] wurde nur in einer Klasse konsequent durchgehalten. Ansonsten zeigte sich, dass die Lehrkräfte bei Erklärungen oder beim Regeln des Unterrichtsablaufes häufig auf das Deutsche zurückgriffen, während die englische Sprache beim Üben von Wortschatz und festen Redemittel, sowie beim Singen von Liedern oder beim Sprechen von Reimen und Chants zum Einsatz kam. [...] Insbesondere Arbeitsanweisungen wurden häufig direkt ins Deutsche übersetzt"* (ROOS 2007: 130). EDELENBOS ET AL (2006: 25) confirm this in their European research study and found that to be fluent and confident in the language is important so that teachers are able to spontaneously and flexibly react to learners' contributions and to involve them in interactive language use, but that *"at the moment, these needs are far from being met"*. This poses a challenge for teacher education.

5 Challenges and perspectives

Teacher education needs to focus on the competences needed to manage learning in classrooms successfully

Teacher education, according to our understanding of professional teacher development, needs to involve school-based teacher education in which student teachers have the opportunity to observe successful strategies of language support performed by model teachers so that they may develop these strategies for themselves as part of their own classroom routines (BIG 2007, Schocker-v. Ditfurth 2003a). We also argue for developing target language competences in an integrated way, with English as the language of communication in all realms of teacher education. One of the reasons why our book is written in English was to contribute to this.

Learners' language development takes time and needs to address learner diversity in mixed ability classrooms

Primary classrooms are constituted with heterogeneous learners who are diverse in many ways: a. o. in terms of individual competence levels, preferred ways of working, or social competences (→ ch. 1; see discussion of issues in Westwood & Arnold 2004). Developing competences in the new language therefore takes time. Teachers need to offer their learners different possibilities of language acquisition so that they may get involved in a way that corresponds to their diverse preconditions, needs and interests. Tasks by their very nature offer choices for learners (→ ch. 3) but there have been a number of further suggestions on how this can be done (Böttger 2006a, 2006b). They range from cross-curricular projects to carousel learning.

Process support requires the development of diagnostic competences

One of the issues in primary EFL is what teachers can do to evaluate their learners' learning process and competences to give appropriate feedback, draw conclusions, and make suggestions for what each individual learner can do to develop. Research on teachers' diagnostic competence is in progress (Arnold 1999, Diehr & Frisch 2006, Groeben 2003, Kubanek-German & Edelenboos 2004, 2005, BIG 2008), even though, given the limited teaching time allocated to primary EFL at the moment, it is difficult to imagine the practicalities of suggestions made. Introducing EFL in grade 1 may therefore offer a promising perspective.

1 Introduction

On the challenges of teaching the language skills in primary EFL classrooms

In this chapter we will discuss how teachers may support the development of the language skills of listening, speaking, reading, writing, and mediating *under the conditions of primary EFL classrooms* (→ ch. 1; for a survey on the models that have tried to describe how the skills are acquired see MÜLLER-HARTMANN & SCHOCKER-V. DITFURTH 2004, ch. 3). This is quite a challenge: usually teachers work with *large numbers of heterogeneous learners* and need to *focus on oral skills development* because listening and speaking have priority over reading and writing at this competence level (BIG 2007; PIEPHO 2001). Since *constant and flexible input, feedback, and support in oral interaction* are required, teachers have to perform a very demanding task (→ ch. 4). Finally, we have to bear in mind that the time of exposure is low with approximately only 120 lessons if English starts in grade 3, while a lot of time and patience is needed to actually develop skills at this language learning level (LEGUTKE 2000: 47f). Therefore we need to have *realistic expectations of the competences that may be developed* under the conditions outlined here. PIEPHO (2001) says why this is important from the learners' perspectives: "*Nichts ist für jeden Lernprozess und für jeden Lernenden (zer)störender als Misserfolge, und die sind meist die Folge von ungeeigneten Anforderungen zum falschen Zeitpunkt. [...] Beim Spracherwerb kommt es immer zuvörderst darauf an, teilnehmen und zeigen zu können, was man kann und möchte [...].*" (PIEPHO 2001: 12).

Procedure: from listening to speaking and from reading to writing

We will discuss skills development in two sub-chapters that outline principles and practices for the skill of speaking on the basis of listening skills and for writing on the basis of reading skills. Our suggestions on primary-specific skills development are based on reported classroom experiences of what learners *can actually do with language* in primary classrooms which we will compare to the skills that curricula have suggested. We will discuss basic principles you will need to consider and will suggest appropriate teaching ideas by referring to selected articles with each of the principles.

2 General principles for developing language skills

Offer activities that are challenging and relevant for your learners

We believe that two principles are basic for the learning of the skills, no matter if they refer to reading, writing, listening, speaking or mediating.

(a) Think of *interesting, surprising, unusual, exaggerated, funny contents* that activate your learners and motivate them to get involved. If the content bores you, it is bound to bore your learners, too. Remember: you do not teach just a new form (English) to express things they already know in German, but you need to present the new form with motivating content. For example, to introduce the speech function: *Talking about my family / my daily routine* you could use the wonderful story of OLIVIA by IAN FALCONER (2000), a very unusual pig, which is a joy to read. Select funny dialogues, stories with a surprising ending and a sense of humor, or songs your learners are eager to learn.

(b) Introduce language in *real contexts* using *lifelike language*, that is, language that real people might use in a particular situation (→ ch. 11). Don't ask your learners to produce language simply because you want them to practice a particular form: some grammar, for example. It would be very strange if learners were asked to answer in a complete sentence if nobody would do so in a real-life situation. Or if learners, asked to talk about zoo animals, would use the chunk *This is a ....* Instead, think about what children might actually talk about at the zoo and which phrases they might use to do so. They might, for example, express surprise about certain animals, saying, *'Oh look, what a big / ugly /... zebra / gnu / ostrich'* etc. – which could therefore be the structure you select to practice zoo animals.

3 From listening to speaking

1 What the curricula say and what learners can actually do in our language-learning context

Standards as defined by curricula

Both curricula that have tried to define minimum standards (BIG 2005) and the different curricula of state governments have stated what learners should be able to do with language when they have finished primary school. Here are some examples taken from the BIG standards which are based on a minimum of 120 lessons, offered in grades 3 and 4 (for the complete list see BIG 2005: 9):

2.1.1. Hören und Hörverstehen

Die Schülerinnen und Schüler können [...] einfache Anweisungen im Unterrichtsalltag verstehen und befolgen, einfache Äußerungen zu vertrauten Themen verstehen und darauf angemessen reagieren [...], Handlungsfolgen verstehen, behalten und das Verstehen des Gehörten nonverbal und/oder verbal belegen.

2.1.2. Sprechen und mündliche Kommunikation

Die Schülerinnen und Schüler können aus ihrer Lebenswelt Gehörtes verständlich wiedergeben [...], vertraute Gegenstände und Tätigkeiten benennen und beschreiben, Informationen geben und einholen, Gespräche beginnen und beenden, Wünsche und Gefühle [...] äußern und entsprechende Fragen stellen, Hilfe und Unterstützung anbieten und erbitten.

2.1.5. Sprachmittlung

Die Schülerinnen und Schüler können einfache Inhalte von Gesprächen aus ihrer Lebenswelt in der Fremdsprache verstehen und anderen in Deutsch und/oder ihrer Herkunftssprache erklären, einfachste Inhalte von Gesprächen, von Texten oder Sachverhalten aus ihrer Lebenswelt in der Fremdsprache vermitteln.

Standards as actually achieved by learners

Recent empirical studies on the competence levels of young learners in Northrhine-Westfalia after two years of English in grades 3 and 4 found that learners exceed their teachers' expectations and performed better in listening than they had expected, with the majority of learners demonstrating high listening competences (GROOT-WILKEN, ENGEL & THÜRMANN 2007: n.p.). When addressed by a speaker, they could understand questions and react appropriately to them, but when they were asked to get actively involved in a dialogue they were less successful and only a minority managed to say things coherently or was able to connect their utterances with structure words such as *and / or* (GROOT-WILKEN,& THÜRMANN 2007: 32f). The authors concluded that learners would readily experiment with language and are not afraid to make mistakes, but that teachers did not provide the time and means to support them to do so (i.e. mainly lack of opportunities to let the children talk, let them learn from mistakes respectively give them positive feedback plus lack of provision of verbs and structure words but instead a focus on teaching nouns). Obviously, developing the oral skills in classrooms in an action-oriented and playful way takes time, requires intensive and varied practice and teaching competences that seem not to be mainstream practice (see also recent results in KURTZ 2008). What are, therefore, the basic principles you need to consider when developing listening and speaking skills?

2 Principles for developing listening and speaking

On the appropriate weighting of listening and speaking

(a) *Find a balance between listening and speaking*

It is generally easier to develop listening skills in a classroom than to develop speaking skills, simply because it is difficult to get a large group of learners to speak at the same time, whereas it is no problem to ask all of the learners to listen and demonstrate understanding by giving them a listening task which they can do at the same time (i.e. listen and do, listen and draw, listen and match). For a long time it has been assumed that learners go through what has been called a 'silent period', that is, that they prefer to listen first and need time before they develop the confidence and urge to produce language. Even though this may be true for some learners, it would be wrong to generalize this: "*Sprachrezeption und Sprachproduktion müssen vielmehr von Anfang an [...] in eine optimale Balance gebracht werden. Dabei sollten die Möglichkeiten und Grenzen jedes einzelnen Kindes berücksichtigt werden. Dies bedeutet [...] dass die Lernenden verschiedenartige unterrichtliche Formen der Beteiligung von Anfang an kennenlernen*" (KURTZ 2008: 7). From research, we know that learners' reluctance to speak can – among other factors – be attributed to the general teaching approach at primary level which does not provide the opportunities and the support for learners to encourage them to do so (→ ch. 2).

(b) *Principles for developing listening*

Apart from the general principles outlined above, it is important that

Provide ample exposure to English and offer varied listening activities with a purpose

you provide as much exposure to English as you possibly can by

- using *English as the means of communication in the classroom* (→ ch. 4)
- using *different media with different (native) speakers* (CDs, videos); the high competence level that learners in the Northrhine-Westfalian study demonstrated with the listening skill was attributed to the intensive use of audio materials in the lessons (Groot-Wilken, Engel & Thürmann 2007: n.p.).

Offer *tasks that give learners a meaningful, varied and challenging purpose of why they should listen to a text* by giving motivating pre-listening activities involving for example hypothesizing or picture prompts (Piepho 2007; → ch. 3). Listening comprehension tasks range from selective, global, or detailed listening (Hoffmann 2005), but learners should always be aware of why they listen to a text (i.e. to identify someone's favorite food, to find the gist of a story or to solve a problem). Offer new language in combination with *gesture, mime and action* as this supports understanding and involves learners physically. Not only is this playful approach motivating for young learners, it also helps them to remember and store new words and takes account of different learner types (→ multi-sensory approach, see Gerngross & Puchta 1996, Gerngross 2004a; examples include action stories, action songs or other listen-and-do activities). Encourage learners *to guess words from the context* and *to predict* about how a listening text (a story, for example) might continue. This way you actively involve them in the process.

(c) *Principles for developing speaking*

Unpredictable learner contributions: an opportunity to learn

Both language acquisition research and practitioner research agree that it takes more than comprehensible input to develop communicative competences of which interactive speaking is a part (→ ch. 2). Through research and classroom observation we are becoming more and more aware that the reasons for the observed lack of oral language production in primary classrooms may not be rooted in learners' preferred forms of participation, but in prevailing approaches to teaching at primary level. Kurtz (2008), in a recent study on how speaking may be promoted in classrooms, observed a strong focus on imitation and reproduction and a lack of interactive learner support (scaffolding) initiated by the teacher when learners tried to communicate something in English spontaneously. What can you do to use the learning potential of these situations?

From imitation and reproduction to production

In the beginning, learners' language production is predominantly imitative and reproductive. It is based on simple models of language use and requires ample exposure to language and listening comprehension. But productive use of language in communicative situations needs to be developed from the start by following the principles below.

Proceed from activities that prepare communication to communicative activities

Learners need models of language use that they can use and adapt to their communicative needs (GERNGROSS 2003). Within the frame the models provide, learners should have the choice to say what they want to say. Examples of different activity types include matching and completing, reconstructing skeleton texts (see below), mini dialogues, construction of sentences or short fictional and non-fictional texts (BLEYHL 2002; GERNGROSS 2003: 12; KURTZ 2004), storytelling activities (BLEYHL 2002; PIEPHO 2007; SCHMID-SCHÖNBEIN 2006a: 5; → ch. 7), or role plays that develop as follow-up activities from a storytelling lesson (PHILLIPS 1999). Here is an example for a role-play we did in a 3rd grade primary classroom in Freiburg on *Clothes Shopping*. The teacher activated learners' pre-knowledge (clothes, colors, sizes) in a meaningful context, by giving them a preparatory homework. She asked them to cut out those clothes from a mail order catalogue which they thought they might want to buy in a clothes shop, and stick them on a handout with the outlines of a shopping bag. This way she considered the vocabulary learners wanted to use. After the clothes items had been practiced, learners got the conversation between two friends who go shopping for clothes as a model dialogue with language production support they could use to practice their role-play:

A *Look, there's a ...*
B *Oh yes, I like it!*
A *Put it on!*
B *It's ... (too big / just perfect / too small)*
A *OK, let's put it back / let's buy it!*

This model dialogue offered learners various choices in what they could say and yet provided the means of how they could say it by using a model dialogue at the same time. The teacher acted as a model, too. She brought along a shopping bag, introducing clothes words by asking learners to guess what she had bought, saying: *I like to go shopping for clothes. Guess what I have in my shopping bag!* As a lead-in to the role play she said what the purpose of the activity was by saying, *And now you learn what to say when you go shopping with a friend!* Alternatively, you could co-construct the model dialogue with your learners by putting them in a situation where they need to say something, i.e. by saying: *This is my boutique! You are my first customer* (choose child). *Good morning, can I help you?* etc. and then collaboratively construct what one could say in this context.

Provide varied age-appropriate real-life situations / contexts in which the children want to or have to talk

As the example has demonstrated, it takes appropriate communicative activities that Klippel has described as follows: *"Zum Üben des kommunikativen Sprechens werden Sprechsituationen benötigt, in denen die Kinder etwas sagen wollen oder aufgrund der Übungsstruktur etwas sagen müssen"* (KLIPPEL 2000: 88). GERNGROSS (2003) lists a variety of activities for teachers to choose from, ranging from games, information-gap activities, role plays, drama, and interviews to sketches.

Use the potential of spontaneous situations in class to communicate in English

It is important that teachers are aware of the potential of situations in which learners want to say something spontaneously and that they know how to provide appropriate support in their interaction with learners (teacher as model → ch. 4). Learners will use whatever resources they have available if they want to communicate something that is relevant and meaningful to them. The following example, reported from classroom observation data by GERNGROSS (talk in Freiburg in April 2008), demonstrates that children, if they want to communicate something, use all kinds of strategies to help them get their message across: they mix or switch codes (German and English), they use simplification strategies (*have got* instead of *she's got*) and actually pick up and make use of new language the teacher offers in the process of communication:

S: *My mother is krank.*
T: *Oh, really? Your mother is ill. I'm sorry to hear that.*
What's the problem?
S: *Have got Grippe.*
T: *Oh, she's got the flu.*
S: *Yes, big Kopfschmerzen.*
T: *Ah, she's got a bad headache.*
S: *She's got a bad headache. Yes.*

You need to create a relaxed atmosphere in which learners feel comfortable to experiment with the new language in many ways. Teachers need to react flexibly and spontaneously to learners' contributions. This asks for a well developed interactive target language competence and a repertoire of appropriate teaching strategies to support this process in a professional way (→ ch. 4). Use whatever situation may come up to talk in English. This may be anything from comments when things go wrong (*Oops – the poster is upside-down*), to classroom management language (*Could you please do this in pairs?*) or, as in the example above, the appropriate reaction to learners' spontaneous communicative needs.

4 From reading to writing

1 What the curricula say and what learners can actually can do in our language-learning context

Standards as defined by curricula

Minimum standards involve the following competences (BIG 2005: 10):
2.1.3. Lesen und Leseverstehen
Die Schülerinnen und Schüler können Wörter lesen, die ihnen bekannt sind [...], Informationen, die [...] bekannt sind, auch aus Texten entnehmen [...].
2.1.4. Schreiben und schriftliche Kommunikation
Die Schülerinnen und Schüler können Wörter und einzelne Sätze [...] abschreiben, [...] unter Zuhilfenahme von Vorlagen [...] auf einfache Weise schriftlich kommunizieren.

2 Controversial views on reading and writing

Current curricula in Germany emphasize the supportive function of reading and writing (Bavaria, Hesse) or introduce reading and writing in a foreign language two years after literacy development in learners' first language has been completed in grade 3 (Baden-Württemberg). Curricula represent the critical views that have been put forward on introducing reading and writing (see below). Since the beginnings of introducing foreign languages at primary school there has been a controversy over *if* introducing reading and writing at this level makes sense (DOYE & LÜTTGE 1977; HELLWIG 1995). To this day, opposing views prevail the discussion, even though there is a tendency to argue for integrating these skills.

Curricula represent a critical view on introducing reading and writing

The arguments that have been put forward against introducing reading and writing may be summarized in three points:

Arguments against introducing reading and writing

(1) The *focus* in primary EFL is on *developing oral communicative competences*. It would be irresponsible to make learners familiar with English spelling, given the already scant time of exposure.
(2) Teachers are worried that it would *put excessive demands on learners* who have to cope with literacy development in their first language or in the language of schooling. Learners should have developed sound competences in their first language (and in the case of immigrant children in the language of schooling) before, so that interferences are avoided (BLEYHL 2002). This argument is supported by referring to the irregular grapheme-phoneme relationship in English, that is, sounds are represented by a variety of different spellings which is why young learners do not recognize graphic representations of familiar English sounds without support. To give an example from DIEHR & RYMARCZYK (2008: 7), for the long /u: /-sound in English we find seven different spellings: *to, too, two, through, threw, clue, shoe*.
(3) Teachers are also worried that *competences in reading and writing could be misused as an additional criterion to select learners* for transition to different secondary school types.

Supporters put forward the following arguments:

Arguments for introducing reading and writing

(1) Learners *want to write in English* (DIEHR & RYMARCZYK 2008, WIGGEMANN 2006) and do so independently and quite naturally, without their teacher asking or supporting them to do so, for the same purposes as they use this skill in their L1. HÄGELE (2008: 9) reports on her learners' attempts to send each other messages in English, to try and read individual words or phrases during storytelling or to take notes of words to help them remember.
(2) As a result of this, learners *may get used to wrong spellings* which may be difficult to change. Therefore it is better not to withhold the correct spelling of words: "*There are many English words which cannot be 'sounded out' and the only way to learn them is by sight, but there are so many that to expect children to learn every word visually and to*

commit them to memory creates an unrealistic learning load to them. It therefore makes sense to offer both phonics and word-recognition" (REILLY & REILLY 2005: 12).

(3) Not only are learners interested in writing, but they are also able to identify, understand and become *aware of the different principles upon which different writing systems are based* (ZAUNBAUER 2007: 46).

(4) Learners are *exposed to written English in their everyday lives,* they live in an environment which is no longer monolingual. KARBE (2001: 31f.) lists a wealth of situations ranging from words and phrases on posters, advertisements or foods that learners are exposed to and use quite naturally. She presents a number of ideas of how this potential may be used in the classroom.

(5) Integrating reading and writing *supports learning*. This argument has been put forward by early research into primary EFL classrooms by DOYE & LÜTTGE (1977) and HELLWIG (1995), and has recently been confirmed (EDELENBOS ET AL 2006: 80). Writing segments the stream of sounds into individual words that may support decoding. SCHMID-SCHÖNBEIN (2006b: 3) presents a nice example from German, in which the following utterance *Woisnderstifdgebliem?* can readily be comprehended if represented in writing: *Wo ist denn der Stift geblieben?*

(6) Closely connected to this argument is the argument for *multi-sensory learning* (CLAUS & GERNGROSS 2003). Writing supports visual and tactile learners.

3 Principles for developing reading and writing

Use the potential of reading and writing to support learning

Research into the potential of integrating reading and writing in primary EFL is only just beginning (RYMARCZYK 2007). In line with BÖRNER (2004) or SCHMID-SCHÖNBEIN (2006b) we argue for integrating writing in the classroom by saying in what way it may support learning. We do so by referring to examples of reported good practice that demonstrate positive effects if certain *principles* are followed and *teacher support* is appropriate.

(1) To support learning, progress from listening to reading and then to writing

Offer the written form of words only after learners are absolutely familiar with its meaning and pronunciation. Otherwise learners may pronounce words following the written example. Reading at this level therefore means recognizing words, phrases and texts that are already familiar from oral communication (BÖRNER 2004: 7, BERGNER 2005).

(2) Provide rich learning environments that motivate learners to read and write in the classroom

Motivating learners to read and write may be done in a variety of ways. Reported positive experiences include labeling familiar objects in the classroom (SCHMID-SCHÖNBEIN 2006b: 4), introducing a message board that teachers and learners may use to publish notes from anything as birthdays to special events (HÄGELE 2008: 11), putting up classroom phrases in the form of speech bubbles that the teacher may refer to when learners say familiar classroom management messages in German (BÖRNER 2004: 7, CLAUS & GERNGROSS 2003: 28), or organizing exhibitions of texts and posters of various kinds that learners have produced (i.e. songs, poems, rhymes or word banks; see example below). Ask learners to produce individual mini-dictionaries, for example pocket dictionaries (STOFFEL 2004). Provide an English book corner where learners are encouraged to read and can embark on some exploratory reading, finding out with the help of the pictures or familiar language what a story is about. Children's books often come with a CD so learners may listen while they are reading along (BIMBERG 2003, BÖRNER 2004: 7, BÖRNER & BRUSCH 2004, ZAADE 2003).

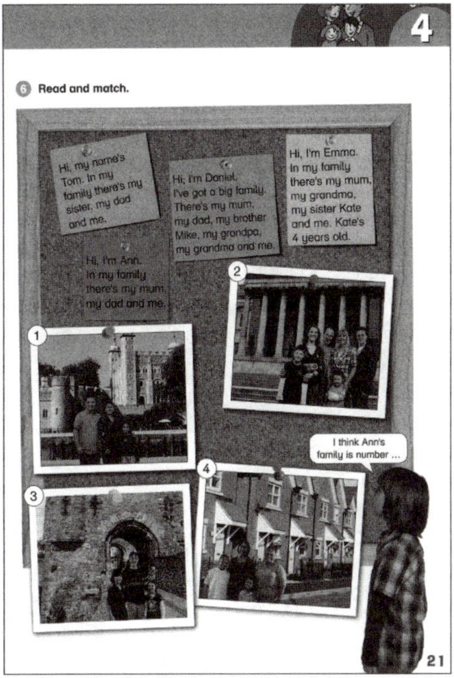

GERNGROSS & PUCHTA (2007). *Playway 3, Pupil's Book,* S. 3, Helbling, Rum/Innsbruck

(3) Integrate learners' everyday experiences with reading English outside the classroom

KARBE (2001: 31f.) lists a number of excellent examples for *language awareness activities*, for example, collecting food items or brand names of which learners are not even aware that they originate from English (i.e. cornflakes or Whiskas – which originates from a cat's whiskers) and finding out what they mean.

(4) Encourage writing based on model texts

GERNGROSS (in a presentation at the University of Education in Freiburg, 2007) argues that *"Schreiben als eigenständige Fertigkeit [Verfassen von Texten] ist in der Grundschule nicht erreichbar, aber möglich und sinnvoll ist die vorbereitende Arbeit für das freie Schreiben"*. To do so, he suggests two kinds of activities:

(a) Copying: matching words / phrases and pictures, gapped texts, crosswords, substitution tables, or jumbled dialogues where learners always may fall back on the correct model, and

(b) Activities that gradually lead learners to writing as a (creative) skill that enables them to communicate personal meanings, such as writing cards (Christmas, birthdays, Valentines, invitations), poems, or other mini model texts (which Gerngross calls *creative copying*) that give learners some space and choice to express individual ideas. This activity follows the steps we have presented when we discussed speaking: First you present a model text, then you reconstruct the model text, produce a text, edit, re-write and publish it. The following two examples (see below) illustrate this procedure: Learners, after being familiar with the poem *I'm not scared*, have the choice to fill in the things they are scared of in this model. Other reported examples include work with skeleton texts in which learners get only the first letter of each word and reconstruct the text orally in pairs or in a group (see Claus & Gerngross 2003: 29) or writing stories or letters to a partner class based on model texts (Baumgarten-Millington 1999; Drese 2000; Wiggemann 2006).

Gerngross & Puchta (2007). *Playway 3, Pupil's Book*, S. 25, Helbling, Rum/Innsbruck

5 Perspectives on reading and writing

Teacher support is central

The classroom teacher has *"a central role in any successes which early language-learning initiatives achieve"* (Edelenboos et al 2006: 158). Without a supportive teacher who is patient and has a feeling for what is appropriate for his or her class, introducing reading and writing may have the negative effects that critics have put forward against its introduction. Börner (2004: 7) in an article with the headline *"Dän kamm the neit"* reports the following incident: Celina had embarked on writing a Christmas-tree story in which she transferred the German spelling she was familiar with to English. Even though the text was anything but correct, it is important to give her some encouraging feedback, saying, that when she reads out her story it may be perfectly well understood but as in English the written form of a word often differs considerably from its oral version, an English child would not be able to read her text. He goes on to say that a teacher could comment learner texts, saying something like: *"I know what you mean. Thank you very much for your letter. An English child would write the letter like this"* (ibid).

Experiment with the learning potential of reading and writing skills

Even though many questions having to do with the potential of developing reading and writing at primary level have not been answered yet (see Diehr & Rymarczyk 2008: 6), using these skills makes sense if the above discussed principles are followed. The introduction of EFL at grade 1 (Baden-Württemberg & Northrhine Westfalia) will probably contribute to it. Bearing in mind that the focus must be on developing oral communicative competences at this language learning level, we argue to experiment with the potential that reading and writing may have for the learners. The examples we have reported in this chapter are encouraging proof that it is worthwhile to do so.

1 Discourse and the lexical approach

Integrating sounds, words, and grammar learning in a holistic way

Pronunciation, words and grammar form the basis of the four language skills (→ ch. 5). In this chapter we will look at how these three sub-skills are related and how we can support young learners in developing them. According to the *Common European Framework* lexical competence consists of *"the knowledge of, and ability to use the vocabulary of a language"* which integrates *"lexical elements and grammatical elements"* (COUNCIL OF EUROPE 2001: 110). Discourse is made up of sounds, words and grammar. It has been defined as *"a general term for examples of language use, i.e. language which has been produced as a result of an act of communication. Whereas grammar refers to the rules a language uses to form grammatical units of language such as CLAUSE, PHRASE, and SENTENCE, discourse refers to larger units of language such as paragraphs, conversations, and interviews"* (RICHARDS ET AL 1992: 111). As the larger unit, discourse usually goes beyond the sentence level and includes all kinds of spoken and written texts. When young learners start learning a foreign language though, they first of all work with the concept of the word as *"a discrete unit. Children will ask what a particular word means, or how to say a word in a foreign language, and, in learning to read, the word is a key unit in building up skills and knowledge"* (CAMERON 2001: 73). While young learners only slowly begin to produce discourse, for example by participating in classroom discourse, they use both words and grammar to construct their first utterances and sentences. At first *"younger children, in particular, are not ready for or interested in thinking about the language system or manipulating the language so as to separate lexical items out of structures. They are interested in the meaning and function of new language more holistically, in order to play a game, sing a song, or act out a story"* (PINTER 2006a: 84). Consequently, as PINTER (2006a: 86) continues *"for younger children vocabulary and grammar should be learnt in a holistic way"*. The BIG circle (2004: 11; → ch. 1) supports this when they describe the basic language competences of young learners:

Wortschatz	Grammatik
Eine grundlegende Kommunikationsfähigkeit in der Fremdsprache verlangt einen Mindestwortschatz. Dieser ergibt sich durch die jeweilige Schüler-, Handlungs- und Themenorientierung.	Am Anfang des fremdsprachlichen Lernprozesses in der Schule steht der Aufbau des Sprachkönnens vor dem Erwerb von Sprachwissen. Den Lernenden wird durch eine sorgfältig strukturierte Präsentation und durch vielfältige Übungsformen ermöglicht, das vorhandene Regelsystem der Fremdsprache weitgehend unbewusst aufzubauen.

Learning words includes learning grammar

At the same time though, while focusing on meaning, children unconsciously pick up a lot of grammar. When children talk about their pets, they do not only want to use the English words for their pets (*rabbit, dog*), but want to say something about their color (*a brown rabbit, a black dog*), their size (*a small rabbit, a big dog*) and exchange other meaningful information (*my budgies have got blue feathers, I like/don't like cats, her favorite food is ...*). Instead of using single words, they want to use language chunks which already include a lot of grammatical features (adjectives, plural forms, negation, possessive case) even though they are not aware that these are aspects of grammar (see also → ch. 2). As CAMERON (2001: 72) puts it, *"vocabulary learning can serve as a stepping stone to learning and using grammar"*. And BATSTONE (1994: 8) supports this when he says, *"grammar does not exist on its own. It is inter-dependent with lexis"*. Since sounds and words form the basis of language learning, we can say with LEWIS (1993: 89) that *"language consists of grammaticalized lexis not lexicalised grammar"*. When using this concept of 'lexicogrammar' or a comparable lexical approach in language teaching, the focus is *"on the main carrier of meaning, vocabulary. The concept of a large vocabulary is extended from words to lexis, but the essential idea is that fluency is based on the acquisition of a large store of fixed and semi-fixed prefabricated items [...]. Grammatical knowledge permits the creative re-combination of lexis in novel and imaginative ways"* but only if *"the learner has a sufficiently large mental lexicon to which grammatical knowledge can be applied"* (LEWIS 1993: 15). In the primary classroom we do not focus on teaching cognitive grammatical knowledge, but on raising grammatical awareness (see below). Before we will show how to teach words and how to develop grammatical awareness, we need to decide which words our learners are supposed to learn, how they store them in their brain, and which competences are involved in mastering a lexical chunk.

2 Selecting and storing words

Choosing a vocabulary basis for young learners

Since the number of words young learners can learn is restricted, we have to carefully select lexical items. This selection is based on the frequency, age-appropriateness (which words do young learners need to express their experiences and ideas?) and accessibility of words (are the words easy to learn? This depends on word features such as difficulty of pronunciation, length of words, complexity of meaning; see also ZANGL & PELTZER-KARPF 1998: 14). The English language contains about 54.000 word families (SCHMITT 2000: 2–3). A word family consists of the base of a word, such as 'play' and all its inflected and derived forms, such as 'plays', 'playing', 'played', or 'playground'. The knowledge of the most frequent 2.000 word families facilitates the comprehension of about 80% of any text (NATION 2001). Child native speakers at the age of eight know about 7–8.000 word families, but a *"realistic target"* for young foreign language learners is about 500 words per year *"given good learning conditions"* (CAMERON 2001:

75). For German learners MINDT and SCHLÜTER (2007: 78–89) propose a basic vocabulary (*Mindestwortschatz*) of 121 words for grades 3 and 4, differentiated into 39 content words, such as nouns, verbs and adjectives, and 82 function words, such as personal and possessive pronouns or prepositions. They base their selection on a corpus analysis of English children's (aged 6–12) language use, *"unter gleichzeitiger Berücksichtigung des Wortschatzes Erwachsener"* (MINDT & SCHLÜTER 2007: 67). They add that a productive extension of this basic count should be possible, and KIEWEG (2005: 20) supports this when he says, *"eine radikale Beschränkung auf einen geringen Mindestwortschatz wäre nach meinen Beobachtungen von Fremdsprachenunterricht in der Grundschule unterfordernd"*. Also, it would be helpful to add to this list a corpus of classroom discourse in the primary school.

Storing lexical chunks in the mental lexicon

When children learn these new words or chunks, they store them in what has been called 'the mental lexicon', a term that describes *"the word-store in the human mind"* (AITCHINSON 1992: 59). SCHMITT (2000: 106) says that the mental lexicon establishes *"a spiderweb of grammatical and semantic relationships between a large number of words"*. But how is this web organised? SCHMITT (2000: 39–40) distinguishes between three kinds of associations: (a) clang associations (which are not related semantically, but in terms of sound), such as *ball – wall, mouse – house*; (b) paradigmatic associations, where words are related to other words of the same class such as synonyms (e.g. *large* and *big*) or antonyms (e.g. *hot* and *cold*) as well as derivations, such as prefixes and suffixes (e.g. *un/happy* or *help/ful*), and word combinations (e.g. *blackboard*); (c) syntagmatic associations that generally focus on different word classes such as adjective-noun pairs (e.g. *beautiful picture*) or verb-noun pairs (e.g. *play ball*). Consequently words are stored semantically by association, i.e. the stimulus of a certain word brings up other words. The word *guinea-pig*, for example, could trigger associations such as brown color, small, or cuddle. This depends on how the word was introduced and networked in the classroom, and it depends on the learner's personal preferences and knowledge. As we will show below we need to teach words in these lexical associations and in meaningful contexts, and help learners construct lexical networks because this eventually supports learners when they try to produce language. As NATTINGER (1988: 75) stresses, *"vocabulary is stored redundantly, not only as individual morphemes, but also as parts or phrases, or even as longer memorized chunks of speech, and that it is oftentimes retrieved from memory as these preassembled chunks"*. This will have consequences for how we best present new words. But before we move on to the teaching of words and grammar we need to have a look at the challenges young learners face when trying to learn words or lexical chunks.

3 Challenges when learning words

Based on a number of suggestions, CAMERON (2001: 77) has come up with a list of different kinds of knowledge that is involved when you know a word.

Knowing a word depends on different kinds of knowledge

Type of knowledge	What is involved	Example
Receptive knowledge; aural/decoding	To understand it when it is spoken/written	*Clothes*, for example is more of a challenge than *house*
Memory	To recall it when needed	Her/his car instead of *teacher car* (→ ch. 2)
Conceptual knowledge	To use it with the correct meaning	To use *make* and *do* correctly, as in *making a cake* and *doing my homework*
Knowledge of the spoken form: phonological knowledge	To hear the word and to pronounce it acceptably, on its own, and in phrases and sentences	To hear and produce the voiced and voiceless sounds, such as in *zoo* (in opposition to the German *Zoo*)
Grammatical Knowledge	To use it in a grammatically correct way; to know grammatical connections with other words	*She sings very well* not *she sings very good*; to know that *is* and *be* are parts of the same verb
Collocational knowledge	To know which other words can be used with it	A *beautiful picture*, not a *good-looking picture*
Orthographic knowledge	To spell it correctly	To spell *house*, and not *haus*
Pragmatic knowledge: knowledge of style and register	To use it in the right situation	To know the difference between *Would you like a drink?* and *What do you want?*

While orthographic knowledge is becoming increasingly important in primary school (→ ch. 5) pragmatic knowledge will develop over time when learners get older and find out how to behave pragmatically correct in a different culture (for example, when taking leave, they would say *see you later* instead of *bye-bye*). When learners encounter a word for the first time they are first of all confronted with its pronunciation.

1 Providing ample practice opportunities for pronunciation

Even young learners have problems when pronouncing English sounds

English pronunciation is a challenge for German learners because the spoken form often does not match the written form and because many of the English sounds do not exist in German. As Kieweg (2005: 20) relates, learners often have difficulties pronouncing words even though children basically are quite good at imitating sounds: *"So kann eine ganze Reihe an SchülerInnen die sog. prosodischen oder suprasegmentalen Elemente der englischen Sprache (Sprachmelodie oder die 'Farbe' einer Sprache) nicht mühelos imitieren. Sie zeigen darüber hinaus erhebliche Schwierigkeiten bei den rhythmischen Betonungs- und Dehnungsmustern und bei den Stimmhöhenkonturen"*. Learners also have problems because of the interferences with their L1 (voiced vs. voiceless as in 'zoo'/'Zoo'; see McDermott 2007 for other examples). Consequently when teaching new words, *"pupils need to hear a new word in isolation as well as in a discourse context, so that they can notice the sounds at the beginning and end, the stress pattern of the word, and the syllables that make up the word. They will need to hear the word spoken in isolation several times to catch all this information"* (Cameron 2001: 86). In this example of teacher talk Cameron provides a good example of how to present the word in an isolated form as well as in the discourse context:

> *An ambulance takes sick people to hospital.*
> *Ambulance*
> *Am-bu-lance*
> *Ambulance*
> *Can you see the ambulance in this picture? (child points to picture)*
> *Yes, there's the ambulance arriving at the hospital*
> (Cameron 2001: 86).

Careful corrective feedback to support pronunciation

Learners need to become actively involved, especially through songs and stories which help them focus on pronunciation and intonation. At the same time, it is essential that we accept mistakes when learners try to pronounce new words and that we provide very careful corrective feedback. Jacobs describes what can happen when learners experiment with language. *"Dadurch kommt es zwangsläufig zu mehr Fehlleistungen [in der Aussprache]. Diese völlig neue Erfahrung führte zunächst zu gewissen Verunsicherungen sowohl bei den Lehrkräften als auch bei den betroffenen Schülern. Sofortige und häufige Korrekturen hatten zur Folge, dass sich diese Schüler [...] in ihren sprachlichen Äußerungen zurücknahmen, aus Angst, zu viele Fehler zu machen"* (Jacobs 2002: 69; see Hutz & Kolb 2007 for suggestions of appropriate error correction; see Mindt & Schlüter 2007: 68–77 for specific difficulties German learners have).

2 Developing the meaning of words

At first young learners often lack the world knowledge to grasp the full

The cognitive development influences meaning construction

conceptual meaning of words. The word *head*, for example, can have different meanings, such as the body part, the head of a school or the head of a state. Children will only learn these different meanings over time when they develop their world knowledge. Younger children make syntagmatic associations when presented with a word, for example by connecting a noun with a verb on the thematic level (*ball – play*). Older children on the other hand produce words from the same word class (*ball – game*) which is a paradigmatic association or categorical association since at that stage of their cognitive development they already think more in categories and abstract connections. A ball would then trigger the connection of 'playing with a ball = a game'. Consequently, as CAMERON (2001: 78) points out, there is a shift from syntagmatic to paradigmatic associations in the course of children's cognitive development. This is important since the fully developed mental lexicon is organized into both of these levels of associations, plus the level of clang associations. In clang associations words that sound similar are stored together. (*ball – wall, mouse – house*; see SCHMITT 2000: 39–40). When beginning to think in categories, learners first use *"the middle of a general to specific hierarchy"*. Instead of using *furniture* (the general end of the hierarchy or superordinate) or *rocking chair* (the specific end of the hierarchy or subordinate) they use the middle word or basic level word *chair* because it is the most often used word (CAMERON 2001: 79). Consequently when teaching vocabulary we can start with these basic level words.

Morphological support when creating meaning

The way words are structured also has an influence on how easily learners understand their meaning and retain them. ZANGL and PELTZER-KARPF differentiate between the frequency of basic morphemes, the ease of a word's segmentation, and the transparency of a word:

> ***Auftretenshäufigkeit:*** *Je öfter ein Morphem in einer Sprache zur Ableitung von Wörtern herangezogen wird, desto früher verwenden es Lernende für die Bildung von Wörtern. Für die Bezeichnung von Opposition ist z.B. das englische Morphem {un} (‚happy' – ‚unhappy') viel häufiger einsetzbar als {in} (‚expensive' – ‚inexpensive') oder {dis} (‚satisfying' – ‚dissatisfying').*
> ***Gute Segmentierfähigkeit (Zerlegbarkeit):*** *Wörter, deren Sinneinheiten (Morpheme) deutlich abgrenzbar sind, wie z.B. ‚paint' – ‚painter' werden früher analysiert als komplexere Wörter wie z.B. ‚strong' – ‚strength'.*
> ***Wortdurchsichtigkeit:*** *Formen, deren Gesamtbedeutung aus den Einzelbedeutungen ablesbar ist, werden klar bevorzugt. So geht z.B. die Bedeutung des Wortes ‚appletree' aus den Einzelbedeutungen von ‚apple' und ‚tree' hervor* (ZANGL & PELTZER-KARPF 1998: 14).

Cultural schemata influence meaning construction

A final aspect which is important when talking about meaning is the cultural meaning of words. The paradigmatic and syntagmatic connections in the mental network create certain schemata. Learners bring their own culturally produced schemata from their L1 culture. This can lead to misconceptions, for example when introducing the word *breakfast*. If the cultural background to different forms of breakfast in England is not provided, then learners will connect it to their L1 schema of what a *Frühstück* is. By exploring the variety of breakfasts, learners will realize similarities and differences as to the cultural scripts this word triggers, which is also a first step to developing intercultural communicative competence (→ ch. 8). All of these challenges and the respective support need to be taken into consideration in the teaching of words.

4 Teaching vocabulary

A sequence to teaching words and lexical chunks

When teaching words or lexical chunks there is a certain sequence to be followed from encountering a word, to storing and finally retrieving it, as HATCH and BROWN (1995: 372) explain, based on their research of learners' strategies:

(1) *having multiple sources for encountering new words*
(2) *getting a clear image, whether visual or auditory or both, for the forms of the new word*
(3) *learning the meaning of the words*
(4) *making a strong memory connection between the forms and meanings of the words*
(5) *using the words.*

To enable learners to transfer new words and chunks from their short-term to their long-term memory (the mental lexicon), i.e. to allow for the deep processing of words, they have to encounter the word repeatedly (between 5–10 times) in different contexts. This is crucial because word learning is a long process. KIEWEG (2005: 21) talks about a phase of up to a year since the networks in the mental lexicon need time to develop. Consequently the question of how many words a young learner can acquire in one lesson is wrong, as KIEWEG (2005: 21) stresses: *„Die Antwort wäre eindeutig: 'Kein einziges!', denn mit der Semantisierung beginnt erst der Lernprozess".* Generally one can say that *"the amount of mental work done by learners affects how well a new word is engraved in memory; the more learners have to think about a word and its meaning, the more likely they are to remember it"* (CAMERON 2001: 85). This leads us to the different ways learners need to encounter and deal with words. KIEWEG (2005: 21) sums up the possibilities: *„deswegen bietet man den Lernenden in thematisch attraktiven Lernepisoden eine möglichst große Menge Wortschatz an und benutzt dafür mehrere Lernkanäle, z.B. visuell (Auge), auditiv (Ohr), haptisch-taktil (Hand, Berührung), kinästhetisch (Körperbewegung), olfaktorisch (Nase) und gustatorisch (Geschmack)".* Visual support is therefore important because writing has not been introduced yet, one important source of visual support that is therefore missing. At the same time it is important not to translate the new word, because this will take away the motivation of understanding it and will not support deep processing of the word.

Networking the meaning of words

To help learners store the words in different mental networks they need to explore the meaning of words, and practice and recycle the lexical chunks in meaningful ways. Take, for example, the topic things in my schoolbag. Learners realize that the word *schoolbag* is a compound of two words and they can individually describe what they find in their schoolbag, thus recycling all the words that belong to the topic web of 'schoolbag'. PINTER (2006a: 89–90) uses the example of the word *sandwich* when dealing with the theme parties, since it presents *"an excellent opportunity to recycle possible types of fillings the children might know, such as jam, or cucumber sandwich, honey, fish, or cheese sandwich, tomato or chicken sandwich, etc., or even silly ones such as frog, or snake sandwiches"*. Children can invent sandwiches and design individual menus, realizing in the process how sandwich *"can interact with language they already know"*. (PINTER 2006a: 90). Allowing learners to create silly sandwiches also supports word retention because it creates an emotional anchor where children laugh about their respective wild mixtures. Anything that is strange, funny or surprising will help learners strengthen the storage of words. Having successfully stored the words, learners will then be able to also retrieve the words for language use in meaningful tasks like the one just mentioned.

5 Creating grammatical awareness

The importance of grammar in language learning

As we have shown above grammatical knowledge develops mostly unconsciously when we pursue a lexical approach in the primary classroom. At the same time teachers can slowly guide their learners to the first stages of grammatical awareness. CAMERON lists the main points why grammar is relevant in communication:

- *Grammar is necessary to express precise meanings in discourse;*
- *Grammar ties closely into vocabulary in learning and using the foreign language;*
- *Grammar learning can evolve from the learning of chunks of language;*
- *Talking about something meaningful with the child can be a useful way to introduce new grammar;*
- *Grammar can be taught without technical labels (e.g. 'intensifiying adverb')* (CAMERON 2001: 98).

In the last few years, there have increasingly been calls for a more explicit teaching of grammatical awareness (see for example KUHN 2006, MINDT & SCHLÜTER 2007). The important difference to the traditional cognitive approach of grammar teaching is that now the focus is on language use and not language knowledge. TEUBNER sums up the reasons why such an approach is necessary for young learners (see also KIEWEG 2005):

- *Kinder im Grundschulalter verfügen über die für Bewusstmachung nötigen kognitiven Voraussetzungen.*
- *Ohne Bewusstmachung geht vielen Kindern vieles durcheinander.*
- *Bewusstmachung als Lernhilfe im Englischunterricht der Primarstufe ist vor allem für lernschwache Schüler unerlässlich.*

- *Viele Schüler haben ein Bedürfnis nach bewusstmachenden Hilfen und fordern diese auch* (TEUBNER 2006: 36; she also provides a good historical overview of the debate about strengthening the grammar focus).

Ways of developing grammatical awareness

When learning their mother tongue children receive extensive language input and sufficient time to implicitly develop grammatical awareness. Time and input are restricted in school, hence we need to support learners in discovering the grammatical functions of language. Based on a slightly changed model by KARMILOFF-SMITH, MINDT and SCHLÜTER have suggested a four-phase model that helps learners to slowly move from implicit to a more explicit awareness about grammar. Here is an example:

Stufe	Beispiel	Stadium der Sprachbeherrschung
Implizit 1	T: *Hello* L: *Hello* T: *Good Morning* L: *Good morning*	imitatives Können
Implizit 2	*One of the mouse**s*** *I bring**ed** three dolls*	übertragbares Können
Explizit 1	*one dog* *two dogs* *a cat* *some cats* *the horse* *many horses* *one lion* ...	übertragbares Wissen
Explizit 2	*"Ist das immer so, dass in der Mehrzahl ein 's' steht?"*	formulierbares Wissen

(MINDT & SCHLÜTER 2007: 33)

While learners only imitate the teacher at first (implicit 1), they soon generate their own hypotheses about how grammar functions (implicit 2). In this example they have noticed the regular past tense which they transfer to irregular forms. This is an example of over-generalization. The same thing happens with the plural form (*mouses – bringed*). On the next level (explicit 1), learners already show grammatical knowledge, by producing the correct plural form, and finally (explicit 2) they even identify and make assumptions about a possible rule. While this example is helpful to show the competences learners are capable of developing we need to be careful not to turn this into a formalized teaching approach by trying to cover all four phases whenever we deal with a grammatical aspect, as it is suggested in some of the literature (see DUDEK 2006, MÖGLICH 2006). It is much more important to create and use opportunities in the classroom to help learners discover or notice words in the lexical chunks and make them realize that these words can be substituted by other words, thus enabling them to use language creatively. Teachers need to look out for these chances to use spontaneous learner contributions (see the rule example above) to insert an awareness sequence rather than pre-planning it, i.e. follow the child when it is ready for it. BATSTONE (1994) has described the process of grammar learning in three phases, from (re)noticing to (re)structuring to proceduralizing. While the first two phases cover MINDT'S and SCHLÜTER'S first three phases, it is proceduralizing which also needs to be integrated into the learning process. As CAMERON (2001: 109) says, *"proceduralization is the stage of making the new grammar ready for instant and fluent use in communication and requires practice in choosing and using the form to express meaning"*. As a final step we would like to present some examples of how BATSTONE'S three phases can be supported in the classroom through different tasks.

Language practice activities	**Example**
Noticing (help L. become aware of new structures): 1. Listen and notice	L. listen to a story that includes prepositions. They tick off the prepositions in an easy grid (that visualizes the grammar function) where they have to decide, for example, if the cat is under or on the table.
2. Using hand puppets (→ ch. 9)	L. listen to a story that describes daily activities (simple present). After having listened to the story twice the T. can use a calendar to ask L. to repeat the key events on their own without the story context, thus helping L. to notice the structure. L. can then repeat the routines by filling in an empty calendar.
Structuring (help L. internalise new structures): 1. Questionnaires, surveys, quizzes	L. interview each other about their food preferences, using the full question form. When presenting their findings to the class, L. will need to re-structure the pattern ('Do you like...?') to a new one: *Six people like pizza, Susanne only likes spaghetti.*
2. Information gap activities	Calendar task – finding a time and activity two L. want to do (the two calendars have different entries): *Shall we meet on Friday? No, sorry, on Fridays I...*
Proceduralizing (help L. automatize grammar use): 1. Describing fantasy animals	L. describe their own or a fantasy animal to the whole class. The public presentation (prepared for by rehearsing) will justify attention to correct form, allowing L. to use specific gram. forms.

(based on CAMERON 2001: 114–20, HALLIWELL 1992: 44)

1 Topics and text types

The dominance of listening texts

In the previous chapters we have shown how the primary language classroom comes to life for children through the complex and dynamic interplay of teacher initiatives, tasks, and materials, which constitute what we call learning opportunities. Furthermore, we have pointed out that the children's need to make sense of what they encounter in the classroom, and their willingness to engage in the challenges these learning opportunities entail, depends to a considerable extent on the content to be explored and the way such exploration is structured and facilitated. Content in the foreign language classroom is organized with the help of themes and is made available through texts. In keeping with the nature of the primary language classroom children will, first of all, encounter a great variety of listening texts. These either derive from communicative events in everyday situations (e.g. friends talking on the phone, a family in a restaurant), or appear as orally staged versions of short literary forms such as fairy tales and children's picture books, which, in turn, may trigger oral responses from the learners. Among the text types easily embedded in listening events and followed by speaking activities are: poetic and rhythmic tests such as songs, tongue twisters, nonsense verses, raps, jazz chants, and poems. Before discussing the multi-faceted potential of such texts for the primary EFL classroom and the demands they pose for learners and teachers, we will start off with some general remarks on literature in language learning.

2 The pedagogical relevance of literary texts

1 The role of literary texts

Literary texts unlock the learner's creative potential

The systematic inclusion of literary texts into EFL classrooms has found growing support in recent years. A number of scholars argue that because of their unique nature, literary texts do not only provide authentic data for language learning, but they also provide motivating content that stimulates students' interests. Literary texts can help to unlock the students' creative potential while appealing to their emotions and simultaneously challenging their established concepts of themselves and the world around them. In this way, they represent a rich resource for (inter)cultural learning, because they make readers not only aware of cultural practices and social conditions, but also of thoughts, emotions, and values accessible through the literary representation of human experiences. Finally, literary texts can be the starting point for a great variety of activities fostering the development of all basic language skills (BREDELLA & BURWITZ-MELZER 2004, COLLIE & SLATER 1987, NÜNNING & SURKAMP 2006). The fundamental tenets of such a view of literary texts can best be summarized with the following seven statements. They also indicate implications for the processes in the EFL classroom. We will explore these tenets with reference to the well-known fairy tail of *The Three Little Pigs* (→ ch. 15.2). In the original version, the first two pigs are eaten by the big bad wolf, because they are careless, lazy and use inferior materials to build their houses. Only the third pig, having built a house of bricks, survives the attacks (huffing and puffing) of the wolf. In the most common adaptations of this story for children in Britain and the US, the big bad wolf chases the first and the second pig into the forest after he has blown their houses down. They eventually find safety in the third pig's house. In the original version, the wolf dies in a kettle of boiling water, after he has failed to blow the brick house down, and after the pig has tricked him several times and resisted temptation. In the adaptations, however, the wolf's life is saved.

2 Seven fundamental tenets

The reader brings the text to life

(1) The language learner as a reader should be the center of the teaching process. This statement goes back to what has become known as Reader Response Theory, characterizing literary reading as a highly constructive, and thus creative, process (Bredella 2007). Since children in the primary EFL classroom are rarely readers in the literary sense of the word, we use the term in a figurative sense, including the learner as a listener or viewer of a presentation of a text. The basic assumption is that the "reader" brings the text to life through a number of creative activities: They need to mobilize their prior knowledge, predict events, hypothesize outcomes, compare, and re-adjust assumptions and expectations. The student-reader will have to respond to areas of indeterminacy by filling gaps and text's silences with their imagination. As for *The Three Little Pigs*, the learners have to create the animals and their houses in their imagination. They have to visualize the wolf, but they are also called upon to reactivate their knowledge of the structure of fairy tales. In short, making sense of literary texts depends on the reader's co-authorship. To foster such processes, learners should be allowed and encouraged to develop, voice, and exchange their feelings, experiences, views, and knowledge of both language and concepts before and while being engaged in a text. It is therefore of central importance that the learners are sensitized to the process of co-creation by becoming an active agent in the dialogue with the text.

The relationship between reader and text

(2) Reading a literary text is directed creation. Even if the learner as reader should be the center of the teaching process, it is not implied that the text's unique way of representing human experience should be ignored. Rejecting a radically subjective view of reading, which overemphasizes the individual's creative process, scholars have underlined the *interactive* nature of the relationship of reader and text. The creative realization of the texts' potential is not arbitrary. It is directed by the text. Therefore the teaching process needs to make sure that learners become aware of how their readings are formed through the text (the way it is told, the choice of characters, the arrangement of the plot). (Bredella 2007, Nünning & Surkamp 2006).

Dialogue between readers

(3) Reading in classrooms occurs within a group situation. If the individual students' attempts of making sense of a text are taken seriously, these individual "readings" provide the basis for the negotiation of meaning in the communication between the different readers, first of all in spoken discourse in small group settings, and, of course, in the whole group. BRUSCH has introduced the concept of *Rezeptionsgespräch* (1986), NISSEN speaks of *Lerngespräch* (1982).

It is important to note here that in the primary classroom such dialogue cannot be realized in the target language. On the other hand, it is crucial that meanings are being explored and morals of stories discussed. For such purposes, clearly marked phases in German are appropriate. The challenge for the teaching process is two-fold: dialogue must be brought about between readers and the text and at the same time, a reception must be created among the readers (cf. KRAMSCH 1985). This complex inter-textual relationship between individual readings in the social setting of a classroom is represented schematically in model 7.1

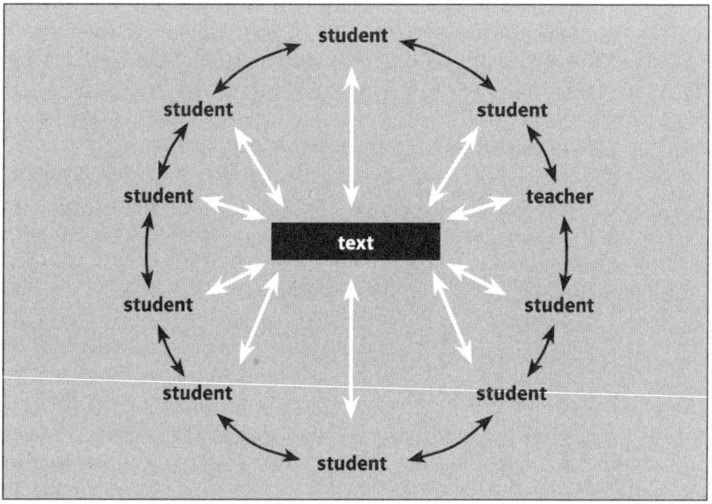

Model 7.1 (cf. KRAMSCH 1985: 358)

The importance of tasks

(4) Sustained motivation is generated more by task than by text and topic. The initial interested response to a text or topic will wear off quickly if it does not lead to an imaginative exploration of the text's potential. As we have argued above, it is the task which makes texts accessible and guides the exploratory process of sense making and negotiation of meaning. Literary texts pose a variety of demands on the learners, ranging from lexical items and register to cognitive and cultural challenges. These challenges may be counterproductive to the learners' engagement, unless they are met with the appropriate support supplementing the tasks.

The importance of learner texts

(5) Learner texts need to be taken seriously. Learner texts, i.e. texts produced by learners, either written or oral, grow out of the special conditions of the individual and collective processes of sense making and negotiation of meaning. They appear in three general forms, as (a) unstructured and structured "reading" responses (learners respond to the teacher's presentation of the story, express surprise, anger, joy), (b) as more or less elaborate inter- and extra-textual variations deriving from writing or creating further sections of stories, completing open endings, inventing new characters, situations and places of action, (c) as more or less elaborate reflections on the learning process. Whereas the first two forms can be realized in the target language, the third form would again require code-switching between English and German: learners might comment on the different scenes they have created in the lives of the three pigs, the media they have used, and the tasks they were engaged in. Learner texts constitute a pedagogically highly significant intertextuality, because they make individual readings accessible to classroom communication (LEGUTKE 2007).

The role of culture

(6) Literary texts allow for the exploration of cultural diversity. As KRAMSCH (1993: 8) has pointed out, if language "is seen as a social practice, culture becomes the very core of language teaching." Including foreign literature, which already represents linguistic otherness, is ideal since it allows learners to experience other cultures and value systems. In the process of relating their own values and world view(s) to those represented in the text, comparing and contrasting them, learners have a chance to change and coordinate perspectives, and thus learn to come to grips with cultural diversity (HALLET 2007). For example, the group might explore reasons why publishers and authors in the US and Britain deviate from the original version of a fairy tale by letting the first two pigs and the wolf survive.

Stories as discourse events

(7) Literary texts need to be integrated into larger thematic and textual units. This statement highlights a second significant dimension of intertextuality: relating a literary text to other text types within a thematic web helps to create a complex learning environment for multifaceted discourse in the language classroom. Learner texts and texts from other domains (historical texts, texts from public media, visual texts) are assembled to express and explore meaning. To bring about such a "play of texts" (HALLET 2002: 29–30, 144–45) is not only the task of the teachers, but also a chance for the learner to contribute to the learning environment (e.g. through texts found on the Internet). It would make sense to place the *Three Little Pigs* and their various adaptations and media representations into the larger framework of exploring fairy tales in German (→ ch. 10).

3 Literary texts in early language learning

1 Short narrative forms: Stories and picture books

The curriculum

Because stories constitute an integral part of human existence, we cannot exist without constantly telling stories. This activity plays a part not only in our private lives (telling people about what we have experienced), but also in the professional world (a teacher recounting a particular classroom event). In each of these instances a story can be seen as part of a larger unit which linguists call discourse. If we take a discourse perspective of a story we are not only examining the oral text produced by the speaker, but also the relationship between the text and the situation in which it occurs. From this point of view, stories are communicative events in which storyteller and listener interact, and where language is not only used in a particular context, but at the same time develops as a result of this contextualized use. We may call this situation a discourse event. (cf. CAMERON 2001: 37). It partly derives from the interplay of the storyteller's intention and his/her linguistic ability to communicate these intentions, as well as the ability and willingness of the listener to collaborate in creating the event by following the storyteller's story-line, accepting the suggested topic, etc. The storyteller will have to build his/her presentation on the prior knowledge of the listener, will react to paralinguistic signals of his/her audience and may (re) direct the message through emphasis, repetition, or omission.

Folk and fairy tales

Experience with folk tales

By the time they start their English classes, most children will have experienced a great variety of these tales. All of them are adaptations of universal folk tales which, before they became fixed in written form, had been handed down in oral form by storytellers. Because of their universal nature and because of the various culturally distinct variations of the old sources, this form of literature provides a particularly rich resource for the primary classroom.

- Drawing on L1 knowledge of formulaic language, children will be able to make sense of formulae such as *once upon a time …, and they all lived happily ever after …*
- By activating their prior knowledge of plot structures such as the three-step quest or trial to be mastered, the three wishes to be made, or the three riddles to be solved, children will succeed in discovering meaning in L2 texts.
- The same is true for building on familiar sets of stock characters (the king, the queen, the good and wicked animals, the good mother and the wicked stepmother, etc.) when children are trying to make sense of L2 texts of this kind.
- Finally, these tales are built on binary opposites. Events and characters illustrate fundamental conflicts (good and evil, danger and safety, greed and the ability to resist temptation).

This 'genre specific expertise of children' (cf. Burwitz-Melzer 2000: 37) will help them to discover and create meaning. Thus providing for a particularly motivating experience of success because children can rediscover what they have already learned in their L1. Furthermore, the culturally distinct variations of the adaptations offer an additional incentive for discovery. The tale of the *Three Little Pigs* is a good case in point.

Action stories

Staging a story

This type of narrative, deriving from the teaching approach known as Total Physical Response (→ch. 4), is best characterized as a dramatic event orchestrated by the teacher. The children's book *We're Going on a Bear Hunt* (Rosen & Oxenbury 1997) may serve as an example here. A group of children is lead on a *bear hunt* and has to overcome many obstacles (high grass, a deep river, a dark forest, a heavy snowstorm), until they finally reach the bear's cave. Scared by the bear, the children run back the same way they came and hide in their beds. Repetitive chunks of language and structures are minimally changed according to the new situation and provide the language input for classroom action as exemplified by the following adaptation of the story by Curtain & Pesola (1994: 256–58):

> *"Let's go on a bear hunt!"*
> *"Everybody ready?"*
> (Class responds "Yes!" or "Yes, ready!")
> *"Let's go!"*
> *"Look at the big wood!"*
> (Make hand gesture for "big", point to visual of woods.)
> *"We can't go around it!"*
> (Make hand gesture for "around".)
> *"We can't go over it!"*
> (Make hand gesture for "over".)
> "We have to go through it!"
> (Make hand gesture for "through", or "straight ahead".)
> (Slap hands on legs rhythmically to represent walking through the wood.) ..."

This type of jointly staged story, directed by the teacher using mainly direct and indirect commands, is obviously only appropriate in specific educational settings. Particularly in classrooms with young learners at the beginning of their language development, this type of approach may serve the important purpose of conveying and creating meaning. This is achieved because this type of story relies and builds on the learners' knowledge of the world (here the concept of a hunt, the specific nature of woods and wilderness, danger and how to deal with it, etc.). At the same time, it takes into account the fact that learners have a rather limited knowledge of vocabulary. This is compensated by the stage director (the teacher) providing supportive gestures and mime.

Children's stories and picture books

Interaction between visual elements and language

The use of original picture books is in many ways appropriate for the primary school, because they offer a wide range of narrative materials. Take for example CARLE's *The Very Hungry Caterpillar* (CARLE 1974) or SENDAK's *Where the Wild Things Are* (SENDAK 1988). In each case, the intricate relationship between visual and textual elements makes these stories interesting for both learners and teachers.
"While picture books do not offer readers the same prolonged identification with a character as longer narrative fiction, what they do offer is a compressed moment in which the character – human, mythical, cartoon or animal – encounters some sort of moral dilemma that needs to be resolved, and in the process the character learns something" (MICHAELS & WALSH 1991: 35). There are many story books for children whose language alone is not enough to make the story comprehensible. The plot becomes clear only in the interaction between the visual elements and the language. Therefore, in order for the listener to understand it, the storyteller has to use the visuals to add the missing parts at the same time as the story is being read or told, e.g. *The Very Hungry Caterpillar* (CARLE 1974). Although a great number of these picture books are suitable for use in a variety of meaningful activities in the EFL classroom, teachers must ask themselves if they are appropriate for learners whose linguistic competence is still limited but who have reached a level of intellectual maturity which requires more demanding content (BURWITZ-MELZER 2007).

The structure of stories

The principle of economy

What makes good stories appealing is the fact that they follow the principle of economy coupled with the principle of coherence: the important elements of the story are connected in such a way that they make immediate sense. *"In those stories which children find most engaging there are only those events and details which further the underlying rhythm"* (EGAN 1986: 25). These organizing features (narrative economy, coherence and story rhythm) provide an important basis for both comprehension and presentation. Even the linguistically rather simple story of *The Very Hungry Caterpillar* (CARLE 1974), has some of the prototypical features we list below. This is achieved in the particular way in which the linguistic and visual elements complement each other. Bearing in mind the examples we have included in this chapter we can now summarize the organizing features as follows: Stories

- have a clear beginning and ending,
- use formulaic language,
- deal with a central theme (narrative economy),
- often use binary opposites (e.g. bad wolf and good pigs),
- present a sequence of often repetitive events (e.g. a three-step quest),
- follow a linear temporal sequence,
- simplify a complex reality in a way which is easy to understand (coherence),
- establish a particular story rhythm,

- combine predictability with elements of surprise,
- have a moral which may or may not be made explicit.

Although these fundamental features apply especially to traditional tales, many of them can be found in other story events as well.

2 Poetic and rhythmic texts

Texts for oral performance

While learners encounter narrative texts predominantly in listening events, in which they might join in orally by co-producing chunks of language (short dialogues, repetitive structures, and taking over the role of a character), poetic and rhythmic texts (songs, poems, raps) are mainly meant for oral productions. Through the combination of sound, rhythm, and meaning in the act of performance, learners not only experience language holistically as meaningful and exciting, but also find ways of continuous oral practice. Repetitions which would be boring otherwise, turn into an enjoyable event, if done in the framework of an appealing song.

- Songs, poems and rhymes are easily integrated in almost any lesson.
- Alliterations, repetitions and rhymes make it easier to memorize new words and chunks; phonetically difficult words can be practiced easily.
- Being engaged in the performance of such texts significantly increases the individual learner's speaking time in the protected environment of a group.
- These types of texts can structure classroom rituals (greetings in the morning, closing the lesson, celebrating a birthday, accompanying the change of weather and the seasons).

4 Selecting and analyzing literary texts

Since it is an important goal of the language classroom to teach children how to make sense of and to communicate in the target language, it is legitimate to use literary texts to introduce and practice specific language features. However, if these texts are reduced to being mere vehicles for language practice, they might not only lose their magic, but children will also be turned off once they experience them as the sugar coating for language work. With this warning in mind we can now turn to the question of which texts to select.

1 Teacher's comfort level

Quality of the text

What EGAN says about stories in his book *Primary Understanding* (1988), is also true for other genres and provides a good entry point into what is meant by this: "*A touchstone of what counts as an adequate story for children might sensibly be whether the adult teacher or researcher will go back to that story for pleasure and be moved by it. As C. S. Lewis rather brusquely puts it: 'No book is worth reading at the age of ten which is not equally (and often far more) worth reading at the age of fifty – except, of course, books of information. The only imaginative works we ought to grow out of are those which it would have been better not to read at all'"* (Lewis as quoted in Egan 1988: 98). Egan's statement should not be reduced to the issue of plot and content, but needs to be read in a wider sense. It also covers aesthetic qualities such as the interplay of words and art work in children's books and, of course, audio and audio-visual versions of stories to be used in the classroom.

2 Appropriateness

Learners' cognitive development and maturity

Equally important are the following questions: Will the text capture the learners' attention, arouse their curiosity, and stimulate their willingness to make a sustained effort to make sense of the text, even if it may be too difficult for them to understand when they first encounter it? The language classroom confronts the teacher with a unique problem here, resulting from the fundamental mismatch between the learners' intellectual development and their linguistic competence. Because the latter is not as well developed as the former, careful decisions need to be made as to which texts the learners can be exposed to without injuring their sense of maturity. Appropriateness, on the other hand, should not only apply to the chosen text, but also to the choice of tasks to be done in the classroom.

3 Authenticity

Learner engagement and text quality

The term authenticity has two dimensions. The first one refers to the *quality of materials*, the second to *the quality of activities* connected with the materials in the classroom. Authentic texts are those which were written for readers whose natural language environment is the target language, and not for foreign or second language learners. Authentic texts, therefore, stand out because they have the quality of natural speech in contrast to reduced speech, which has been constructed for teaching purposes only. The important question is whether such texts are accessible to learners. Starting from the particular mixture of the familiar and the unfamiliar elements of a text, the teacher needs to decide whether it should be shortened or simplified. The challenge, though, is to keep the intrinsic qualities of the text: its magic, its appeal, and its potential for enjoyment. In a discussion on authenticity, Breen (1985) relates the concept to the text brought into the classroom (our first dimension), to the learners' involvement with the text generated by the learning tasks (our second dimension), and to the social situation of the classroom which constitutes the learning environment (→ chs. 2 & 3). For us, it is the learners' involvement and the tasks done in the classroom which are important. With the focus on learner engagement with the text, it does not matter whether a text is authentic (i.e. written for native speakers) or whether it was written specifically for teaching and learning purposes. What matters is what learners do with it: e.g. respond non-verbally and/ or verbally to the teacher's presentation of the story, miming events or producing a relevant piece of artwork.

4 Structure

Plot, setting, conflict and solution

Especially narrative texts need careful analysis. The elements we have listed above provide the necessary orientation. CAMERON points out critically: *"Most often they lack a plot; instead of setting up a problem and working towards its resolution, the characters just move through a sequence of activities. Teachers should not assume that such non-stories will capture children's imagination in the same way that stories can do"* (2001: 162). Analyzing the structure of a text will not only support the teacher's efforts to determine its quality and decide whether it might appeal to the learners. It will also help them become aware of the text's teaching potential.

5 Teaching and learning potential

Six interrelated dimensions

Six interrelated dimensions need to be considered here:
The psychological dimension: A teacher may choose a text simply to provide their learners with a moment of enjoyment. These emotions could be created by a story or a poem (its form and content) or by the experience of success and achievement that the presentation of the text brings (e.g. a rap song). Learners feel encouraged and rewarded because they can comprehend what is being presented to them or they can successfully present the text themselves.
The educational dimension: Literary texts carry meaning for the children to discover and lessons for them to learn. Of interest here is whether, and in what way, the text represents human experience, whether children can relate to it, and what can be explored in terms of values, morals and cultural learning. It would be a pity to sacrifice this educational dimension for the sake of language training. Since it is seldom possible to deal with the deeper meaning and the message a text conveys in the target language, the teacher would have to hold a conversational phase in a circle session in German.
The linguistic dimension: A text can be analyzed from three different perspectives. The lexical perspective focuses on lexical items. Here the teacher needs to decide which of them need to be pre-taught before the learners encounter the text, and which should be further emphasized and practiced. The structural perspective, on the other hand, looks beyond the single word and focuses on chunks of language (e.g. repetitive elements, which can often be transferred to contexts beyond the text (→ ch. 6). Finally, the textual perspective looks at language use from a discourse point of view, i.e. it goes beyond particular chunks of language and tries to assess the relationship between narrative and dialogic elements as they occur in the text. Stories and children's books, for example, contain extensive dialogue or have narrative passages which can be adapted for dialogue, and so they have a particularly rich potential for teaching and learning. Learners in elementary schools are not expected to tell stories themselves. It may, however, be useful to invite them to act out key dialogues from the story in follow-up activities.

The skill dimension: Since children experience English in primary school primarily in its spoken form, the development of listening skills plays a dominant role. However, children may produce spoken language when they interact with the teacher in the process of storytelling. In spite of this, students will rarely be asked to re-tell a story because a very high level of linguistic competence would be necessary to complete such a task after listening. On the other hand, they could learn poems or songs by heart. In any case, the teacher needs to be aware which of the skills might be involved and in what way they might be developed. Although the literacy skills of reading and writing play a less prominent role in the primary classroom, they should not entirely be overlooked here. Written words or networks of words could supplement the text and thus function as anchors for comprehension prompts to retell parts of a story, to act out some key dialogues, or to present a poem. The teacher might also decide whether they want to make a print version of the text available for individual reading in the classroom's reading corner.
The social dimension: This means that the teacher will try to decide whether a text is suitable for cooperative action either during the presentation or during the follow-up activity phase.
The curricular dimension conceptualizes a text as part of larger units that go well beyond the language classroom and embrace other subject areas such as the Arts, Social Studies and Physical Education. This curricular dimension is very important for a number of reasons (→ ch. 10). On the one hand, a thematic connection of this kind gives the teacher opportunities to explore some of the deeper meanings of a text, which cannot be done in the English lesson alone (for example, cultural meaning, values, morals, social rules and roles, similar stories in other cultures etc). However, if a teacher has dealt with a particular topic in other curricular areas, learners will have the necessary knowledge to help them understand content in the foreign language. Finally, the thematic connection will help learners to understand different, often separate, curricular areas better and thus support their cognitive and emotional development. A good example to illustrate this point is CARLE's *The Very Hungry Caterpillar* (1997). This story could either lead to an exciting exploration of the metamorphosis of insects, or the teacher could explore the topic before they present the story (for further details of thematic webbing → ch. 10).

6 Media: Visual and audiovisual support

Modes and media

Since media will be dealt with in chapter 9, a few remarks will suffice here. An interesting question that follows from the selection of a text refers to the media form in which it is available for classroom use. A classical fairy tale might be chosen both in a well-illustrated story book and in an animated film adaptation such as our example of the *Three Little Pigs* because of its multi-modality (→ ch. 9). In other words, this criterion asks for the availability and quality of visual and audiovisual material and considers their appropriate use in the classroom.

5 Approaches to literary texts

Principles for classroom action

Throughout this chapter we have referred to how short literary texts can be approached in the primary EFL classroom. Returning now to the seven statements which opened this chapter, we can submit a set of principles which should guide classroom work.

- *Prior knowledge:* The children's ability to make sense of new and unknown texts depends on the way their prior knowledge can come into play in the interactive processes. Prior knowledge encompasses micro-level questions of vocabulary as well as macro-level issues of conceptual and cultural knowledge.
- *Discourse events:* Literary texts come to life in discourse events, where processes of presentation and comprehension interact. The language classroom needs to provide a great variety of such events.
- *Co-authorship and co-production:* In relation to literary texts, the learners should be thought of as active agents in creating meaning. Their contributions range from non-verbal expressions and short verbal utterances during a story telling session to mini (learner) texts in written (drawings, cartoons, captions) and oral form (role plays), from presenting a poem verbally to illustrating the written text.
- *Cooperation and group experience:* Even if individual learners should be enabled to recite a poem in public or act in a role play derived from a story book, such individual performances necessitate the protective space of small and large group activities preparing and thus empowering the learners for individual language use.
- *Tasks*: Once again the crucial role of appropriate tasks needs to be emphasized. Even the most exciting literary texts will not speak for themselves. Rather, they need to be made accessible to the learners, they need to be staged in the classroom, framed in thematic units and related to the world of the learners, so that their magic, power and meaning can be explored and enjoyed.
- *Intertextuality:* Approaches which connect the English lesson with other subject matter foster a stimulating "play of texts" even in primary school. Literary texts are particularly suited for cross-curricular endeavors.
- *Multi-skill approach:* Even if the primary emphasis is put on the development of listening skills, working with literary texts should go beyond a single skill approach and include not only speaking, but at least some forms of reading and writing.
- *Multi-sensory learning:* Last, but not least, the inclusion of literary texts in the primary EFL classroom is called for because such integration fosters multi-sensory experiences crucial for language acquisition (→ ch. 2).

1 ICC: The main goal of language learning

The aim of ICC – the 'intercultural speaker'

In this chapter we will look at the main goal of foreign language learning, which is intercultural communicative competence (ICC), and what we can do to start developing this complex aim in the primary language classroom. According to the *Common European Framework*, every learner is already *"competent in his or her mother tongue and the associated culture"* when they enter the classroom for the first time (Council of Europe 2001: 43). The learners bring different mother tongues and cultural identities into the classrooms which are increasingly becoming multilingual and multicultural. Learners express their identities through language. Consequently, foreign language learning integrates linguistic and cultural learning. For this reason, the monolingual native speaker model cannot be the dominant language model anymore (see Kramsch 1998). Instead we need a model which integrates this linguistic and cultural diversity. It has been named "intercultural speaker" (Byram 1997: 31–2). For Kramsch (1994: 138), a language learner is an intercultural speaker if s/he has developed the following competences

1. *communicate appropriately with native speakers*
2. *get to understand others*
3. *get to understand themselves.*

The challenge of ICC – what children can do

When learners use the foreign language they want to talk about things that are related to their own cultural upbringing, their hobbies, ideas, or dreams. When talking to a speaker from another cultural background, learners do not only need to be able to express these ideas in a linguistically appropriate way, but they also need to listen to and try to understand what the interlocutor has to say. They have to be open to and interested in the conversation, and since language is culturally grounded, they have to relate to this person's cultural background. Understanding might also involve aspects such as empathy, tolerance, and a change of perspective. *The Common European Framework* (Council of Europe 2001: 43) and most of the primary curricula (see, for example, Ministerium für Kultus 2004: 69) ask for the development of ICC. But learning to become an intercultural speaker is a life-long process and in primary school we can only begin to develop this competence on a very simple level. Before we present a model of how to analyze and teach ICC, we will ask to what extent children can actually deal with cultural differences, and how German primary schools have attempted to integrate cultural learning into foreign language teaching in the past.

Doyé (2005: 4–7) has pointed out that often, teachers who try to make things as easy as possible for young learners, *"neglect the cognitive dispositions of primary school children for explicit linguistic information as well as their readiness to occupy themselves with people and objects that are strange or unfamiliar to them; in other words, with foreign cultures"*. Consequently we need topics and tasks that help develop ICC in a child-appropriate way (*kindgemäß*, as Kubanek-German 1996 says). Research has shown that even at the age of five children are able to see themselves as part of an ethnic group and that at the age of seven they are able to question stereotypes (Marschollek 2003: 4). In a longitudinal study over two years with more than 700 primary school children, Marschollek (2003: 6) has found out, *"dass der Unterricht die Persönlichkeitsentwicklung der Kinder fördert, sofern er ihnen immer wieder gezielt die Möglichkeit eröffnet, über Sprache(n), Menschen und Kulturen zu reflektieren"*. At the age of 8 the *"child is conscious that each individual is aware of the other's perspective and that this awareness influences self and other's view of each other"* (Selman in Doyé 1999: 37). This is crucial since the development of ICC depends to a large extent on the ability of becoming aware of different perspectives.

2 Teaching culture in the primary classroom: A short history

***Heimatkunde* and *Landeskunde* is insufficient**

The traditional concept of *Heimatkunde* concentrated on the children's close surroundings of their home town before dealing with the region, the nation and the wider world, i.e. it followed the principle of moving from the known to the unknown or foreign, from one's own culture to other cultures. But today children do not live in a mono-cultural environment anymore. Instead, they often live in a multi-cultural environment where 'things foreign' are very close to them: they are in touch with other cultures through the people who live in their neighborhood, through their peers, mass-media, or tourism. International migration brings children from different cultures into the classroom, even globalization affects children, for example, when we think of the toys children play with (see Kubanek-German 2003: 143–49). Consequently we need to integrate young learners' environments and prepare them for intercultural encounters in their direct surroundings. This is why we need a more complex cultural studies approach in the foreign language classroom than the traditional *Landeskunde* approach which just concentrates on basic cultural information (for a general discussion of the *Landeskunde* approach versus the cultural studies approach see Müller-Hartmann & Schocker-v. Ditfurth 2004: 110-12). Kubanek-German (2003: 102) outlines the challenges that come with migration, Europeanization, and globalization: *"Kulturelles Lernen lässt sich nicht mehr wie vor 30 Jahren auf elementare Informationen über Großbritannien und die USA [...] und eine aufgeschlossene Haltung gegenüber diesen Ländern beschränken. Vielmehr umfassen die Aufgabenbereiche bereits für die Grundschule Informationen im Sinn der klassischen Landeskunde, Erziehung zu einem europäischen Bewusstsein, global education/ Verständnis für eine Welt, interkulturelles Lernen in der Schulklasse, cultural awareness und gegebenenfalls binationales Lernen für eine Begegnung, wobei die Gewichtung von der jeweiligen Konzeption abhängt"*.

Encountering foreign languages and cultures in- and outside the classroom

During the last 20 years, German primary schools have designed different EFL programs to tackle these challenges, the most important ones being *Lerne die Sprache des Nachbarn* along the German/French border (PELZ & WECKMANN 1989) and the *Begegnungssprachenkonzept* in Nordrhein-Westfalen (KUBANEK-GERMAN 2003: 111–13). In the latter it was intended to open a window to other languages and cultures, creating an awareness for the equal value of all languages. The focus was not on teaching communicative competences in the language of encounter but on learning about cultures, especially those that were represented by the learners in the classroom. Those components of the program were usually taught in German and there were no extra lessons provided in the curriculum to teach the language of encounter: *"Begegnung an Sprachen soll Interesse an Sprachen und Freude am Umgang mit ihnen wecken, die Gleichwertigkeit der Sprachen und Kulturen bewusst machen und dadurch einen Beitrag zur interkulturellen Erziehung leisten; [...] sie soll zum gegenseitigen Verstehen erziehen und dazu beitragen, dass bei den Kindern Vorurteile und ethnozentrische Denkweisen nicht entstehen"* (KULTUSMINISTERIUM NRW 1992: 2). The main problem was that these lessons had no explicit focus on a particular language. Communicative competence was not fostered (see also KUBANEK-GERMAN 2003: 111–12 for a critique of this concept). This is quite different in the across-the-border projects along the German/French and the German/Czech border where learners learn each others' language and then use it in carefully planned encounters. Teachers often consider direct encounters (*Austauschpädagogik* or *pédagogie des échanges*) as the best form of cultural learning which is why it has been promoted as the main approach for foreign language learning (see for example BAUMGRATZ-GANGL 1993). Research has shown though that often learners come back with new stereotypes or that they tend to generalize single events (see MÜLLER-HARTMANN & GRAU 2004: 2–3). Consequently, such encounter programs need long-lasting institutional support, teachers' training, and careful planning to be effective.

The situation today – integrating language and cultural awareness

Today, competence-oriented foreign language courses are the standard in Germany. They attempt to integrate both the development of language and cultural awareness approaches to intercultural learning, using the diverse cultural potential that our learners bring to the classroom and the opportunities through real and/or virtual encounters (for an overview see DOYÉ 1999: 19–22). This approach integrates the development of language and cultural awareness in a process of cultural discovery, through which *"Kinder daran gewöhnt werden, das Entdecken und die Entschlüsselung von Fremdartigem als bereichernde Freude zu empfinden"* (PIEPHO 1998: 36). Only if the seemingly normal can be experienced as different can children develop cross-cultural awareness by comparing languages and cultures. PIEPHO presents the example of a learner posing the question *"Are turkeys from Turkey?"*, which demonstrates this learner's awareness of language, since he realizes that both words have the same stem. On a cultural level this question led to a project of finding out about turkeys in Germany and other countries like the U.S. And when learners asked if turkeys are also eaten in Turkey, cross-cultural learning ensued. As PIEPHO (1998: 37) describes it,

> *plötzlich war das Thema Essen (food) nicht mehr nur ein unverbindliches Sammeln von Wortschatz mit ebenso unverbindlichen Äußerungen mit I like/I don't like. Vielmehr war nun, auch durch ein Kind aus jüdischem Elternhaus, das Thema: We eat/We never eat…, is kosher/not kosher, […]. Jewish/kosher butchering war auch für Kinder mit islamischer Religionszugehörigkeit ein Thema.*

The focus here is not on cultural knowledge, but on taking advantage of the opportunities that come up spontaneously in the classroom from the learners' perspectives. PIEPHO shows that awareness of other cultures in the classroom leads to new questions and opportunities for learning that often are initiated by the learners themselves. The same thing happened in an English lesson where numbers were the topic and the learners remarked, "*Wenn wir die Zahlen jetzt auch auf jugoslawisch und türkisch lernen, dann können wir überall einkaufen*" (FELBERBAUER 1991: 13). At the same time awareness-raising might lead to a different view of classmates ("*Der Minoir kann das aber sehr gut! Für ihn ist das schon die dritte Sprache die er lernt!*" See FELBERBAUER 1991: 12), and it might provide positive learning experiences for children who have difficulties in other subjects because of their L1 ("*Jetzt traut sich sogar die Shezana fragen, weil auf Englisch kann sie es genauso gut wie wir!*" See FELBERBAUER 1991: 11). These examples show that language and cultural awareness are closely related and that they need to be taught in an integrated way. Instead of merely teaching cultural facts we need to focus on the process of teaching a complex set of competences. Even though young learners are only beginning to develop ICC, we need a comprehensive model to help us as teachers to understand the different aspects that are involved in teaching language and culture. BYRAM's (1997) model of ICC does just that.

3 Teaching ICC: A model

BYRAM'S model of ICC

By applying BYRAM's model to the primary classroom we will show which competences may be reached at that level and how to go about it. We will start by presenting two examples of cultural learning.

a) Schools around the world (textbook)

In *Bausteine Magic 4* (PIEPHO 2005: 4–7) the first chapter deals with schools around the world. After having matched six countries on a world map with the respective flags and a short text which describes school activities, learners learn about a day at school in Sengerema, Tanzania (ibid. p. 6). Four photos show children walking to school which takes one hour, sitting in the classroom with 50 pupils, playing with friends and being involved in Hadithi, a subject where learners act out stories that they have been told. Additionally, one child describes his school day in a letter. The task is: "Read the letter and look at the photos. What's different? What's the same?"

b) The Teddy Bear Project (tele-collaborative project)
The Teddy Bear Project has the following goals: "*The aim of this project is to team pairs of schools and have them exchange a teddy bear or other soft toys. The bear then sends home a diary by e-mail describing its adventures, the places it has been, as well as the things it has seen and done. The project aims to enhance understanding and acceptance of diverse cultures*" (www.iearn.org.au/tbear; see also www.pestalozzischule-weilburg.de/teddybear/index.html for learner texts, and http://www.goethe.de/lhr/prj/wdt/deindex.htm). The sending class prepares the teddy bear for his trip to a primary school in Australia, for example, designing a passport, packing his little backpack and adding a small dictionary and sun lotion against the strong sun in Australia (see ELLERMANN 2007 for these and more ideas). Learners in the receiving class take the teddy bear home, to the dentist or any other daily event in the week the teddy bear visits. They take pictures of these situations and then write about the teddy bear's experiences in a web blog (see ELLERMANN 2008 erscheint), diary or in e-mail letters. The main task is to exchange a number of mails/letters with a partner, using the word fields they have learned so far. This includes season's greetings, birthday cards, valentine cards, and descriptions of daily activities at home or in school.

	Skills interpret and relate	
Knowledge of self and other; of interaction; individual and societal	**Education** political education; critical cultural awareness	**Attitudes** relativising self; valuing other
	Skills discover and/or interpret	

(BYRAM 1997: 34)

In his model of ICC, BYRAM integrates the five basic competences of communicative language teaching, grammatical, discourse, sociocultural, and strategic competence, as well as the competence of mediation (see SAVIGNON 2001: 17, and MÜLLER-HARTMANN & SCHOCKER-V. DITFURTH 2004: 20–6 for an overview).Young learners in the primary classroom will be able to develop these different areas to a certain extent with the help of age-appropriate tasks and the support of their teacher. While the different parts of the model have to be seen in relation to each other, we will present them here individually.

Affective level or attitudes

The central aspect of the affective level is openness towards the other culture and curiosity to enable learners to de-center from their own perspective. In our two examples learners will become curious about children's lives in the other culture through the authentic photos in the course book and the cuddly toy from Australia which arrives in their classroom, as well as the e-mails, blog entries, and pictures of their partners, telling them about the adventures of the animal they have sent. By experiencing the other culture in an authentic way (instead of just finding drawings in a textbook), learners can relate to the life of their peers, which is the first step to making comparisons to and de-centering from their own experiences.

Cognitive level or knowledge

On the cognitive level, learners deal with cultural information that forms part of the traditional *Landeskunde* approach. Learners engage with their auto-stereotypes (positive/negative stereotypes a person has about his or her own culture) and hetero-stereotypes (positive/negative stereotypes somebody has about other cultures). By looking at the flags and different countries in the course book the learners realize that English is spoken in many different countries. Through the photos and letter, they learn a lot about school life in Tanzania which might already question some of the stereotypical images they have about Africa as being only a very poor continent with suffering children. Yes, the classroom is small and there are 50 pupils in it, and they have to walk one hour to get to school, but they also have fun playing with their friends or participating in the Haddithi lesson, and they all learn English like the learners in Germany do (see O'Sullivan & Rösler 2005 for another example that works with story books). As Kubanek-German (2003: 150–51) points out, we need to get closer to the age-specific, authentic culture young learners are occupied with: TV, comics, English news for children (*Children's Express* in London, for example. For a discussion of Culture with a capital 'C' versus popular culture with a small 'c' see Müller-Hartmann & Schocker-v. Ditfurth 2004: 110–11).

Skills of interpreting and relating

On this level, learners relate texts from different cultures to each other. They try to find cultural similarities and differences, for example, by comparing school life in Tanzania to their own school life (see task above). In a simple task, learners have to move pictures of cultural objects/aspects from Tanzania and Germany into two circles which overlap. They can negotiate what appears in both cultures (the English book, a ruler, etc) and move it into the part that overlaps and other things that do not (such as Kiswahili, German school uniforms, etc) which go into the individual parts of the circles. The subject of Haddhiti will present an interesting aspect of relating and interpreting since, on the one hand, it is clearly Tanzanian, but on the other hand, the German learners experience a similar approach in their story-telling sessions when they do role-plays or short simulations. While the comparison will be done in English, this discussion might need to be done in German, but it helps learners put into perspective and relativize the concept of us versus them (see Doyé 1999: 32–34 for other examples), which is crucial for identity formation. The same is possible in the *Teddy Bear Project* when learners compare the different timetables of their schools, learning in the process which subjects are important in their partners' school in comparison to their own school.

Skills of discovery and interaction

This is the most demanding skill level because it involves real-time interaction. A discovery approach generally allows learners to find out about similarities and differences of another culture as shown above. While the course book is limited in this regard, the *Teddy Bear Project* offers a lot more because many learner texts will arrive in the classroom that can be searched for cultural discoveries, i.e. the fact that in Australia it is summer when here it is winter. Or they might discover the fact that in Australia the partners have emus on their farms. That way they discover important phenomena in the other culture. During study visits (see below), for example, ethnographic observation tasks (looking out for sounds, smells, images, colors of a new place) help learners discover new aspects about a culture. In a classroom with different cultures, children might discover their own non-understanding when confronted with a native speaker of English. This experience could enable them to become aware of what learners from other cultures experience, as in this case FELBERBAUER (1991: 11) describes: *"Jetzt weiß ich wie es dem Ali gegangen ist. Er hat dich genauso wenig verstanden wie ich den Amerikaner, als er das erste Mal bei uns in der Kasse war"*. Bringing native speakers to the classroom creates real-life interaction and confronts the learners with all the demands a communicative situation entails, such as the accent of the native speaker or the speed they speak at in English. Role plays and simulations in the classroom facilitate this kind of foreign language interaction (→ ch. 5 for how to prepare learners for creative oral or written discourse; also see below for task support).

Critical cultural awareness

Even young learners can begin to develop critical cultural awareness (see our example at the end of this chapter). Dealing with another culture always involves the evaluation of that culture which might quickly lead to the use of stereotypes ("us versus them"). To be able to eventually deal critically with one's own and the other culture, learners need to develop competences in all of the above levels of ICC. We agree with DOYÉ (1999: 58), though, who stresses that critical cultural awareness does not really concern young learners yet, but it does concern their teachers who need to develop a clear idea of how far tolerance can go to avoid the danger of cultural relativism – where anything goes when choosing and working with educationally appropriate topics.

4 Issues when teaching ICC

1 Working with course books

Analyzing course books

Most modern course books include cultural material, (see, for example *Bausteine Magic 4* by PIEPHO 2004) but often they are not helpful in facilitating cultural learning. When analyzing learners' textbooks we need to check whether the diversity of the target culture(s) is represented as to its people, animals and landscapes (see BURWITZ-MELZER & QUETZ 2000: 22–3). Often we find pictures of white children only and most of the time fantasy drawings replace real drawings or pictures. For example, while choosing the politically correct term Shoshone for the story of Sacagawea, a brave Shoshone girl (instead of using the term Indian or Native American), the textbook *Discovery 4* (BEHRENDT, CHRISTMANN & MAYER 2005: 30-1) alludes to the diversity of Indian cultures in the U.S. It would have been even better, though, to include photos of Shoshone children today to allow learners to relate to peers. By working with the images learners have of Indians, making them draw a picture of a typical Indian, hetero-stereotypes can be tackled by comparing these pictures (usually of Indians with feathers, bow and arrow, and a rudimentary language, see LUTZ 1985 for examples) to photos of contemporary native children either in the textbook or by using material on the internet. Tasks for such comparisons between daily life in Germany and the target culture(s), are rarely to be found, and often the peer group's language is missing (→ ch. 11). BURWITZ-MELZER and QUETZ (2000: 23) conclude that often *"die Themen der Schülermaterialien verweisen auf ein traditionelles Landeskundekonzept, das(s) die fremde Kultur bzw. fremden Kulturen schematisch und homogen darstellt"*. Course books that focus on ICC, like *Bausteine Magic 4* (PIEPHO 2004) or *Ginger 2* (HOLLBRÜGGE & KRAAZ 2003) choose a different approach, *"da sie in fast jeder Unterrichtseinheit interkulturelle Themen ansprechen, eine große Bandbreite von Einzelthemen behandeln und die Erfahrungen der gesamten Lerngruppe in die Gespräche über Gebräuche, Werte und kulturelle Ansichten integrieren wollen"* (BURWITZ-MELZER & QUETZ 2000: 24). This includes a discussion about foods from different cultures, imitating and comparing animal voices in the learners' different L1s, or talking about sports that are not known in Germany (see also → ch. 11 and CURTAIN & PESOLA 1994: 175–95). The use of stories is another important text genre for developing ICC (BURWITZ-MELZER & QUETZ 2000, PIEPHO 1998, → ch. 7), and the internet provides still another source for authentic cultural material (see LEWIS 2003). As a consequence we also need to look for cultural learning material in the experiences of our learners (see examples above) and by initiating projects that focus on the development of ICC.

2 Working in projects in- and outside the classroom

Project work

Since ICC is a complex aim, we have approached it with a long-term perspective in mind which will need to last throughout our learners' time in school. Projects allow teachers to focus on this long-term process of developing intercultural competences. We can differentiate between projects that take place in the classroom, when native speakers are invited, or when a tele-collaborative project is initiated, as well as those that happen outside the classroom. For example, when visiting a partner school (see also storyline projects; → ch. 3).

Bringing native speakers to the classroom

a) Facilitating authentic cultural experiences in the classroom
One way to facilitate authentic cultural experiences is to invite a native speaker or another speaker of the target language to visit the classroom and prepare questions for the visit with your learners. While the teacher will need to do some translating and mediating, learners will profit from listening to an authentic accent, learning about life in the other culture, and be able to ask all the questions they have (see KUBANEK-GERMAN 2004: 137–39).

Letter exchanges and tele-collaborative projects

b) Moving beyond the classroom
Even though young learners' language competence is still limited, first exchanges with other speakers of English are definitely one possibility of practicing their English and finding out about similarities and differences of the daily life of peers in other cultures, as a number of projects show (see CLAUS 2003, DRESE 2002, ELLERMANN 2007, forthcoming, LEWIS 2003, MARSCHOLLEK 2003, OTHMER 2007, WASCHK 2001, ZEIDLER 2007). Language production during such projects needs to be carefully scaffolded (see suggestions for writing in → ch. 5; most of the textbooks today provide examples of e-mail letters; e.g. CANDY et al. IKURU 4. 2004: 43, BREDENBÖCKER et al. SALLY 4. 2006: 36). LEWIS, for example, describes the process for a tele-collaborative project about school. Learners are asked to describe a typical school day by answering questions like, "*When do you arrive at school? How do you get there? Do you stay in the same room or do you switch classes? When do you have breaks? What do you do after school?*" Using a word processing program, the teacher creates "*a template for a schedule. You can do this as a table or in form of a questionnaire. [...] Write key words and sentences on the board for the children to refer to. They will only need to write individual words to fill the chart*" (LEWIS 2003: 32, see also WASCHK 2005: 97 for another example). The routines are exchanged with the partner school and then the learners compare them, finding similarities and differences, such as different lengths and kinds of lessons, or the fact that American learners switch rooms every lesson etc. Two other project forms that are quite established by now is *Das Bild des Anderen* (see www.europeanschoolsproject.org/image) and the *Teddy Bear projects* (see above). Other subjects can be easily integrated into tele-collaborative projects (for an example see → ch. 10; to find partners for e-mail projects, see MÜLLER-HARTMANN 2003, and LEWIS 2003).

Visiting partner schools

Another, more complex, and for some contexts perhaps a rather visionary, approach is the visit to a partner school in England. OTHMER (2007) describes the visit to a British school by 4th grade learners. Such a visit demands intensive preparations and clear tasks of discovery on arrival in the new cultural context to enable learners to orient themselves and to cope with the situation linguistically. During the visit it is important to have regular class meetings without the partner class to allow learners to voice their impressions and questions about the experiences they have had. These visits, just like tele-collaborative projects, offer many opportunities for discovering and collecting language items as well as cultural experiences which can be analyzed and presented later at home in the classroom. We would like to close with an example that shows to what extent learners are able to develop ICC. Project work includes a product orientation where learners present their findings. In this project, learners develop role plays for the presentation of their experience when they come home. Not only do they show their growing language competence, but also a beginning critical cultural awareness.

Erste Fassung der Kinder	Durch die Lehrkraft modifizierte Fassung
Arne: I no wear school uniform. I don't like the school uniform. The colours are bad, bad, bad!	Arne: Mum, I don't want to wear my school uniform. I don't like it. The colours are ugly!
Fiona: Put the school uniform on. I'm Mum and you do it. The friends do it.	Fiona: Put it on! You have to wear it. Everybody does!

(Othmer 2007: 9)

1 Introduction

The overall pervasiveness of media

This chapter will foreground some key functions of traditional and digital media. Entering any primary EFL classroom in Europe will reveal the overall pervasiveness of different media: Post-it stickers name furniture in English, posters present stock phrases of classroom language, flash cards arranged according to topics are available in boxes, a blackboard and a CD-player are standard equipment ready to be used any time. A growing number of classrooms have at least one computer with internet access, and smart-boards are increasingly available. These media are generally referred to as technical (non-personal) instructional media, encompassing the board, course books and all sorts of realia (toys furniture, shopping utensils). As we will see in this chapter, media can only unfold their functions for language learning when seen in connection with the teacher and the learners (sometimes referred to with the rather awkward term "personal or non-technical media"). In the literature, media are often grouped according to the different senses they relate to, such as the visual (e.g. flash card), the auditory (e.g. CDs), and the audiovisual (film); see Freudenstein 2003: 394–99. Accordingly, media are connected to the fostering of particular skills: The audio cassette, the film, as well as satellite and cable TV allow students to improve their listening skills and their proficiency in non-verbal communication by watching speakers of English in action. Throughout the book we have made explicit and implicit references to the use of media. It is now our task to tie these elements together. The potential of media for language learning is not only determined by its specific properties, but also by the particular role a medium plays in the interactive world of the FL classroom. The latter will be our main reference point for the next section.

2 Properties and functions of media: Focus on the language classroom

"If-then-statement"

As we pointed out in chapter 1, language classrooms constitute an arena of unique subjective and inter-subjective realities, which are worked out, changed, and maintained by both teachers and learners. The basic assumption underlying this construct of a language classroom is the rather simple "if-then-statement." If the goal of classroom work is to help learners become competent users of the target language outside the classroom, then this very capacity must be initiated, fostered, trained, and experienced through activities in the here-and-now of classroom life. For this purpose, learners and teachers jointly observe and explore communication inside and outside classroom walls, whereby the learners' own experiences of trying to use the foreign language to create meaning is at the center of awareness. During this process, the classroom takes on different shapes or configurations which can be conceptualized with the following six metaphors.

In each of these configurations media serve particular purposes supporting the classroom's central goals.

1 The classroom as simulation and stage

The creation and simulation of worlds

The very nature of the classroom's space for action is artificial in the sense that it is not the world of the target culture, and, therefore, has its obvious limitations and constraints. Yet, in spite of this artificiality it allows for the creation of a simulated world whose objects not only receive new names (the tables, walls, the board, the light switch), but where *interactive and mutable relationships* are carried on in a different code. This means that, among other interactions, the everyday routines of classroom life are acted out in the target language (→ *classroom discourse*, ch. 4). Traditional forms of media such as the board, the CD-player, and the poster have long been used by teachers as tools to create such simulated spaces, building on the ability of learners to co-create this new space with their creativity and imagination. The language classroom, therefore, is more than a physical location. Rather, it needs to be seen dramaturgically as a stage for engagement. There is no existential need to carry out learning routines and classroom discourse in the target language. It is a matter of having agreed on new rules stating the experimental use of the language here and now in order to learn how to use it later. From this perspective, the classroom appears as an ensemble of mini-situations constituting an ongoing simulation which needs a stage for realization (used, and, at the same time, co-created by all participants). Here children explore their communicative abilities by using media themselves (a menu in a role play, a transparency of a floor plan of an apartment when talking about their home, a hand-puppet telling a story about a treasure island).

2 The classroom as detective agency

The learners are challenged to unlock the foreign code

The theory of communicative language teaching (CLT) has conceptualized the foreign language classroom not only as an arena for experimental language use, but also as a world within which texts are available for listening, watching, reading, and interpretation (see Candlin 2003). Again, media are the tools the teacher will use to make interesting topics accessible to learners and voices from the target cultures available for appropriation. Seen from the children's point of view, classrooms therefore resemble detective agencies, because the learner-detectives are challenged to unlock the foreign code. Such decoding not only depends on the learners' ability to bring their own experience and knowledge of the world to the foreign texts, but also on the support the teacher provides through different media. Once the children have grasped the gist of a story staged by the teacher with the help of a sequence of pictures, the presentation of the same story on CD spoken in normal speed by a native speaker may pose a new challenge for the detectives and, at the same time, foster a tremendous sense of achievement for them.

3 The classroom as training ground

The greater the variety of training the more effective its outcome

Without continuous and systematic training, learners will not develop the envisaged competencies. Training is not only strenuous, but must be undergone repetitively and regularly. The greater the variety of such training, the more effective is its outcome. Variety is achieved both through changes in the activities and through the use of appropriate media. Almost all of the above mentioned skill-getting and skill-using activities (→ ch. 5) require media support: A speaking and sound discrimination activity can be best supported by a CD, learning words can be based on a memory game or on picture bingo, working on a role play presentation "On the phone with friends" can be improved considerably if recorded and played back to the learners with a digital camera. On the training ground, media not only support and frame learning, but also render learning activities more interesting, challenging, and thus more effective. It is, however, not the medium as such, but the quality and content of the activity, which makes the difference in learning (→ ch. 3).

4 The classroom as studio for text production

The two functions of learner texts

Even if primary school children do not write complex English texts independently as older students do, they will nevertheless create a variety of texts, by means of which they support their actions (a shopping list for a role play or a poster for a fashion show), formulate textual messages (a get-well card to a friend), or express what they have understood from a story the teacher has read to them (a picture sequence reconstructing the story line). What is important here is the fact that learners partially assume control of media for their communicative purposes. These learner texts have two major functions. On the one hand they are not primarily produced for the teacher to assess the learner's success or failure in mastering the input. Rather they are produced by learners for their own benefit to communicate their own meaning, however limited the expressive potential might be. They are contributions to a mutual process of creating meaning. On the other hand, as we will discuss later when commenting on the use of portfolios (→ ch. 12), such learner texts are, of course, expressions of the learners' present stage of communicative competence, and as such give evidence of what has been achieved. Therefore, they also play an important role in assessing learning outcomes.

5 The classroom as window to the world

New dimensions of the FL classroom

The metaphor of a window denotes the fact that classroom walls can be opened to allow for direct encounters with speakers of the target language. Since the early 1980s, CLT has emphasized this connection to the world outside as a crucial element of the classroom's architecture. Before the advance of the personal computer, this connection could be maintained by class correspondence projects (letter, cassette and video exchanges), through visits of L2 speakers to the classroom, and through exploratory projects in the immediate environment where the target language is used as a means of communication (youth hostels, international schools, hotels, railway stations and airports). Although these possibilities have been focused on and used successfully by communicative language teachers for many years, they are not easy to put into practice and thus have remained a sideshow to mainstream language teaching (see: LEGUTKE & THOMAS 1999). The invention of the personal computer and its rapid development into a multimedia machine linked to the internet has the potential to offer new dimensions to the language classroom, as we demonstrated with the *Teddy Bear Project* (→ ch. 8). An authentic audience, which has been lacking in most traditional classrooms, is now easily accessible. The interaction, brought about by computer-based activities potentially enhances language learning and promotes communication even in such early phases of language learning. However, the negotiation of meaning and critical cultural awareness will depend on factors that go beyond technology. We will return to these issues later. For the time being it needs to be emphasized that the spatial dimension of the language classroom extends beyond the physical location of a particular school to the world outside. Traditional and new media provide the windows where the inside and the outside merge to constitute a learning environment with great potential for the growth of language competence.

6 The classroom as workshop for learning

Language learning awareness

Finally, the classroom is the location where children learn the acquisition of languages. While becoming competent in the use of English, they develop language learning awareness that paves the way to learning still other languages. Also, this dimension of the classroom heavily depends on the multifarious use of media: creating a word box not only serves the purpose of learning English words, but also makes the learner aware of how words are built and how they are best learnt. One important medium, no doubt, is the portfolio; challenging children to take stock of what they can do in English. The learner texts assembled in the portfolio's treasure chest (the dossier) serve as stepping stones to presenting language and learning achievements (→ ch. 12).

3 Multimedia and intertextuality

1 Multiple connections

Three pedagogically relevant implications

If media are understood as integral components of the dynamic world of a primary language classroom, where they perform specific functions, as explained above, three pedagogically relevant implications need to be stated here:

- First of all, it is obvious that media must not be looked at in isolation, but rather in the way they are interdependently related to each other.

Therefore classrooms represent *multi-media* environments for language learning. "Multi-media" here simply means the integration of multiple forms of media. This is exactly what happens in the teaching and learning process: listening texts are being used in connection with printed texts which again relate to visual texts, graphics, animation, and even full-motion video.

- The second implication underscores the fact that media must not be separated from their content, i.e. from the meaning they carry. This meaning is either decoded in the process of sense-making and negotiation, or it is created through the participation in classroom discourse, as we will show in the next section. Different media allow making texts accessible in different modes (visual, auditory, print): a picture card in the context of other picture cards represents the story line of *The Three Little Pigs* and thus prepares learners for the teacher's narration of the story, which in turn might not only be followed by the presentation of the story by a native speaker on a CD, but also by a cartoon version on film or from the Internet. Since these texts are interdependent we can speak of the classroom's *intertextuality*.
- Finally, media are always connected to the people who use them for specific purposes. For this reason they are part of the discourse world of the classroom. Even if the teacher will necessarily play a dominant role in creating the learning environment, learners are by no means excluded from media use, when trying to make themselves understood, for instance. The interconnectedness of media, texts in different modes, and the people who use them can be seen in the following example:

2 "A fashion show"

Students and teacher in action

The following example is taken from the project E-LINGO, www.e-lingo.de; the lesson was recorded in the state of Hesse, March 2004.

The 24 children (in Grade 3 at the beginning of the second half of their first year of English) appear in a fashion show representing a target task of a 45 minutes lesson. The tables and chairs have been removed to make room for a catwalk. An audience is seated along the catwalk; background music gives the event an additional air of importance. Students working in pairs (one in the role of the model, the other in the role of host/ show master) stage one show after another. While the model dressed up in fancy clothes moves along the catwalk the host holding a mike introduces the model and describes their outfit. The hosts speak without any linguistic prompts, but generate their texts from memory. A round of applause concludes each presentation before the next pair takes over. Although differences between the learners in terms of speaking competence (pronunciation and intonation, range of vocabulary) are obvious, all teams succeed in completing this target task. From the body language, you can tell that the learners are completely engaged in their activities. The teacher keeps in the background. No German is spoken. In the following lesson, the show will be repeated. Host and model will, however, switch roles.

Skill-getting and skill-using activities

A sequence of skill-getting and skill-practicing activities precedes the fashion show. The activities focus on the revision of vocabulary (*colors* and *clothes*), the introduction of new words (*clothes*), the introduction and practice of phrases and chunks (*introducing a model, describing a model*). Almost all of the activities depend on the integrated use of media as will be shown with reference to the two activities *describing a female clown* (2 min, 10 sec.) and *describing a male clown* (2 min. 25 sec.). The teacher sits on a table, to her right is a girl dressed as clown with a hat, glasses, a red nose, jacket, scarf, gloves, and fancy boots. On her left, on a second table close by, is a boy clown in similar dress. The children forming a semi-circle on the floor are asked by the teacher to describe the woman clown first. The teacher in her opening stimulus emphasizes the personal pronoun *she* several times, *"tell us what* ***she*** *is wearing, what* ***she*** *is wearing..."* and holds up a flash card with the word *she*. Before initiating the description of the male clown, she makes learners aware of the gender difference "she" and "he", and holds up the appropriate flash card *he*. During both practice phases, when the children describe the clowns in simple sentences, the teacher praises the students and corrects mistakes. Several times she directs the learners' attention to word cards on the wall for the colors and to a poster mind-map of clothes. Although this phase is hard work for a lot of students, they are very engaged and enjoy this form of practice.

3 Multi-modality and classroom discourse

Interconnection of media

This short example not only demonstrates how media are interconnected in the dynamic world of the language classroom, but also how teachers and learners shape this world not only by the spoken and written word, but by simultaneously using visual objects (pictures) and artifacts (clothes and other props such as noses, glasses, lip stick, and face paint) as representational resources in the process of teaching, learning and creative expression (i.e. the practice phases and the fashion show). Teacher and learners appropriate these resources, imbuing them with their own personality (e.g. facial expression, voice, gestures, and body posture). The world of the classroom, therefore, is best characterized as multi-modal, because here the linguistic and non-linguistic means of expression supplement each other, the visual and the verbal combine in a presentation. The staging of a fashion show by the learners, together with its preparatory phases and a follow-up to examine and assess the experience is a telling example of what we call *classroom discourse*. In contrast to the traditional use of the term, which is restricted to the organizational aspects of teaching and learning (e.g. handing out of scissors, or having learners assist in cleaning the board), classroom discourse in its wider meaning denotes much more, i.e. a task-based and theme-centered process of sense-making and learning. This process takes shape in different modes, with a variety of texts made accessible through a combination of media (Hallet 2008).

4 Computers

A powerful tool

The steady increase of access to computers in educational settings has also enhanced the possibilities for teachers and learners in primary school if the medium was situated in the dynamics of the EFL classroom. In each of the above mentioned configurations, it can serve as a powerful tool for both learning and communication.

- *A tool for accessing resources:* A growing number of institutions, publishing houses, and individuals have provided a wealth of multi-media resources to be used either directly by children, if they have access to computer labs in schools or at home, or by teachers for classroom use. The BBC website *Cbeebies* and the site *LearnEnglish Kids* of the British Council (→ ch. 15.2) may serve as representative examples here. A wide range of stories, songs, language games, as well as craft activities can be found on these sites, all of them realized as multi-modal and interactive textual arrangements for learning and exploration. For the teachers, up-to-date digital add-ons offered by many publishers can not only compensate for the loss of topicality of course books, but also broaden the teachers' repertoire of tasks and activities.
- *A tool for accessing peers from other cultures:* Furthermore, computers enable teachers and learners to overcome traditional constraints of classroom learning by providing them with various channels for interaction with speakers of the target language in different cultural environments, as we have pointed out above (→ ch. 8). *The Teddy Bear Project* is a good example that e-mail ventures need not be restricted to older and more competent learners, and have earned their place in the primary classroom (Müller-Hartmann 2003). Children not only try to understand peers from different parts of the world, but also make themselves understood in the target language by using written and spoken language (audio files), as well as pictures and films.
- *A tool for learning:* Part and parcel of any modern ensemble of materials around a core textbook are digital language trainers, which aim at supplementing classroom work for individuals and groups. Again, we can find a range of skill-focused activities ranging from vocabulary training to listening, reading and writing. Although publishers generally make claims as to the high quality of these digital resources for language learning, careful assessment is called for (→ ch. 15.2).

5 The hand puppet

Most publishers have included a hand puppet in their multi-media kits supplementing their textbooks. On the surface, it seems so appealing and easy to use, yet it poses a number of challenges which have not received appropriate attention in the literature. (For further reference see: Haudeck 2000, 2001, Möller 2007, Hassheider & Scheffler 1995).

1 Reasons for the use of hand puppets in primary EFL

Mediator between teacher and students

The use of the hand puppet can be justified under four mutually supportive and interwoven perspectives based on two assumptions: As a representative of one of the target cultures it is a fluent speaker of English with no knowledge of German. Secondly, it has a vita and a distinctive character.

- *Psychological perspective:* The hand puppet serves as an important mediator between the teacher and the students. On the one hand, it needs to become a member of the learning community; students will gradually discover its vita and its character. Likewise, the puppet will get to know the children. During this process of familiarization, it will become a *partner* who is close enough to the children to express their voice, or it may inform the teacher of what is going on among the children (one child is missing). Most importantly, it invites the children to identify with the puppet and thus delegate their own voices to it. Because of its superior language competence, it can be much more expressive than the children. At the same time, the puppet can stimulate the shyer children's willingness to speak in public, because speaking to the puppet can be far less intimidating than speaking to the teacher. On the other hand, the puppet has the role of a *co-teacher*, helping the children to communicate with and through the English language. In this role, it might even assist the teacher in managing the interaction during class time (making sure that students stay on task), or it might support the students by giving prompts, whispering the missing word or the chunk.

Ideal partner for the teacher

- *Linguistic perspective:* Since communicative exchanges between teacher and students will be rather one-sided linguistically in the first years, the hand puppet is an ideal partner for the teacher to engage in meaningful dialogue. The playful staging of mini dramatic situations provides a rich context for language in action. Within such situations, new words can be introduced, expressions (chunks) repeated, intonation patterns demonstrated, or polite and impolite behavior recognized. Even if the puppet is primarily *the teacher's partner for extended discourse*, the students are not excluded from interacting with it. On the contrary, quite often the teacher-puppet interaction will be broadened in scope to include the children. Where a lot of traditional dialogues during the elementary phase of language learning are communicatively dubious, even ridiculous (e.g. asking about each others' names and hobbies, when everybody knows the answer), a dialogue with the hand puppet on such topics could make more sense. After all, it is a new member of the community. Entering and exiting the classroom stage, the puppet provides opportunities for a wide range of language related activities for students and teachers which can take the form of almost ritualized events: calling the puppet, greeting it with a song, informing it about the current birthdays, days of the week, the current weather conditions.

Valuable helper to the teacher

- *Educational perspective:* Based on the assumption we made earlier, the hand puppet can be a valuable helper to the teacher in bringing aspects of the target culture(s) to life. It could introduce cultural products (such as food, and clothing, as well as songs and stories), present cultural symbols (such as flags and insignia), and, of course, exemplify cultural practices (forms of greetings, eating habits, school rituals). At the same time, the puppet is a stranger to the world of the children. What is perceived as common practice and not questioned by them, might appear strange to the puppet. It needs, therefore, to be introduced to cultural representations, and as a consequence, it will struggle with misunderstandings. It will, no doubt, be surprised sometimes how things are done in the world of the children, and will ask all sorts of questions. Connecting the hand puppet with central issues of intercultural learning does by no means imply that it should be overburdened with this function. However, it certainly provides an opportunity to integrate the intercultural dimension into the daily language work.

Students as participant observers

- *Learning perspective:* This reason is closely related to the linguistic dimension and draws our attention to the fact that learners following the mini-dramatic interactions between the teacher and their puppet act as participant observers of contextualized language use, i.e. of discourse events (cf. Cameron 2001: 37). Time and again they will be exposed to short units of language, which lend themselves to re-enactment because they carry meaning. This does not only happen in the classroom. There are reports of students copying the dialogues experienced in class at home with their siblings and friends, using their own hand puppets (Haudeck 2001). This kind of participant observation is an important stepping stone towards learning to engage in discourse with others. The creative re-enactment of a pleasurable experience serves as a bridge to this goal. What is experienced, repeated, and re-enacted could easily become the center of attention during 'focus on language sessions' when learners discover language forms and begin to understand how language works.

2 Quality, choice and training

The personal medium

Experts agree that a hand puppet not only needs to meet a number of criteria to function as a partner in classroom discourse (big enough to be seen by all the children, moveable, expressive eyes), it also requires considerable training on the part of the teacher. In addition, the teacher's creative potential and imagination are called for when inventing its character and vita (cf. Möller 2007). Since the puppet is a personal medium with its history and character, it needs a home in the classroom from where it enters the stage and to where it exits: a basket, a shelf in the cupboard. It goes without saying that the use of the hand puppet cannot succeed without the teacher having a good level of language competence. Even the fluent speaker will need some time to become familiar with the medium.

3 Issues and limitations

The puppet's final exit

Hand puppets will, no doubt, eventually lose their appeal with the growing age of the children. The acceptance of the puppet by the learners depends to an important degree not only on the skills and creativity of the teacher, but also on the puppet's character and maturity. On the other hand, the teacher should be ready for the puppet's final exit, which might be embedded in a sequence of farewell events. Several authors suggest that learners should be encouraged to take over the role of the hand puppet once they have learned to master certain phrases and expressions (e. g. HASSHEIDER & SCHEFFLER 1995). This move, so they argue, could boost some learners' motivation and help them overcome inhibitions, because the mask of the puppet provides the necessary protection for shyer students. Although we agree with the argument that the security given by a role can have a liberating and supporting function for many learners, the difference between drama activities and the use of the hand puppet should not be blurred. In order to preserve and maintain the puppet's distinctive character, which incorporates its superior language competence, one could, with some justification, argue against such a transfer of the puppet to a learner. A viable alternative for the teacher would be to invite the students to bring their own puppets to class and have them meet the hand puppet and the personal puppets of other learners. The hand puppet, no doubt, represents a particularly powerful tool for authenticity, yet it should be kept separate from other tools which also add to the creation of pretense: the students' cuddly toys, the paper mask and the assumed role.

6 Issues and directions

Pedagogy first, curriculum second, media third

A critical look at the history of foreign language teaching reveals a recurrent tendency of scholars to overestimate and idealize the power of media for learning and teaching. In 1948 EDISON claimed *"that the motion picture is destined to revolutionize our educational system and that in a few years it will supplant largely, if not entirely, the use of textbooks in our schools"* (Edison in RITTER 1996: 40). In the 1960s and 1970s the language lab was seen as a revolutionary step toward effective learning, and at the turn of the century the computer was imbued with excessive expectations as to its effect on learning. Findings from research on the use of information and communication technology (ICT) support a more balanced view as to the surplus value of technology applications (cf. KERN 2006, RÖSLER 2007). It is not the individual medium, nor technology alone that guarantees communicative success and/or positive learning outcomes. Rather, they will depend on the choice of appropriate content that engages learners, on the definition of pedagogical goals to be pursued, and, of course, on the design and implementation of meaningful tasks providing a framework for interactions that focus learners' attention and challenge their points of view. As RÖSLER summarized in a review of research on e-mail in language learning *"[t]he medium is not the message because if people have nothing to say to each other then it doesn't really make any difference in which medium they don't say it"* (RÖSLER, 2000: 18).

It remains a challenging task for further research on the new dimensions ICT has opened for the language classroom (e.g. the social web and the smart board) to be first and foremost concerned with issues of pedagogy, and then to be guided by curricular considerations. Only when the critical parameters of pedagogy and the curriculum have been established can the inclusion of media be addressed (LEGUTKE 2008).

1 Introduction: Clarifying terminology

Combining language and subject matter teaching

Cross-curricular teaching is the idea of teaching different subject or content matter such as music, sports, art, biology or math in a foreign language. It is one of the most promising approaches to teaching a foreign language in primary school because it allows learners to focus on content matter. This may involve tasks such as performing a play, playing a game in sports, solving a math riddle, or describing how beans grow. The learning of the language happens *"incidentally"* (CAMERON 2001: 192, BURMEISTER 2006: 197), while the learners' focus is on content. This approach also integrates strategy learning of different subject areas, such as observing and describing an experiment in biology. In Germany the idea of using the foreign language to teach subject matter started in the 1970s (for an overview of the historical development in the German school system see MÜLLER-HARTMANN & SCHOCKER-V. DITFURTH 2004: 152–53). When dealing with cross-curricular teaching, we need to clarify the terminology, because different terms abound that describe seemingly similar concepts, but need to be differentiated according to their specific context and approach.

CLIL, immersion programs, and cross-curricular teaching

Concepts frame the relation between the focus on teaching the foreign language and the subject matter differently. In Europe, teaching content in a foreign language is usually called *"content and language integrated learning"* (CLIL – the German equivalent is *Bilingualer Sachfachunterricht*). In North America, it is called content-based second language instruction (see BURMEISTER 2006: 196–96). But CLIL covers different concepts as EDELENBOS et al (2006: 93–94) point out

> *CLIL is an umbrella term with many definitions. It is a keyword which is appearing increasingly and can be interpreted very broadly, from teaching a 15-minute sequence about apples as part of a lesson on fruits, to teaching some topics within a year in the foreign language, to teaching one or more subjects in the other language. [...] If the term CLIL refers to programs with at least 50 percent of subject matter teaching in the other language, 'immersion' is also used.*

Consequently we can talk about a continuum, *"an dessen einer Seite Programme mit vorwiegend sprachlicher Zielsetzung und an dessen anderer Seite vorwiegend auf Sachinhalt zielende Typen einzuordnen wären"* (BURMEISTER 2006: 198). While there are a few immersion programs in German primary schools (see BURMEISTER 2006: 199–216, and ZYDATIß 2000: 20–30 for a description of schools and the specific characteristics of immersion programs, → ch. 14), most primary schools in Germany and Austria use *"cross-curricular teaching [...] a version of bilingual education and subject-teaching which not only teaches the language required for school learning, but also teaches subject knowledge through the newly acquired language and promotes thinking skills* [see table 10.2] *as well"* (PROCHAZKA 2006: 133). Since teaching in primary schools is organized by the integrated topic approach (*Klassenlehrerprinzip*), teachers are supposed to also teach English in an integrated way (see the *Bildungsplan* of Baden-Württemberg as an example, MINISTERIUM FÜR KULTUS 2004). As RYMARCZYK (2006) has explained, we can basically differentiate between exporting the language to another subject, such as sports or math (subject-based approach) or we can import the subject to the English lesson (theme- or topic-based approach). Teachers can flexibly handle the weekly 90 minutes they usually have for English, and even extend it considerably by combining the two approaches. *"Behält man sich den 'topic-based approach' für die 90 Minuten des regulären Englischunterrichts vor, so lässt sich über den ‚subject-based approach' noch ein Plus an Englisch über die Woche verteilt in den Stundenplan integrieren"* (RYMARCZYK 2006: 3).

2 Purpose and principles of cross-curricular teaching

Using language meaningfully and stretching languages resources

In cross-curricular teaching the focus is not on language learning, but on working on the content matter of a particular subject or several subjects. The language is used as a medium of communication to solve subject- and task-based problems. Let us have a look at an example of a cross-curricular project on animals in the zoo which covered biology, math, geography, sports, fine arts, and English (RYMARCZYK 2005: 6).

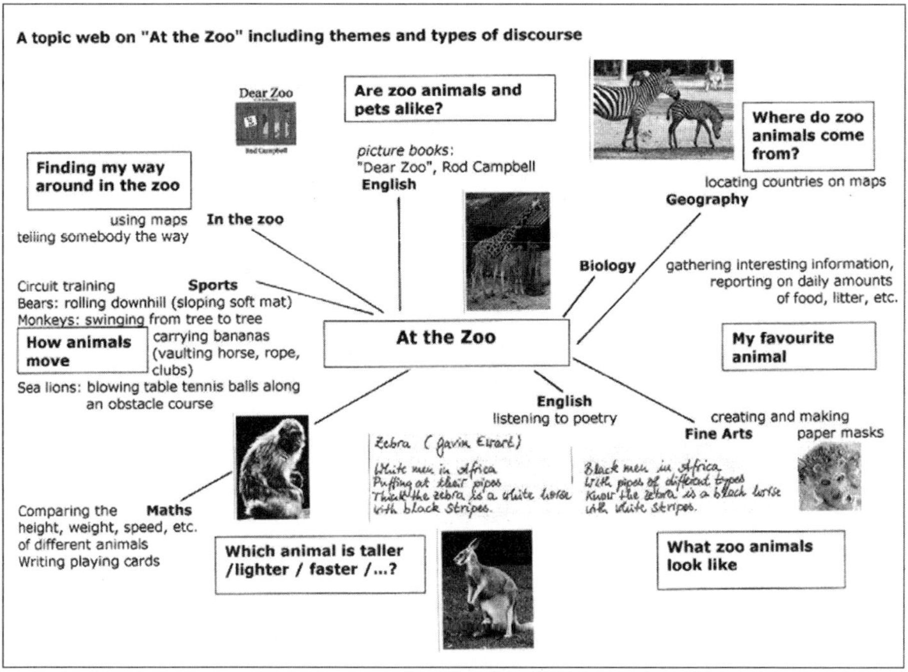

"At the zoo" from RYMARCZYK (2005). Primary English, 6, S. 6

The project deals with a motivating subject, that of zoo animals, which is presented in a discovery-oriented and problem-oriented approach (see also Mayer 2005). Learners are engaged with the rich language material in many different ways as they discover and express meaning. They find out which countries and continents the animals come from by looking for countries on the map, and they solve the problem of giving precise directions by having different groups of learners try to find the quickest way to the lions' cage on the zoo's map. In the process, learners stretch and develop their language resources. By trying to communicate their personal meanings about a topic, what bears can do in the wild, for example, learners will need to be precise in terms of content and language (for example: What can bears do? They can swim *in* the water, they can sleep *in* a cave, or hide *in* the forest, but they climb *onto* a tree. See also table 10.1 on the topic 'potatoes'). As Cameron (2001: 192) stresses, *"motivated by real interest in a topic, they may struggle to communicate their knowledge to someone else [...]. Stretching resources in this way pushed the child into the ZPD [→ ch. 2] and can be very productive for learning"*. When dealing with a topic like potatoes in different subjects, learners use language in many different functions, but they also use it repetitively (e.g. names of countries, nationalities, or the use of the imperative; see table 10.1), thus stretching and recycling their language resources.

Subject	Activity	Example language focus
Math	Counting and weighing	Numbers, how much/ how many?
Geography	Potato maps	Names of countries, nationalities
Art	Potato printing, decorating a card	Colours, shapes, writing invitations
History	Where potatoes came from	Past tense, countries, nationalities
Craft	Making a potato vehicle	Parts of a vehicle, how far...?
Drama	Potato puppet role-play	Dialogue for giant potato story
Physical education	Potato races, pass the potato	Imperative, instructions
Home education	Potato recipes	Imperative, instructions, tastes

Table 10.1 (based on Vale & Veunteun 1995: 41)

Supporting a learning-centered approach through strategy training

Since cross-curricular learning integrates language learning and different subject matter learning, it enhances the overall development of children's conceptual abilities, and it allows learners to develop cognitive, meta-cognitive and social strategies as well as motor skills (see table 10.2).

Strategy (general)	Examples of strategies	Use of strategies in classroom
Cognitive strategies	Comparing, counting, classifying, ranking, predicting, problem-solving, measuring, hypothesizing	Learners bring potatoes to the classroom which can be weighed and compared (who has got the biggest/heaviest).
Meta-cognitive strategies	Reflecting on how to learn sth. or prepare for sth.	To prepare for a presentation we can learn a text by heart, say it out loud, tell/present it to a friend
Social strategies	Helping others with language or content problems, being patient, showing tolerance toward language mistakes of others, giving positive feedback, offering advice	Offering advice: *'Why don't you...?'* *'You could...'* Giving positive feedback: *'That's nice...'* *'I like...'*

Table 10.2 (based on BREWSTER & ELLIS 1992: 129–45, CAMERON 2001: 196)

Choosing appropriate cognitive input

Learners can *"benefit from bringing existing skills and understanding to bear on new areas,"* applying the knowledge and strategies they have learned in other subjects (HALLIWELL 1992: 131). At the same time, learners deal with different text genres and discourse styles. In the example "At the zoo", learners listen to poems, read picture books, look at maps, solve math problems, and could even look for information on the internet to find out more about the animals. Consequently, cross-curricular teaching supports a learning-centered approach (→ ch. 2) because learners are challenged to use their language capacities to apply different study skills and to develop learning strategies (see table 10.2).

In cross-curricular teaching, the creation of a rich learning environment (see above the topic web "At the zoo") is especially important to help learners deal with and understand cognitive subject matter in the foreign language. Basically, all subjects can be chosen. Depending on the stage of learners' cognitive development, it is helpful to start out with subjects that are not very challenging cognitively, such as sports, music and art.

Using a multi-sensory approach

In the beginning, cross-curricular learning is often characterized by extensive code-switching, since learners want to get a message across but they are still missing the respective language resources. Thus receptive skills are more important at first. BUTZKAMM (2005) argues for an intensive usage of L1 alongside the foreign language. Others have shown that while learners code-switch because the necessary vocabulary is missing, they still try to express themselves in the foreign language. This also demands a high tolerance of mistakes, especially in early cross-curricular teaching. The rich learning environment offers opportunities for learners to express themselves even with a rather restricted L2 proficiency, as long as the teacher at first does not expect more than "minimal output" (see RYMARCZYK 2003: 272). To scaffold content input in the foreign language, the teacher can vary her/his expressions by paraphrasing or by looking at issues from different perspectives and commenting on them, providing rich language input (BURMEISTER 2006: 205). But there are also other ways of scaffolding learners' understanding and language production. Since learners have to deal with sometimes complicated subject matter, *"something other than language must carry meaning"* as HALLIWELL (1992: 132) says. Concepts have to be visualized with the help of pictures, charts, graphs and diagrams (see BREWSTER & ELLIS 2002: 138–140; HALLIWELL 1992: 134–37 for examples), and learners need to be supported by allowing them to do things. For example, by participating in experiments. Consequently, multi-sensory learning is the key to making new concepts less language-dependent. CURTAIN and PESOLA (1994: 155) make the following suggestions:

1. *Make increased use of visuals and realia.*
2. *Provide for hands-on involvement of learners.*
3. *Increase the number and vividness of examples.*
4. *Establish a clear, meaningful context.*
5. *Draw on learners' past experience and previous learning from the curriculum.*
6. *Make sure of rephrasing and repetition.*

Employing a task-based and project-based format

If the topic (see table 10.2 on the topic 'potato') is being dealt with in different subjects, repetition of content, concepts and vocabulary help the learners to understand the relevance of the topic, and the contact to content matter and contextualized language is increased at the same time (BURMEISTER 2006: 205).

3 Features of good practice

Finding a topic and brainstorming activities

We have already outlined many of the features of good practice in cross-curricular teaching in earlier chapters of this book. (→ chs. 3, 4, 6 and 8). As has been pointed out above, combining a topic- and subject-based approach on the basis of a task-based frame seems to be the most promising, because it looks at an issue from a different perspective. This may take the form of a project offered by different subjects (see also the story-based and story line approach in → ch. 3). For more examples see BECHLER and DOFF (2005 – a project on dinosaurs in the natural sciences and English), OECHSLE and GLATZ (2005 – a project on growing beans in biology and English), or RYMARCZYK (2006 – a project in art and English).

Finding appropriate materials

There are various ways of choosing a suitable topic for cross-curricular teaching. You may take a topic from the general primary school curriculum, or the topic may develop from what children are concerned with: *"It may arise from the children's 'news' or from something buzzing in the wider community; it may come from a subject other than English, from discussion or reading"* (GARVIE 1991: 121). These could be topics about me and my body, my family, my home, our street, and my town (see DINES 2000: 74–76). Consequently, the teacher involves the children when choosing and developing the subject matter; deciding with the learners which questions or issues they want to pursue. As a first step, brainstorming techniques, such as mind-mapping or topic-webbing, are helpful to cover the various aspects of a topic, such as objects, actions, processes, typical events, places and discourse types (for examples see BREWSTER & ELLIS 2002: 132–34, CAMERON 2001: 187–90 and CURTAIN & PESOLA 1994: 202–03). *"A topic web is a free exploration of ideas – you would be unlikely to attempt to cover all the ideas first noted. By laying out ideas in this way, however, you can check for balance and identify the structures, activities and resources required"* (HOLDERNESS 1991: 21).

At first, good cross-curricular materials were hard to come by for teachers who consequently had to design their own. Now, there are some good examples of course books on the market that follow a cross-curricular approach, such as *Supermouse* (BAUMANN ET AL 2005), the first cross-curricular primary course book, *Discovery* (BEHREND, CHRISTMANN & MAYER 2005), or *Magicland* (HANCOCK, REED, SCHOCKER- V. DITFURTH 2003). *Supermouse* pursues the concept of *"'maximum' impact on curricular learning with 'minimum' requirements in the new language"*, integrating math, music, arts and crafts, and sports with foreign language teaching (PROCHAZKA 2006: 134). Primary journals provide a host of suggestions (e.g. *Grundschulmagazin Englisch*, *Grundschule Englisch*, and especially the new journal *Take off!* which has an explicit cross-curricular approach; see also BAUMANN, LEWIS & PROCHAZKA 2000 for materials) and story books, such as Posy SIMMONDS' *Lulu and the Flying Bears*, are another rich resource. In the latter, the little girl Lulu visits the museum and is taken by two cherubs on a flight through famous paintings where they experience a number of adventures (see RYMARCZYK 2006 for task suggestions). The internet provides another source for materials. Since tele-collaborative projects are theme-based, they facilitate many opportunities of integrating language work with projects in different subject areas. At the same time, they help learners develop intercultural communicative competence, as the following example shows (→ ch. 8). An American kindergarten teacher posted the following request on the St. Olaf list (http://www.iecc.org/):

> Aloha,
> We are a kindergarten class in Koloa on the island of Kauai in the state of Hawaii and our country is the United States of America. We are studying the seasons and since it's usually warm and sunny here in

> Hawaii, the color of our leaves don't change so we don't know what Fall leaves look like. We hope that you can help us by sending us some Fall leaves and in return we would send you some shells from our beautiful beaches. Please let us know if you can help by contacting our librarian, Jennifer Cramer. Her e-mail address is jenny@aloha.net

Structuring the learning environment

This project is truly intercultural because both sides contribute from their specific cultural context. It can become the center of a cross-curricular project about the seasons which integrates subjects such as art, biology, and geography, providing a real-world connection. It also enhances a multi-sensory approach, supporting young learners' preference for the visual, haptic, and kinesthetic by involving them to collect leaves or, looking at and touching the shells. On the language level, the project could consist of an exchange of short introduction letters, the exchange of the desired products and a thank-you note. As a project outcome the shells can be exhibited in the school, providing a map and information where they came from in English.

Generally, opened-ended tasks in a project format are supportive of a discovery-based approach. Instead of just having learners match pictures and words on transport, for example, they could engage in an experiment: rolling a toy car along different surfaces, trying to find out which surface is best, etc (see Holderness 1991: 24). Learners need to have a choice to deal with issues they are interested in, and they have to be able to make decisions in the process. For example, by presenting the material for designing a potato vehicle or puppet, learners will need to make choices in terms of the subject matter, but also in terms of language use. Cameron (2001: 195) describes this process as follows: The learners *"are asked to decide which materials they want, using simple phrases in the group decision-making: 'do we need string? how many potatoes do we need?' The group then prepares a representative who is sent to the teacher to ask for those things: 'please can we have four potatoes and some string?'. The teacher can support the representatives in their language use, and may send them back to the group to check more precisely what is needed. Each stage in this decision-making process will generate repetition of the vocabulary about the materials, as well as other simple but useful phrases, which the teacher will need to model"*. As can be seen from the examples, cross-curricular teaching lends itself to the production of displays, posters, simple web sites, or story-books, as well as performances by acting out stories or by documenting a project for an audience inside or outside the school, such as another class, teachers or the parents.

Providing a final checklist

In summary, Cameron (2001: 198) provides a comprehensive final checklist of the most important features of cross-curricular teaching:

- *careful choice of theme to involve all children;*
- *detailed planning, using brainstorming and webs;*
- *linking content with activities and discourse types;*

- *pre-planned organization of materials and activities;*
- *teacher and class decide together on 'guiding questions' that structure activities;*
- *building in 'choice points' where children are guided in making decisions over direction, activity or timing;*
- *management of classroom activity and use of resources;*
- *attention to amount and type of language use during activities;*
- *regular monitoring of each child's involvement and success in activities and language use, by teacher and children themselves;*
- *use of final products to motivate and involve all children.*

1 Introduction: Why use course books?

Different functions of course books

Why is it important to pay so much attention to course materials that we allocate an extra chapter for discussing them? Why should we evaluate, and, if necessary, adapt them? The answer is because they play such an important part in the teaching of a teacher's "hidden curriculum" (NEUNER 2003: 400). EDELENBOS and VINJÉ (2000: 145), in the context of researching early start programs in the Netherlands, conclude that it *"is safe to say that the materials in use are the primary factor controlling the teaching of English."* EDELENBOS ET AL (2006: 153) say *"that textbooks are a manifestation of an influence of theory of education and research and therefore function as change-factors"*.
Good course materials can be of invaluable help to teachers. But what are good materials? And do the majority of teachers use course materials? We assume that they do because their teaching load including correcting homework, talking to parents or attending staff meetings leaves them very little time to write their own texts and think up activities. Course materials provide teachers with "building blocks" to work with; they help to plan and structure lessons and they give learners a sense of system and cohesion.

Different points of view

Of course, primary school teachers' views on the relevance of course materials differ. They range from those who are totally dependent on their course book to those who create their own curriculum. At one end of the spectrum there are teachers who painstakingly do all the texts, activities, tasks and exercises etc. with their classes and who become extremely worried if they miss a footnote. At the other end of the spectrum there are teachers who rely completely on either authentic materials they have collected or materials they have written themselves. They argue that no one set of course materials can be ideal for all classes. Consequently, they adapt and produce materials for each individual class they teach, including the use of a course book as a kind of 'quarry'. Such an approach is extremely time-consuming, as it requires a very high level of linguistic and methodological competence as well as careful planning. A third group of teachers neither use materials nor do they create their own materials or collect texts and activities in a systematic way. They use whatever material they happen to have and follow a kind of 'patch-work approach' without following any plan or curriculum. Needless to say, learners who are exposed to patch-work teaching have no opportunity of experiencing a sense of system and cohesion. Thus, the feeling of security and systematic continuous progress which is important for any kind of learning environment does not exist.

A good course book is important but does not guarantee 'good practice'

Countless visits to classrooms have shown that most teachers who are successful in motivating their pupils and whose learners achieve a high level of competence rely on course materials, but use them wisely and selectively, not exclusively. *"It is worth arguing [...] that however good a textbook may be, it is highly unlikely that a learner-centered approach can possibly work with young children if it is based solely on a textbook. Good practice in teaching [...] seems [...] to require some flexibility in approach, in order to [...] cater for each individual child's actual environment, interests and needs and to exploit unpredictable opportunities as they arise"* (EDELENBOS ET AL 2006: 153). It takes confident teachers to do so, and consequently teachers who are able to choose tasks and materials to meet their students' needs (→ ch. 3).

2 Defining course materials

Course materials support learners to do tasks in the new language

What do we mean when we talk about course materials? Today materials for foreign language teaching at the primary level usually consist of a pupil's book, a workbook (often also called activity book), a teacher's book and CDs. There may also be OHT transparencies, a video, a hand puppet, flash cards, picture cards, a CD-Rom and other additional materials, such as tests or a portfolio based on the course (→ ch. 9). Course materials translate the framework of the syllabus into concrete texts, activities, tasks, exercises and methodological guidelines. They provide a cohesive framework for what teachers should do in the classroom and state what the learners are expected to do. In doing so, they make an implicit statement about the nature of language learning. Up-to-date materials are based on the assumption that competence in the foreign language is not achieved by instructing the children *about* the new language, but by doing tasks and activities *in* it.

3 Criteria for good course books

Criteria to focus on the quality of activities, of language and of the teacher's guide

When a number of well-known materials writers were asked about how they set about writing, many of them apparently replied that they follow their intuition rather than any particular specification of objectives, principles, and procedures (PROWSE 1998). Obviously, their intuition must be based on experience. However, we believe that materials development must also be informed by basic principles and criteria that we know account for the quality of language learning at the primary level. They may be identified by considering the following three areas:

(1) the quality of *activities* that need to consider what we know about how children learn foreign languages (→ chs. 2 and 3);
(2) the quality of the *language used in activities* that needs to exemplify examples of natural and authentic language as it is used in everyday communication;
(3) the quality of the *teacher's guide* to give teachers ideas of how to support language learning in the classroom.

Principles derived from these areas may then be used to evaluate and compare materials currently in use when a school is planning to introduce a course book or to guide the design of materials that teachers develop themselves.

1 The quality of activities

Activities need to make an impact on learners

For a detailed discussion on criteria for appropriate activities, we would like to refer you to our chapter 3 on tasks. But we would still like to discuss basic criteria here that go beyond what informs task-design from a language learning perspective. We agree with TOMLINSON (1998), who, following his summary of the basic principles of second language acquisition relevant to the development of materials for the teaching of languages, says materials need to qualify in one basic respect: they should achieve *impact*, which he defines as having *"a noticeable effect on learners; that is when the learners' curiosity, interest and attention are attracted. If this is achieved there is a better chance that some of the language in the materials will be taken in for processing"* (p. 7). According to Tomlinson, materials can achieve impact through:

- novelty (e.g. unusual topics, illustrations and activities);
- variety (e.g. breaking up the monotony of a unit routine with an unexpected activity; using many different text types taken from many different types of sources; using the voices of a number of different speakers on a CD);
- attractive presentation (e.g. use of attractive colors; lots of white space; use of photographs);
- appealing content (e.g. topics of interest to the target learners; topics which offer the possibility of learning something new; engaging stories; universal themes; local references).

PIEPHO (2003: 60f.) has criticized course books generally for failing to have impact on learners because they do not provide space for learners' own ideas, arguments, and interpretations. Dialogues, he argues, are reduced to unrealistic 'fill in' exercises that do not take individual language development and individual needs into account. What we get is anything but texts that surprise, involve, or trigger dispute and personal comments. He therefore believes that course books rarely provide content that motivates learners. Judging from our own classroom experience, the situation PIEPHO criticizes is definitely changing. Recently published materials offer learners quite a selection of texts that trigger immediate response: Sixteen children rushing about, shouting in their mother tongue, "Can we act out the story?" are proof that there are texts that surprise, involve and motivate (reaction reported on watching the video taken from *Playway 3 DVD, Cartoon Story "The Woolly Hat", Activity Book Unit 6.4.*)

BUZAN (quoted in STEINBACH 1995: 13), following the same line of argument, adds another criterion for material that has an impact on learners. Children remember new words better if presented in contexts that are *unusual or absurd* or that *exaggerate* or that are presented with *a sense of humor.*

The impact of materials on learners also depends on whether learners perceive a task as personally relevant, meaningful and useful to them. This is why course books need to include what Nunan has called 'target tasks' or 'real word tasks' (NUNAN 2004: 2-4): They relate to learners' own lives and interests and are rehearsals of performance outside the classroom in that they mirror the things people do in everyday life. The following activity illustrates this nicely:

Listening to a dialogue and creating your own dialogues.
In their fourth year of learning English children deal with the topic *"Through the week"*. In this unit there is a listening comprehension activity. Two children talk about what to do and where to go. The learners listen to the dialogue *"What can we do?"* and perform the task of putting numbers on the correct pictures.

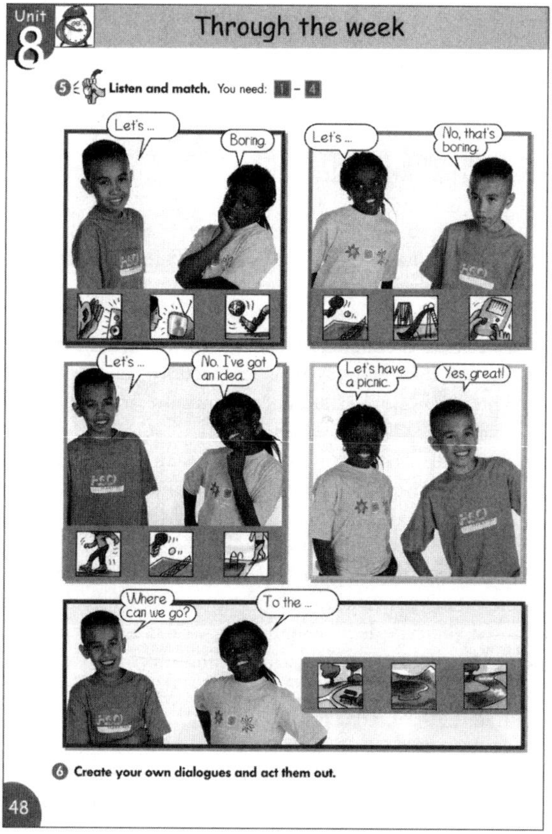

GERNGROSS & PUCHTA (2002), *Playway to English 4: Pupil's Book*, Ausgabe 2002, Helbling, Rum/Innsbruck

After they have completed the task, the learners are asked to create their own dialogues using the dialogue as a model text. They can get into groups and talk about what they are going to say. Therefore the task should provide a blank square in which children can fill in the activity they would like to suggest to make it meaningful to them. The teacher's role is that of a facilitator who offers advice when asked, or helps with words the children want to use, but have not learned yet. While this task would be classified as a 'real world task' as it is performed for one-to-one use outside the classroom, another task type, that of a 'pedagogical task,' cannot be directly transferred to communicative situations outside the classroom. Pedagogical tasks structure meaningful classroom interaction processes and generate negotiation to stimulate internal processes of acquisition (e.g. *information-gap activities*).

Ballinger, Davis, Gerngross, Hladnig, Puchta (1993):
Conrad and Company 2: Pupils' Book. Longman: Harlow, S. 38.

The children work in pairs. Without letting their partner see, they "hide" the animals in the picture of the room by putting the initial letters of the animals into the circles. Pupil 1 asks Pupil 2 where the animals are in their picture. Pupil 1 marks in red their position on their own picture. Then they swap roles. When they have finished they compare pictures.

Take care to analyse activities in detail

Do not be distracted by glossy colorful illustrations but look at activities in detail to find out if they qualify as content that may have an impact on your learners. There are quite a number of course books on the market that have a marked absence of any sense of humor and are guaranteed to bore your learners (and you!) to death. This may not only be true for the print version of materials, but also particularly for audio materials that may have been produced in a rush which clearly affects the quality of dialogues or songs, for example. For a survey on current course books for primary EFL see *Grundschulmagazin Englisch* (2006) and individual evaluations of course books handed in by primary EFL teachers, often based on their classroom experience with the course book they have evaluated (Bailey 2006, Beck 2006, Duda 2006, Esser-Mirbach 2006, Geisler 2006, Hüttner 2006, Kitz/Göb-Endres 2006, Mayer 2006, Pielen 2006, Scholz 2006, Thielen 2006). Let us now turn our attention to the kind of language we ought to expose our learners to.

2 The quality of the language

Language to exemplify examples of natural, everyday communication

It is obvious that the quality and quantity of *language that learners are exposed* to in a classroom affect what is available for pupils to learn. Language input comes from two sources: the course book with its accompanying media (i.e. dialogues and stories on CD or on video), and the input of the participants in the classroom – the teacher and the learners. If we wish to evaluate the quality of course books in this respect we must take a closer look at two elements in course materials:

(a) When children learn a new language, they ought to be able to use it as a means of communication. In what way do the texts in the course book and the tasks and activities which accompany them provide *natural examples of why and how children and adults communicate in the foreign language?*

(b) The quality of teacher talk is crucial to support learners in their language acquisition by helping them to understand and to communicate. Klippel (2003: 57) distinguishes between two basic roles: *the teacher as instructor* when they are presenting new language or providing practice opportunities and *the teacher as a partner in communication* when teacher and learners exchange information or opinions, if only at a very elementary level. In what way can the teacher's guide offer support that is useful to teachers in both roles (→ ch. 4)?

Much of the language found in course books does not qualify as an example of natural everyday communication

"Concocted, made-up language can be perfectly viable but it should be modelled on naturalistic samples" (Carter 1998: 86). It is one of the main purposes when developing course materials to expose learners to examples of language currently in use, that is, with features which are characteristic of authentic discourse in the target language. This statement may sound simple and straightforward, but it is not so easy to define what 'language in use' actually means. Let us therefore look at some examples of language use we found in primary course books:

Example 1: Priesack & Wilson & Wilson (2002): *Sunshine 1, Activity Book*, Milan: Mondadori, S. 26.

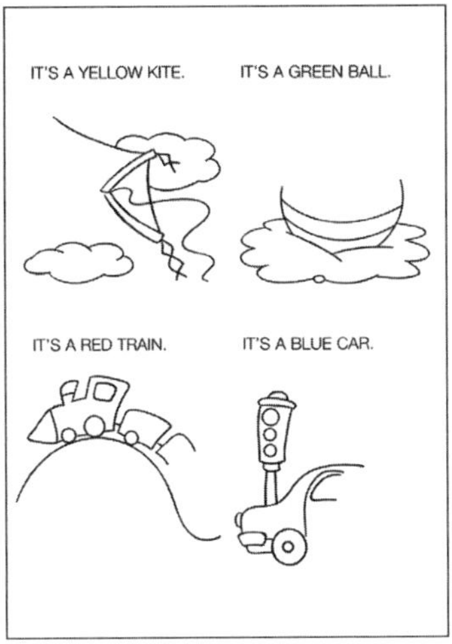

Example 2: Agostinelli et al (1997): *Busy Moments 1. Workbook.* Rafaello: Monte San Vito, S. 28.

Examples 1 and 2 cannot be considered to be examples of natural everyday language in use. In example 1, toys were randomly selected and named using *'It's a ....'*, quite out of context. If we ask ourselves what children really say when they get out their toy boxes and show their toys to each other, we would probably come up with something like: *'Look, this is my new ...'* or *'Do you like my ... ?'*. They would definitely *not* say the obvious to their friends, e.g. *'It s a yellow kite. It's a green ball.'* The language used in example 2 is slightly better, because children might actually use the structure *'there are'* when they are describing the contents of a toy box. But again the hidden purpose of this activity is obviously too form-oriented to make it a relevant and meaningful activity for learners' *real-life needs*. Agostinelli designed this activity in order to practice numbers and the structure *'there are'*, but the activity does not really provide learners with much motivation, because there is not a minimum of challenge. The learners have to function properly in the field of grammar, but this exercise does not give them a chance to express their own communicative needs. It also uses language at the expense of meaningful and relevant content. These examples demonstrate that even today, some course books define progress as progress by grammar. Progress as defined by topic and speech functions (i.e. providing ideas about what children *can do* with language) still seem less relevant. Language is reduced to unrealistic examples that do not take account of individual learners' communication needs.

The language in course books: a positive example

There are, of course, many course book authors who try to make sure that they focus on the *communicative purpose* of the language they present: they think about what children would like to express with a structure or a set of words and in which situation they might do so. Example 3 illustrates this rather well:

Tapescript:

Eddie:	*Look! It's a rabbit.*
	And there's a bird.
Rose:	*Oh! It's a cat.*
	And here's a dog.
Queen:	*Look! It's a tortoise.*
	And here's a fish.
King:	*Aagh! It's a rat.*

HANCOCK, REED & SCHOCKER-V. DITFURTH (2003): *Magicland 1: Class Book.*, S. 7, Langenscheidt: München

In order to learn the words to go with the topic *pets*, the children are offered the context *pet shop*, where they are allowed to say things that real children might actually say in that situation, such as *'Oh look, there's a …!'* to express astonishment. Even minimal language such as *'Aagh! … a rat!'* to express disgust is included. Having said this, the dialogue does not seem to have been modeled completely on natural samples of language either. Children would not normally say *'Look, it's a rabbit.'* They would probably leave out the *'it's'* and say *'Look, a rabbit.'*

Conclusion: course book to contribute to real language use

[A]ll language is used in a context and develops as a result of contextualised use [and …] people use language for real purposes […]. Discourse as real language use is the target of teaching: we want children to be able to use the foreign language with real people for real purposes (CAMERON 2001: 37).

Course book writers can make a real contribution to help make this happen.

3 The quality of the teacher's guide

Teacher's guide to support classroom management and teacher talk

English is probably not the mother tongue of most primary school teachers, and many may not have been adequately prepared by their inset crash courses to develop sufficient competence and confidence in the foreign language to use it as a flexible means of communication in the classroom.

With this in mind, it seems particularly important to look at the ways in which course books may support quality in teacher language input and discourse. If we look at teacher's guides, we will find that different course book authors approach the issue in different ways. While it may be helpful for inexperienced teachers to get detailed suggestions about what they can say to introduce an activity etc, the question is how teachers will manage to deal with detailed step-by-step information in an actual classroom situation, as is done in some teacher's guides. In the classroom, teachers may be faced with more than twenty learners, and all kinds of things are happening at the same time. This is a situation where flexible responses to the demands of the moment are required. If the teacher's guide contains a lot of detail, it will probably be quite difficult to react spontaneously to unpredictable learner contributions. Many things teachers might have to say in the course of a lesson cannot be planned in advance. While we agree that it may be helpful to give teachers ideas of how to introduce the characters of a story, how to create suspense before listening to a text, or how to make the purpose of a follow-up activity clear, we do not consider it to be very helpful to give teachers a detailed list of what to say and even what to expect learners to say because language learning in a large group is hardly predictable – and more often than not, teachers need to be able to give flexible responses to unpredictable learner output.

4 Five basic questions to ask when deciding which course book to choose

Select a course book with a view to adopting one for a particular class

To conclude this chapter, we would like to present a selection of five basic questions concerning objectives, content and activities which are relevant when deciding whether or not to introduce a particular course book to a class. Needless to say that this can only be done by considering who your learners are and what the curriculum demands. What counts at the end of the day is that a good course book invites children to browse through it simply because it is a joy to do so (Börner 2007).

TIPP

Basic questions:

1. *Are the purposes of the course material clearly stated?*
2. *Will the children be able to easily recognise the purposes of the course material?*
3. *Does the subject matter of the materials encourage affective involvement and is likely to have an impact on learners so that learning is facilitated?*
4. *Do the texts convey a message or information, or are they just vehicles to practice certain structures or vocabulary?*
5. *Are the texts authentic or modelled on naturalistic samples of texts and speech?*

1 Classroom assessment: Towards a definition

Key terms: evaluation, assessment and tests

The classroom-centered approach we have pursued so far generates the key questions of what knowledge and skills learners will acquire from their engagement with topics, tasks, and texts, and how their growth in knowledge and skills can be assessed. Before we can attempt to offer a few answers to these questions, some clarification of the terminology seems to be called for. In the following we will not use the term evaluation. Even if evaluation includes assessment, the former is a very broad term concerned with a wide range of aspects that impact educational processes. Evaluation takes into account not only the role and impact of the institution, the curriculum, the materials, and teacher performance, but also children's attitudes, parents' opinions and political ideologies. Assessment, on the other hand, has a more restricted focus and encompasses two major forms: testing and classroom assessment. Testing uses structured, statistically valid means of assessment conducted by researchers from outside the classroom (→ ch. 2), or authored by external test organizations such as the *First Certificate of English* (FCE), administered by the University of Cambridge Local Examinations Syndicate, or the *Test of English as a Foreign Language* (TOEFL), administered by Educational Testing Services in the USA. Classroom assessment is best subdivided by the persons who are responsible for the activities. We therefore distinguish between teacher assessment, peer assessment, and self-assessment. Classroom assessment in its various forms tries to fathom learner knowledge and skills, and may also focus on attitudes, understanding, and motivation. If it accounts for achievements at the end of a course or a unit, it is called summative, because of its product-orientation. If, however, assessment takes place continuously with the aim to diagnose learners' stages of development and therefore is guided by principles of process-orientation, it is called formative. In any case, it involves different forms of data gathering (observational, written, and oral data) and data interpretation. In the following, we will address classroom assessment by discussing questions of purpose (why should we assess?) and procedure (how, when and how often should we assess?). (For further reference see: Cameron 2001, Genesee & Upshur 1996, Harris & McCann 1994, Rea-Dickins 2000).

Assessment to serve teaching

Although we agree that assessment must serve a number of important purposes beyond classroom work (such as providing achievement accounts to feeder schools, the larger community of a county or a state, or informing the parents), we are mainly interested in what Cameron calls a reasonable requirement of assessment, i.e. *"to serve teaching, by providing feedback on pupils' learning, that would make the next teaching event more effective, in a positive, upwards direction"* (Cameron 2001: 215). To serve teaching, of course, for us entails: serving and fostering the learners' language growth.

2 Teacher assessment

1 Types of teacher assessment

No doubt, the teacher is the central agent of classroom assessment. They have to create the appropriate atmosphere, select appropriate tasks for the learners, analyze the data, and provide feedback – a challenging task since established paper-and-pencil formats of assessment (which in the German school context are mostly referred to as "tests") have only very limited value in the primary classroom, where the emphasis is on the oral skills (→ ch. 5). Let us consider the *Fashion Show* again, because it represents an excellent opportunity for the teacher to assess learners' performance while they are acting in the role of host/show master (→ ch. 9). The teacher could informally observe learner performance. Such informal observation is easy bread and butter of any language teacher. When it comes to giving feedback, however, the situation becomes more demanding. Since in our case one pair of students follows the other, the teacher would have to wait with their feedback until the end of the lesson. With 13 groups in a row this informality is not very practicable, and might not only turn out anecdotal, but, in fact, be unfair unless some formal organization is used. On the other hand, immediate feedback would certainly destroy the flow and dynamics of the event. In the next sections we will show that assessment practices (content, focus and procedure) not only need to be formalized to a certain extent, but also need to meet a number of quality criteria.

2 Quality standards

Validity and reliability

Although the first two criteria, validity and reliability, derive from test theory, they also apply to classroom assessment (cf. Genesee & Upshur 1996). It is valid when it assesses what is claims to assess. The validity criterion therefore asks us to think very carefully about what exactly we want to assess. If, in our case, the task requires the learners to take over the role of a show master and introduce the models by describing their clothes, the assessment would not be valid if the learner was assessed only in reference to standard pronunciation. While validity makes us aware of what is assessed, reliability emphasizes how well it is done. The question here is whether the assessment would produce the same results, if it were taken by the same learners at a different time, or if it were conducted by a different teacher. We can already see that reliability is very difficult to achieve if we move beyond standardized paper and pencil assessment. In our case, the assessment not only depends on the teacher's competence to stage the role play, the atmosphere they create, and the emotional support they provide, but also on the criteria they employ, his or her experience with assessing oral performance and, of course, the professional training they have undergone. In addition, the situation of the children might impact reliability if they were assessed at a different time of day, e.g. following a strenuous PE lesson. Cameron also points to this conflict between issues of validity and reliability: "*The most reliable assessment will be pencil and paper tests in which each item measures only a single aspect of a skill and which give each testee a numerical mark. But the most valid assessments will be those that collect a lot of information about performance on several aspects of a skill*" (CAMERON 2001: 225).

Practicability and fairness

The second set of criteria is of equal importance. Practicability makes us aware that classroom assessment must be doable given the constraints of the institutional context (e.g. 25 students, two lessons per week, space available). It may sound feasible in terms of validity to include a great number of different aspects of learner performance which could easily be employed if the teacher had a group of ten learners or if they could do it with the support of a co-teacher, but which is impractical under standard conditions. Since assessment affects children's motivation and sense of themselves as learners, it can be an encouraging or a discouraging experience. Fairness, the fourth principle, must be taken very seriously. Because learners differ, they need to be granted many different opportunities to show what they know and what they can do in the language. Fairness not only presupposes, for instance, that learners have encountered the tasks and situations employed during assessment in their classrooms, but also that different stages of individual development are being catered to (e.g. a learner who is new in class or started late in the program). In addition, gender issues come into play here. Tasks need to involve boys as much as they do girls. Finally, the fairness principle calls for predictable and transparent procedures: learners have a right to know what they are being assessed upon. It goes without saying that these four potentially conflicting principles need to be balanced, which can best be achieved when site-specific assessment designs are negotiated by local teams of teachers responsible for similar groups of learners.

3 Assessment tasks

Great variety of assessment tasks

As we have argued in chapter 3, tasks provide and frame the opportunities for learners to do things with language. Consequently, they also provide the space of action within which they can demonstrate this. Tasks capture the interesting content learners are willing to engage in and relate to the texts learners deal with and produce. Furthermore, they integrate several skills, even if they focus on one particular skill. As to the social arrangements, assessment tasks can be performed by all learners simultaneously (e.g. in phases of summative assessment) or by individuals and small groups one after the other (in formative assessment).
Listening tasks: After the *Fashion Show*, the teacher could conclude the unit (describing and promoting people) with the following listening and comprehension task: learners are exposed to a recording of a fashion show in which several models are introduced. Supported by a worksheet representing different fashion models, the learners have to indicate individually

which of the models are being introduced. This could be concluded by means of a color dictation: the teacher tells the learners which clothes should be colored, and in what way. Most modern textbooks offer a considerable variety of such listening tasks, among them: card games, bingo games, listen and match activities, and action stories (for examples of tasks cf. CLAUS et al 2008: 15–20).

Speaking tasks: Whereas the above listening tasks can be administered simultaneously to all learners, speaking tasks require a clear focus on one individual and are more demanding to analyze in terms of learner performance. During the *Fashion Show,* the teacher observes the learners in action and takes notes after each performance. The interesting question is, of course, what the focus of the teacher's observation is and what criteria and rating scales they use.

Semi-formal situations

Recent case studies on formative classroom assessment of speaking skills indicate that speaking tasks can turn into effective tools for learning and teaching if the following conditions are met (DRESE 2008; for examples see CLAUS et al 2008):

(1) In order to be fair to the needs of all learners, teachers need to use a great variety of speaking tasks ranging form monologic reproduction of short texts to dialogic and group interactions, some of them having the teacher as prompter, helper, and/or partner.
(2) Learners need to be familiar with the tasks and should be made aware that they are being assessed. Such awareness can trigger a willingness to perform under the safe conditions of the classroom.
(3) Formative assessment should be administered on a regular basis so that outcomes can inform teaching and provide the information for regular feedback.
(4) If designed properly, such assessment tasks can easily be implemented in the classroom in one or two lessons. While the class is engaged in some kind of silent activity, the teacher calls individuals or groups of learners to a designated area in the classroom to administer the assessment procedure.

Such assessment scenarios display an elaborate level of formality and therefore enhance the reliability of the procedures.

4 Data gathering, documentation and feedback

The complexity of assessing speaking skills

Effective assessment tasks require adequate tools for data gathering which help the teacher frame their observation, support the interpretation of the learner's performance, and guide the feedback to the learner. This is true for any assessment task and is the most demanding when it comes to assessing speaking. When constructing or selecting the task, the teacher needs to be absolutely clear what they want to focus on. Standards and state curricula provide the necessary orientation (→ ch. 13). In addition, the most recent generation of course books for the primary school offers a range of sample assessment tasks for the teacher to choose from. Let us again consider *The Fashion Show*, and focus on some dimensions of the skill "speaking". We can distinguish at least four levels of competence:

(1) On the pragmatic level, we could state whether the learner can open the show, attract the attention of the audience, introduce their model, describe the model, and close the performance.
(2) On the linguistic level, we might be concerned with the range and choice of vocabulary, the use of structures and chunks, and issues of pronunciation and intonation.
(3) On the level of fluency, we want to state how fluent the learner presents their text.
(4) On the level of performance, we are interested in the way the learner delivers the text using body language and other means of expressiveness, but also in their use of strategies. How do the learners cope with task demands in view of their limited linguistic means?

Each of these achievements can be expressed by means of a can-do statement. Having selected these aspects is not enough, however, because it is as important to assess the degree and/or quality of the performance on each level. Is the learner always fluent, or does their fluency differ? Do they use more complex structures? Finally, the question is whether the teacher wants to relate the learner's performance to previous events in order to diagnose progress. One can easily see how under classroom conditions, matters of validity clash with the criterion of practicability. To support practicability, and at the same time do justice to the complexity of the assessment event, several types of observation sheets and checklists have been developed and are now part and parcel of teacher handbooks (for examples cf. DIEHR 2005, DRESE 2006, DRESE 2008, CLAUS ET AL. 2008: 12, 14, 24).

3 Peer and self-assessment

1 The concept of self-assessment and the portfolio initiative

The European Language Portfolio (ELP)

The notion that learners can profit substantially in their language development and in their ability to learn when given the chance to contribute to assessment is not new (OSKARSSON 1980, 1986). Concepts of self-assessment in language learning have recently received a major boost through the portfolio initiative of the Council of Europe (COUNCIL OF EUROPE 1997, 2000) and through general education research on alternative forms of assessment (WINTER 2004). Language portfolios can be defined as a *"systematic collection of student work that is analyzed to show progress over time with regard to instructional objectives"* (O'MALLEY & VALDEZ PIERCE 1996: 5). Examples of student work may range from drawings and written texts to learning logs and reflections on achievements. As with other professions, where portfolios are used, for instance by artists or architects, the documents represent the holder's subjective view of his/her accomplishments, which needs, of course, to be completed by other points of view (e.g. of the teacher). On the basis of the *Common European Framework of*

Reference (Council of Europe 2001), which defines levels of language competence, the Council of Europe has adapted the portfolio concept and defined two key goals for the *European Language Portfolio (ELP)*: its reporting function should give evidence of the holder's language achievements and thus promote mobility in Europe. Its pedagogic function should validate the wealth of different languages and thus promote multilingualism. To achieve these goals, guidelines for a prototype of the *ELP* were developed which led to a number of national and regional adaptations. The *ELP* consists of three parts: (1) *The Language Passport* provides on overview of the individual's proficiency in different languages including formal qualifications. (2) *The Language Biography* helps the learners state what they can do in a language and give evidence of intercultural experiences. (3) *The Dossier* offers students the opportunity to document and illustrate achievements reported in part 1 and 2 (Council of Europe 2000, Schärer 2003).

2 Features of a junior portfolio

Three aims of *Mein Sprachenportfolio*

Junior portfolios or primary school portfolios have been created in various European countries and several German states as an attempt to put the three parts of the *ELP* prototype into child-appropriate form (for examples → ch. 15.2 Resources). The project group responsible for *Mein Sprachenportfolio*, the junior portfolio for the State of Hesse, (Legutke & Lortz 2002b) summarized its three aims as follows (Legutke 2002a: 105f):

(1) To give evidence of the language skills children have acquired or learned within and/or outside formal education. Particular attention should be paid to heritage languages represented in a class (reporting function).
(2) To introduce children to the idea of self-assessment by exploring appropriate ways of becoming aware of their language learning biography, their skills, their strengths and shortcomings, their willingness to learn, and their learning strategies (pedagogic function).
(3) To support the children during their transition process to secondary schools and to prepare children for the use of the ELP (presentational function).

Whereas the first functions are in keeping with the general requirements of the ELP prototype, the third function has been seen as an important and unique feature of the junior portfolio. (→ ch. 13).

3 Reasons for using a junior portfolio and challenges for self-assessment

Findings from observational studies

Current research into the use of junior portfolios in different German states and reports from teachers have confirmed several expectations of the various project groups, but have also uncovered a number of challenges which need further exploration. Some of them will be briefly touched upon here (for details see Christ 2004, Claus et al. 2008, Kolb 2007, Legutke 2002a, 2006, Lippelt 2002).

(1) The portfolio is a powerful tool to move the learners' subjective view of accomplishments into focus, which is best achieved by means of reflective dialogue as a continuous element of classroom work. Portfolio work therefore affects the entire pedagogy of the EFL classroom and not only the few lessons during which the learners work on the portfolio. To learn how to assess themselves properly, learners need continuous guidance how to do so. Appropriate preparatory tasks need to be built in on a regular basis throughout the course (for examples cf. Claus et al. 2008).

(2) The fact that portfolio pages help learners become aware of what they can do with reference to different skills (*"Ich kann meine Lehrerin verstehen, wenn sie ein Spiel erklärt, ich kann einen Clown beschreiben, ich kann über meinen Tagesablauf berichten"*) is seen as a positive move away from a narrow orientation towards learner deficits (deviations from a native speaker norm). On the other hand, the descriptors for competences offered by most portfolios are not satisfactory, because they are extremely difficult to formulate in child-appropriate language.

(3) Especially the research by Kolb (2007: 311ff) has underscored that portfolio work can provide a unique space of reflection ("Reflexionsraum"). Kolb isolated four salient strategies children employ when working with portfolio pages for self-assessment. (a) Children refer back to a lesson. Achievement is equated with "we have covered this topic." (b) Children look for confirmation through others (teacher or peers) by creating a situation where this is rendered possible. (c) Children invent ways of self-testing. For instance, they use a page representing the word field "food" with pictures and matching words by covering all the words with small pieces of paper to check whether thy know the respective words by looking at the pictures. (d) Finally, children, once they have been accustomed to methods of self-assessment, tend to refer to an inner representation of their competence. They imagine themselves in situations where they have acted successfully; for example, when presenting a clown in a fashion show.

(4) Closely related to the previous point is the development of learning awareness. Observations during the implementation of the page *"Wie ich meine Sprachen lerne"* of *Mein Sprachenportfolio* (Legutke & Lortz 2002b: 10–11) give an indication how creatively learners go about learning vocabulary. Their strategies range from monologic reproduction to dialogic realization (*"Ich sage sie [die Wörter] mir im Kopf auf, bis ich sie richtig weiss [sic]". „Am nächsten Tag sag ich mir Die Wörter noch einmal auf". „Ich merke mir Wörter, indem ich mir die passenden Bilder merke". „Wenn ich meiner Mutter die Wörter lese und sie später aufsage dan [sic] hab ich sie auswendig gelernt." „Ich sag sie meinem Kanarienvogel auf". „Ich sag sie meinem Teddybär vor, dann kann ich die Wörter"* (cf. Christ 2004).

(5) Portfolio work supports the growth of learner self-awareness and confidence as several studies have confirmed. Such growth is best repre-

sented by the following learner statements: Aishe (9) *"Englisch ist so, dass ich was Knuspriges essen würde. Ich sehe das Welt ist sooooooo bunt. Ich schreibe ein Gedicht auf Englisch, auf einmal schwebe ich in der Luft. Eigentlich mag ich kein Englisch, trotzdem ist es soooo schön"* (Kolb 2007: 297). Michael (9) after he had completed one self-assessment task: *"Englischlernen ist wie stark sein, weil stark sein ist wie gut lernen. . . . Ich fühl mich dann stark, sehr stark"* (Kolb 2007: 297). Fadime, after she had worked through several pages of *Mein Sprachenportfolio: "Ich fühle mich, dass ich Englischkönigin bin!"* (Kolb 2007: 299).

(6) A particularly interesting tension between benefits and challenges can be stated for the use of the dossier, often referred to as the treasure chest (*Schatztruhe*) in the junior portfolio. Although scholars agree that the treasure chest should be filled with a great variety of learner texts and documents that could give evidence of the learner's achievements, very little attention has been given to the questions as to how these documents can be used successfully. Findings from a recent case study indicate very strongly that the presentational value of treasure chest documents is enhanced if learners have gained experience and practiced how to use them, either in dialogic situations or with an audience, e.g. the teacher or a peer. (Rau & Legutke 2008). This is particularly important during the phase of transition from primary to secondary schools (→ ch. 9). As part of the *Teddy Bear Project* (→ chs. 8 & 9), a girl has received an e-mail from a pen pal in New Zealand. She has printed the text and creatively decorated it in the treasure chest. In a presentational situation she could either read out the e-mail, or use it as a stimulus to introduce either her pen pal or her friend. Unless such presentation has been practiced, very few students will be capable of using the text to demonstrate language accomplishments. These findings are also supported by Drese 2008, who focused in her study on the value of semi-structured assessment of speaking skills.

Most of the available studies and reports support the insight that the main question is not how a portfolio could be integrated into main stream primary EFL classrooms, but rather how classes need to be pedagogically conceptualized and appropriately realized to allow portfolio work and self-assessment to unfold its potential for learning. Chapter 13 will return to some of the issues related to this insight.

4 Challenges and future directions

Current and future research. Guidelines for classroom action

This chapter has introduced different assessment formats and demonstrated a few ways how learning and language growth can be fostered. At the same time, it has touched on a range of assessment issues that pose considerable challenges to teachers, as expressed in the following table

Assessment	Task types	Record keeping	Advantages	Challenges
Teacher Assessment (TA) Informal	Variety of tasks (speaking and listening)	Checklists	Easy to realize	Not very reliable, possibly unfair
TA: Semi-structured	Variety of tasks (speaking and listening)	Checklists and structured observation sheets	Valid and fair	Time constraints, possible conflict between reliability and fairness
TA: formal "tests"	Paper and pencil tasks	Test scores	Easy to do, reliable	limited validity and fairness, very limited use in the primary classroom
Peer assessment	Partner tasks	Observation sheets	Highly supportive of learner engagement	Training required, demand of social skills
Self-assessment	Portfolio tasks	Self-assessment sheets	Promotes confidence and learning awareness	Requires committed and qualified teachers

These challenges are rendered even more demanding by institutional and systemic pressures. As the introduction of FL in primary schools was not matched with adequate teacher education, many teachers have not yet had a chance to develop the necessary diagnostic skills for classroom assessment (→ ch. 4). This lack of professional competence is particularly worrisome in an educational system which allocates children to career-bound streams of schooling after grade 4. The question whether a learner is suitable for the top stream can easily override the pedagogically more relevant question which supports a learner needs to continue growing in their language competence. There are no easy and straightforward answers to these challenges. What is encouraging, though, is the fact that classroom assessment has moved from a side-show to center stage in the professional debate. Experts, making use of recent European research, have begun to formulate guidelines for classroom action (BIG 2008). In addition, recent studies in the complex world of German primary classrooms have investigated practicable and highly effective ways of both teacher assessment and self-assessment that serve teaching and foster learner growth. Although the findings of these pioneer studies cannot be generalized for standard practice, they set the parameters for future work in teacher education (cf. Diehr 2006, Drese 2008, Kolb 2007).

1 Interface between the primary and the secondary school: Transition or gap?

English in the primary school – and then?

Although the introduction of foreign language learning into primary schools has been hailed as a major achievement in European education (→ ch. 1), it has been accompanied by a range of challenges at the institutional level that have affected the individuals (teachers and learners). The challenges can be grouped around the following key question: if more and more children start learning a foreign language at an ever earlier age, how is their education to continue into secondary schooling? The answer does not seem to be easy, because the question of how the knowledge and skills that have been acquired in primary school may be recognized, consolidated and expanded once children have reached secondary schools has become a major point of the educational debate. We will present some of the issues in the following sections. Since research on the crucial interface of primary and secondary English programs is in progress, our insights are primarily based on teacher accounts we have compiled in many seminars all over Europe. In addition, the outcomes of a German inter-state project we will refer to below in detail give us many new insights (also cf. Burwitz-Melzer & Legutke 2004). The chapter will conclude with an overview of strategies and initiatives which have been proposed to meet some of the challenges.

1 Gains vs. losses

Approaching the challenges: seven dichotomies

With the introduction of primary EFL programs, teachers in the secondary school have lost a chance to participate in a highly rewarding experience in their professional lives: opening the world of a new language and culture to children who tend to embark with great enthusiasm on this exciting venture. When children arrive at secondary school today they have not only already gone through this exciting phase of initial contact with the new language with a different teacher, but they also expect that their experiences will be recognized and appreciated. Primary school teachers, on the other hand, have gained a new and exciting field of work yielding a range of very rewarding experiences. It seems difficult for some secondary teachers to accept this loss and discover the new chances this change might entail.

2 Innovations vs. established routines

Teaching English in the primary school has been accompanied by Europe-wide efforts to develop methods and materials that can accommodate the needs of young children and do justice to their learning potential. In particular, innovative methods for fostering listening and speaking skills have resulted from these efforts, based on holistic and communicative principles. These ideas and practices, willingly accepted by primary school teachers, seem, at least to some extent, to challenge established teaching routines of secondary school teachers, who feel that they are pressured to change. Indeed, to build on what learners bring from the primary school, it is absolutely necessary that teachers, especially in the first few weeks, continue with routines established earlier (such as opening routines, routines of classroom discourse, circle sessions, story telling routines, and routines of changing the lesson's pace) and use task formats for listening and speaking the learners are familiar with. In this sense, primary school programs have exerted considerable pressure on secondary teachers to change, which, for understandable reasons, is not always appreciated, because teachers are required to rethink their established practice.

3 Expectations vs. reality

There are considerable misconceptions about what can actually be achieved in a standard primary English program where children usually are offered two 45-minute sessions per week in grades 3 and 4. Secondary teachers tend to view the outcomes of these programs from what may be achieved in their own context where in grade 5 children have contact with English four to five times a week (at least 45 minutes per session). This means that the exposure time in grade five exceeds the total contact time in primary school. Although expectations need to be adjusted to these conditions, there is no reason to downgrade what is possible. However, expectations need to be portrayed realistically and accessibly by primary teachers, as we will show later.

4 Generalists vs. language specialists

Primary school teachers are generalists, whereas secondary English teachers are trained specialists with a degree in the teaching of English, which, of course, includes advanced language studies. Although there are no reliable figures available for all German states, it is quite reasonable to assume that only about 20% of these generalists have received some form of systematic training in the teaching of English either through university programs or through in-service teacher education. This leaves a substantial group of teachers who lack the appropriate teaching and language skills which would allow them to manage the learning process, as we have outlined throughout this book. The lack of basic language and teaching skills on the part of some primary teachers accounts for the recurrent skepticism of secondary teachers as to the quality of primary programs, but this does not justify discarding their achievements altogether. Major efforts by the state educational institutions, such as teacher qualification programs, are called for to compensate for these shortcomings.

5 Relative homogeneity vs. mixed ability

No group of learners is homogeneous, of course, but before primary English was introduced, secondary English teachers could work with relatively homogeneous groups of learners in the initial phases of the English lessons. This has changed dramatically. Since secondary schools draw learners from different feeder schools, with possibly different foreign language programs, the heterogeneity of the learners is much more obvious right from the start. The loss we addressed above is thus aggravated by the fact that teachers now have to come up with methods that accommodate mixed ability groups – a task secondary school teachers usually have not been qualified for. Instead of meeting these new challenges by adjusting their methodology, teachers might resort to simply ignoring the new situation, and start from scratch again. This, of course, would mean a major loss for the children and could easily have demotivating effects.

6 Standards vs. native speaker norms

From the very beginning, early language programs have been guided by outcome-oriented principles which emphasize language growth and learner competence. This means that the main focus of assessment is to describe and appreciate what learners can actually do with the target language (e.g. introduce a pen-pal, → ch. 12) rather than to state in how far they conform to a native speaker norm (e.g. correct use of plural "s"). This is not to say that all secondary teachers are only guided by native speaker norms. However, we have come away from many seminars with the impression that it seems to be much easier for teachers to respond to deviations from the norm than to describe achievements. In this way, primary English language teaching is in keeping with what the Council of Europe had in mind when they published the *Common European Framework of Reference* (Council of Europe 2001). Furthermore, primary ELT is compatible with the current move towards standards for educational processes, which again has moved learner competencies and achievements to center stage. Teachers are encouraged to assess achievements and provide the necessary support so that the standards can be met by all learners (Hallet & Müller-Hartmann 2006, Vollmer 2006). Comments of secondary teachers during in-service training indicate quite clearly that a change of perspective in this respect has not taken place yet, that is, the shift from focusing on learner deficits to an awareness of learner achievements is still in progress. Instead, there are recurrent complaints towards primary English programs that the learners violate native speaker norms or that they have not learned enough.

7 Self-assessment vs. teacher assessment

Since the achievements of children coming from primary school are mostly related to listening and speaking skills, the challenge for the secondary teachers is enormous. Listening and speaking skills are quite difficult to assess in large classes and this process might not have been addressed in teacher education courses at the university. But secondary school teachers are expected to broaden their diagnostic tools and their range of assessment tasks. If children bring along a portfolio, and if they have been trained to demonstrate their language abilities (→ ch. 12), the portfolio could certainly support the teacher's assessment. But they would need to know how to use it. Again, a change of perspective is called for. Only if the teacher accepts the children's subjective view of their learning as a valid contribution to their diagnosis of achievements can self-assessment supplement teacher assessment for the benefit of the learners. On the other hand, it cannot be denied that self-assessment is still rather alien to German schools, which explains why teachers find it difficult to integrate this tool into their daily work. (cf. WINTER 2004).

2 Chances, strategies and perspectives

Complex issues and multi-faceted answers

The complex and multi-layered issues and challenges connected with the interface of primary and secondary English programs require multi-faceted answers. Some of these answers, which have emerged from the current debate and from a number of state and inter-state projects, will be summarized here, among them the most comprehensive initiative launched between 2003 and 2006 by the project *"Sprachen lehren und lernen als Kontinuum"* (funded by the *Bund-Länder-Kommission der Ständigen Konferenz der Kultusmisnister der Länder*, BLK). Possible solutions will be presented according to the various levels of who is responsible: the national/state level, the regional/school/local level, and the level of the individual teacher.

1 The state/national level

(1) Although the German states have agreed on standards for foreign language learning at secondary level (HALLET & MÜLLER-HARTMANN 2006), no such national standards are currently available for primary school foreign language learning. A national consensus on what children should achieve at the end of primary school would certainly help in building programs that are committed to support all children. Coincidentally, a blueprint for such standards has been submitted by the BIG circle (BIG 2005), which could provide guidance for state and regional institutions.

(2) Language curricula need to be rewritten so that they embrace the primary and secondary level and define the continuous growth of language development. The basic language portfolio (*"Grundportfolio"*) developed by the BLK project, does justice to this demand by systematically building a bridge from grade three to six (→ ch. 15.2).

(3) All major course book companies in Germany have reacted to the new situation and have built-in pick-up tasks in their English course books for the fifth grade which allow teachers to work with what learners bring to class from the primary school.

(4) In order to make sure that these standards, curricula, portfolios and new course books are recognized, and their implications transferred

into day-to-day practice, intensive in-service teacher education programs are necessary, which need to bring teachers together from both levels of education. The programs should be based on documented classroom experiences and cover the core topics of methods of mixed ability teaching, documentation and diagnosis of learner achievements, and classroom assessment. Several proposals for such seminars have been submitted (BLK 2006a, KIEWEG 2004). State institutions are, first and foremost, responsible that teachers are granted the space and the flexibility in their professional lives to attend appropriate and quality programs.

2 The regional and local level

(1) Most promising are the initiatives at the regional level, where feeder schools cooperate with their respective secondary schools. Such cooperative ventures should not only provide the opportunity to visit classes at both types of schools, but also make sure that realistic expectations are built on detailed reports of the primary schools regarding their resources and curricula (topics, language functions and stock chunks of language), but also their methods of classroom assessment. Secondary school teachers, on the other hand, need to explore classroom routines and learning arrangements of their colleagues to discover how they can build on what learners are familiar with (BLK 2006b).

(2) Regional activities depend very much on what happens at the individual school. Because the challenges cannot be met by the individual teacher alone, decisions need to be made at the school's administration level that touch on methods for teaching mixed ability groups, task-based language learning, and on assessment tasks and criteria. Sharing experiences of success and jointly searching for solutions to day-to-day problems will make up some of the core activities.

3 The individual level

Even if the three levels of responsibility cannot be separated, since they supplement each other, it eventually comes down to the individual teacher and their willingness and ability to meet the challenges. Primary English teachers can best prepare the learners for the next phase of their language development by helping them to become aware of their knowledge and abilities and by training them to demonstrate their skills in semi-formal encounters (→ ch. 12). To reach this goal, they need to address a number of key questions. Among them are:

- Do I know what my learners should know and be able to do in English once they have reached the end of primary school? (e.g. the topics they can handle, the chunks of words they have available, the learning strategies they use)
- Can I describe their skills in detail and give a record of possible achievements to other teachers? (e.g. they can follow the classroom discourse in

English, they can understand simple stories, introduce their friends, describe their favorite animal)
- Can I give account of the methods I use to support my learners development to other teachers? (e.g. methods of introducing and practicing words, use of routines, use of TPR activities, use of the hand puppet)
- Have I shown my learners how they can present their knowledge and skills to other people? Have they learned how to use their portfolios?
- How would I assess my language competence? To my view, have I reached a level of competence which allows me to react spontaneously to the learners and manage the learning process in the target language?

Secondary school teachers need to be ready to answer to the following questions (a selection):
- How can I expand the topics the learners have covered so far? (e.g. learners discover in the course book texts and topics they are familiar with)
- How can I consolidate previous knowledge and speaking/listening skills? (e.g. recreate situations from the primary classrooms, and then add new, possibly more complex but similar situations from the course book)
- How can I broaden what learners already know and are able to do orally into reading and writing? (e.g. let children demonstrate their speaking skills in describing their favorite animal, use the learner texts as models for writing)
- How can I build on language structures that have been learned implicitly in chunks and make the items more explicit for conscious learning? How can I do this holistically and inductively?
- How can I maintain the learners' willingness and eagerness to continue learning, even if the classes are more demanding?
- Which of the routines the learners are familiar with do I want to continue, and which need to be discontinued? (e.g. singing an opening song, using circle sessions, using a lot of visuals, managing the classroom in English)
- What are appropriate methods to teach mixed ability groups?

Small is beautiful

As can be gathered from what we have discussed throughout this book, there are no easy answers to these questions, because teaching English in the primary school, and beyond, is a demanding task. The challenges for the teachers at the transition between the primary and the secondary levels are even greater where institutional support is lacking and/or insufficient, and teachers feel left alone. On the other hand, it would be irresponsible to wait for the institutions to shoulder this responsibility, because the children have a right to be supported in their language growth, and it is primarily for their benefit that the programs are organized. Even in contexts where institutional support is insufficient, it is always more productive if teachers follow the principle of "small is beautiful," and try to discover what is possible for the children, instead of being too concerned with what cannot be done, because this or that is missing.

1 The importance of pre-school education: Literacy development and multilingualism

The current debate

The last chapter of our introduction will be devoted to the current debate on whether second/foreign language learning should become part and parcel of pre-school education. Although the drive to integrate languages into kindergarten and pre-school is not new (SCHMID-SCHÖNBEIN 1978), the debate has gained momentum in recent years. On the one hand, it has found expression in partly polemic articles in the education sections of serious news magazines and daily papers arguing for and against very early language instruction (→ ch. 15.2). On the other hand, researchers have taken up the topic (e.g. SCHOTTE-GREBENSTEIN 2006), professional journals reserve full issues for it (e.g. *Frühes Deutsch* 2006), and new guidebooks for pre-school teachers who want to teach English (*Erzieherinnen*) have appeared (LEIDNER 2007). In the debate, two models for implementing language learning can be distinguished: a course model based on mini-lessons and an immersion model. Although these models differ considerably, as we will explain below, they have in common the fact that they do not represent mainstream initiatives supported by state educational authorities and institutions, but by private parents' groups and associations, i.e. by private sponsors and foundations. Before we introduce these two models, we will briefly touch upon some of the reasons that explain the growing interest of parents and experts in pre-school learning.

Three reasons why pre-school education is discussed

There are at least three complex and interrelated reasons why pre-school education has moved to a prominent position on the educational agenda. (1) Because of the radical changes in demography due to global migration, pre-schools and primary schools have become the most multi-ethnic, multicultural and multilingual institutions, and therefore require new approaches to language and literacy development and cultural awareness (ANSTATT 2007, also cf. HU 2003). (2) The initiatives of the Council of Europe for a three-language policy for all European citizens (mother tongue plus two additional languages, and the strong recommendations to start language education as early as possible (→ ch. 1) coupled with research data from immersion programs (see below) have heightened the awareness that the pre-school years of children constitute an ideal time for language experiences and language growth. (3) The findings from the PISA studies (BAUMERT et al. 2001) have triggered a growing concern in Germany that established modes of early childhood education (as traditionally offered by the German kindergarten) are no longer capable of meeting the learning needs of multi-ethnic groups of children and do not prepare all children adequately for the demands of schooling. Therefore, not only a new professionalization of pre-school teachers is called for, but also a fundamental re-evaluation of early childhood education including issues of literacy development.

Blueprint for early childhood education

A representative example of this new orientation in Germany is provided by the blueprint for early childhood education of the state of Hesse jointly published by the Ministries of Education and Social Affairs (HESSISCHES SOZIALMINISTERIUM & HESSISCHES KULTUSMINISTERIUM 2007). The 149-page document discusses a comprehensive list of competences for children from 0 to 10 years of age. Language and culture related aspects play a central role. Under the heading *"Kulturelle Offenheit"* the blueprint argues: *"Zwei- und Mehrsprachigkeit sowie interkulturelle Kompetenz können Kindern helfen, sich zu weltgewandten, weltoffenen Persönlichkeiten zu entwickeln. Gemeinsame Lernaktivitäten, bei denen sich Kinder mit verschiedenem kulturellem Hintergrund begegnen, sind geeignet, um interkulturelle Kompetenz einzuüben. Die Kinder werden neugierig auf andere Kulturen und lernen Andersartigkeit zu achten, auch wenn sie sie nicht vollständig verstehen"* (ibd. 32). Various dimensions of intercultural competence are covered in great detail such as curiosity and openness, awareness of otherness and ability to accept differences, appreciation of heritage languages, and the ability to act and learn in multilingual contexts, to name just a few (ibd. 49; also → ch. 8)). Even if the blueprint does not explicitly call for the introduction of a particular foreign language into the various pre-school locations, it provides a general framework and a coherent set of arguments for foreign language education. The arguments put forward and the competences addressed by the blueprint are very similar to those presented in the BIG standards for foreign language learning in primary school that we have referred to throughout the book (BIG 2005). The following discussion of two basic models for teaching English to very young learners needs to be seen against the background of these general trends in early childhood education.

2 Very young children learning English: Two instructional models

1 The course model: Mini English lessons

The most common model

The most common model used with pre-school children all over Germany is best described as a course model (for details cf. SCHOTTE-GREBENSTEIN 2006). The model is based on mini-lessons of various length distributed over the week. They are either integrated into the daily routines of a kindergarten, if pre-school teachers are available to take over the task, or offered by a growing number of private and commercial language schools, often staffed with native speakers catering to parents who can afford to pay for this special service. In addition to the pioneering course materials and guidelines for pre-school teachers *English for Mopsy and me* (FÖHLICH-WARD & SCHMID-SCHÖNBEIN 1999), a range of materials is available through publishers or via the internet and private language enterprises, if a kindergarten has the means to obtain the necessary licenses for the programs from the private schools and language offices. The materials combine listening texts, songs, and games, and usually include a variety of visual and digital media and a hand puppet. The underlying philosophy of these resources subscribes to a holistic and highly interactive methodology. Although the mini-lesson programs have become quite well established in many German cities, it is very difficult to judge how efficient they are. The only available case study for the time being (SCHOTTE-GREBENSTEIN 2006) confirms informal reports that children display a lot of enthusiasm for learning English. They not only show a very positive attitude to the learning tasks, but also develop elements of language awareness and language learning awareness: *"So kann ein sechsjähriges Mädchen bei der Einführung der neuen Vokabel 'Easter bunny' sofort 'easter egg' bilden, womit sie ein unbekanntes Wort durch ein ihr bereits bekanntes Wort ersetzt hat."* (ibd. 93); children explain that they learn by repeating words or by singing them, or that they speak a word silently by moving their lips before speaking aloud (ibd. 94). Also, pre-school teachers and parents in the study show very positive attitudes towards the programs and seem to agree that children are not overburdened by the mini-lessons. Since the language competence of pre-school children having attended such mini-lessons has not been researched so far, claims concerning course results need to be handled with a grain of salt. Indeed, it is an important task of future research to assess the development of language competence with reference to contact time, resources, language input, methodology, and teacher performance.

2 The pre-school immersion model

The language bath

The second model is based on the idea of a total language bath, hence the term "immersion." Children are "immersed" in a second language, which means that everyday communicative exchanges are realized in the target language (e.g. English is used for breakfast, for helping children brush their teeth, during play time, story telling, introducing nap time). If at least 50% of the instruction is done in the target language one speaks of *partial immersion, total immersion* on the other hand involves 100% target language use. Advocates of the immersion model in Germany refer to more than 30 years of research on French immersion programs in Canada which has provided consistent findings as to the success of the programs. CUMMINS summarizes these findings: *"In early immersion programs, students gain fluency and literacy in French at no apparent cost to their English academic skills"* (CUMMINS, online: 2; CUMMINS 1999; for overview of research cf. GENESEE 1987, JOHNSON & SWAIN 1997). Backed by these findings German supporters of the immersion model criticize the mini-lesson course model as inefficient and a waste of time because of the extremely limited language contact being provided to learners. Instead, they offer the immersion approach as the appropriate answer to early language education (WODE 1998, WODE 2002a, b, c; more details and a list of schools and initiatives under: www.fmks-online.de).

The Altenholz model

A concrete reference point for the discussion on early immersion in Germany is the well-documented pilot project in Altenholz/Kiel (Wode 2002 a, b). This model operates with the principle of "one language per person". Of the legally required two pre-school teachers per group of children, person A only speaks English to the children whereas person B speaks the common language all children understand (German). But person A knows enough German so that the children can address her and she can negotiate activities with person B. Wode makes a strong point that person A should be a native speaker of the target language. It is important in the model that all key activities that the children favor and enjoy should be conducted in the target language, whereas the common language is used for managerial purposes. Data from the Altenholz project show that by the end of the three years of kindergarten learners have acquired comprehension skills which by far exceed their speaking skills. Spontaneous language production, on the other hand, is rare, because the children know that their teachers understand German. With the help of controlled production experiments, however, using hand puppets and picture cards, insights could be gained into the children's production skills. It became obvious that these skills actually had been acquired once the children had entered a bilingual primary school which also operates with an immersion model. An amazing language growth could be observed, which showed that pre-school immersion can lay a solid foundation for a continuation of language learning: *"Dass vergleichbare Fähigkeiten auch für andere Strukturbereiche vorhanden sind, ergibt sich aus der geradezu explosionsartigen Entwicklung des Englischen innmerhalb des 1. Schuljahrs in den Bereichen Wortschatz, Flexionsmorphologie, Syntax und Diskurs […]. Ausgelöst wird dieser Schub durch den Zwang zum mündlichen Klassengespräch"* (Wode 2002b: 28). The immersion model, therefore, makes the most sense, if it is conceptualized as the first step of immersion education which is continued in primary school (Burmeister 2006). Such primary immersion schools, however, only represent a minute minority in Germany, where about 100 are presently in operation. 27 of them can be found in Berlin. There are immersion schools for German-Spanish, German-Japanese, German-English (9x), but also for French, Greek, Portuguese, Turkish, Russian, and Polish (for details see: www.fmks-online.de). Quite a number of these immersion schools in Germany are private schools and ask for substantial fees, such as the Frankfurt International School.

3 Issues

In order to assess the educational value of these two models of early childhood language education, at least four issues need to be considered. They are best summarized with the following questions:

- Who has access to these programs?
- How are the programs continued beyond pre-school?

- Which methods and material are available?
- Who is willing to and capable of educating the pre-school teachers?

1 Access

Selected and privileged group of children

At the moment, only a very selective and privileged group of children has access to either of the models. SCHOTTE–GREBENSTEIN, providing a comprehensive survey of initiatives that follow the course model, comes to the disillusioning conclusion: *"Derzeit geht die Förderung von Fremdsprachen im Kindergarten von Elternhäusern mit hoher Bildungsambition aus. Die an Englisch im Kindergarten teilnehmenden Kinder kommen vorwiegend aus Elternhäusern mit gehobenem sozialen und kulturellen Hintergrund"* (SCHOTTE-GREBENSTEIN 2006: 184-5). Apart form the fact that the immersion model is extremely exceptional in Germany, it needs to be recognized that the results of the Altenholz pilot were obtained with a predominantly monolingual group of German children. No pilots have been reported about multi-lingual groups of children, which today have become dominant in many urban and even rural areas. What is missing so far are immersion programs that consider all children of a given area. In conjunction with these pilots, the impact of factors such as diverse cultural and linguistic backgrounds, social status, and economic status of parents would have to be researched. Unless these issues are addressed, it is difficult to avoid the impression that a privileged group of monolingual German children is granted the chance of "explosive language growth", whereas the much more difficult and thus more demanding group of children with less developed literacy skills in German and/or their heritage languages is left out. For this reason, it is most important that more comprehensive proposals for pre-school immersion programs must be conceptualized and piloted which grant learning opportunities to all students, no matter what language and cultural background they have.

2 Continuity

No systematic follow-up

Most of the questions we have raised in the previous chapter can be asked here again. Only the advocates of the immersion model explicitly address the issue of continuity, since for them the pre-school programs provide the necessary basis for immersion education in the primary school. Less obvious is the interest of those who propagate the course model. Since most German primary schools start in grade 3 with their English programs, there would be no systematic follow-up for two years. Given the rather limited contact time and the fact that there are no regional programs that would include all children of a given area, the question is more than justified whether such mini-lesson programs are really worth the effort. On the other hand, they seem to stimulate not only the learners' cultural and language awareness, but also to some extent their language learning awareness.

3 Curricula, methods and materials

Lack of a comprehensive curriculum

Even if there are interesting materials on the market which seem to meet the learning needs of children and stimulate their interest, so far no curricular guidelines are available that define possible outcomes, and thus define learner competences. These guidelines should, on the one hand, capture what can be achieved at pre-school level, as well as indicate how the competences will be further developed in the primary school. The above mentioned blueprint of the state of Hesse could be seen as a step in the right direction, but more concrete explications are needed for early language education. These will necessarily have implications for new materials supporting continuous learning. Although most of the currently available materials subscribe to a communicative philosophy, there is no common understanding of the appropriate methodology for early language learning. Again, further discussion based on research seems necessary.

4 Teacher education

Lack of qualified teachers

As we have underlined continuously, it is the teacher who matters. Their competence (→ ch. 4) will ultimately guarantee the success of the learners. Where are the qualified teachers for early language learning programs? Who is going to educate them? Who is going to pay for native speaker teachers from English speaking countries if one advocates the presence of such teachers in immersion education? There are no indications at the moment that state institutions are willing to invest into teacher education for early language programs when funds are already rather limited for teacher education at primary level. From our point of view, it is unacceptable to promote language education at pre-school level without seriously considering teacher education.

4 Chances and perspectives

Programs for the future

Even if the German state educational systems are still far away from being willing and able to implement foreign language education at pre-school level for all children, the privately funded projects we have touched upon here and the few primary school initiatives following an immersion format clearly point in the right direction – toward the future. The research findings reported from these projects strongly support the arguments we have summarized in chapters 1 and 2 of this book: children show not only great enthusiasm for learning a new language, but also are highly successful if offered appropriate contact time with the language and if they are involved in meaningful and stimulating activities. Most importantly, there are no indications that children are overburdened by the language programs. Literacy in the language of schooling (German) and competence in a foreign language can grow side by side – at least for some groups of learners. Furthermore, these programs provide a fundamental stepping stone for children towards developing elements of ICC and therefore towards becoming multilingual citizens. Finally, the studies and reports corroborate other findings that emphasize the centrality of a well-qualified teacher, an argument we have continuously presented in this book.

The key question

The key question, of course, is whether the goals promoted by private initiatives should become a central concern of language policy. We subscribe to the view that they should not be given priority for the time being. Other, more pressing challenges need to be addressed. As long as the state and regional systems have not provided the important prerequisites for adequate teacher education (university education and in-service education), as long as state programs are inconsistent in terms of standards and good practice, as long as the interface between the primary schools and the secondary schools has not taken forms that support the children's language growth (to name only a few of the pressing issues), pre-school foreign language programs will have to remain a side show of our professional endeavors.

On the other hand, this last chapter has argued that the general debate on educational reform cannot exclude early childhood learning from its agenda. This is particularly important, since the foundations of literacy development in the language of schooling (in our case German) will be laid in this phase. Furthermore, pre-school education can help children to appreciate and value the languages they bring to class. New directions in pre-school teacher education will not only have to address teachers' competencies in dealing with the multilingual reality of German pre-schools, but also provide for the necessary linguistic and cultural competences as fundamental prerequisites for successful teaching.

1 Bibliography

AITCHINSON, JEAN: *Introducing Language and Mind.* London: Penguin 1992.

ANSTATT, TANJA (Ed.): *Mehrsprachigkeit bei Kindern und Erwachsenen: Erwerb, Formen, Förderung.* Tübingen: Narr 2007.

APPEL, JOACHIM: *Diary of a Language Teacher.* Oxford: Heinemann 1995.

ARNOLD, KARL-HEINZ: „Diagnostische Kompetenzen erwerben. Wie das Beurteilen zu lernen und zu lehren ist." In: *Pädagogik* 7–8, 51 (1999), P. 73–77.

ASHEUER, URSULA: „‚Oops, I did it again!' – Der Umgang mit dem Fehler im Englischunterricht." In: *Englisch in der Grundschule und darüber hinaus: Eine praxisnahe Orientierungshilfe.* Ed.: Christoph EDELHOFF. Frankfurt a.M.: Diesterweg 2003. P. 131–142.

BAILEY, MARIA: „Playway. Spaß am Lernen." In: *Primary English, Fachbeilage des Grundschulmagazin Englisch* 1 (2006), P. 14–15.

BAILEY, MARIA & GISELA SCHMID-SCHÖNBEIN: „Classroom Management: Gut organisiert Englisch unterrichten." In: *Primary English* 3 (2005), P. 3–5.

BATSTONE, ROB: *Grammar.* Oxford: Oxford UP 1994.

BAUMANN, GUDRUN, ELIZABETH LEWIS & ANTON PROCHAZKA (Eds.): *Language Teaching Across the Curriculum. Subject-Based Approach.* Books 1 + 2. Wien: Pädagogisches Institut des Bundes in Wien, IFU 2000.

BAUMERT, JÜRGEN et al (Eds.): *PISA 2000 – ein differenzierter Blick auf die Länder der Bundesrepublik Deutschland.* Opladen: Leste & Wudrich 2001.

BAUMGARTEN-MILLINGTON, CLAUDIA: „Grundschulkinder schreiben ihr erstes Buch auf Englisch." In: *Englisch* 34, 1 (1999), P. 1–3.

BAUMGRATZ-GANGL, GISELA: „Bildungs- und sprachenpolitische Perspektiven eines zukünftigen Europa." In: *Sprache, Kultur, Identität – Selbst- und Fremdwahrnehmungen in Ost- und Westeuropa.* Ed.: ASTRID ERTELT-VIETH. Frankfurt: Lang 1993. P. 240–249.

BECHLER, SABRINA & SABINE DOFF: „Dinosaurier und ihre Lebensweise." In: *Primary English* 6 (2005), P. 13–17.

BECK, ROSEMARIE: „Supermouse. Ein Lehrwerk mit ICT-Activities." In: *Primary English, Fachbeilage des Grundschulmagazin Englisch* 6 (2006), P. 14–15.

BECKER, CARMEN: „Projects go primary. Kreatives und produktives Handeln fördern." (Basisbeitrag zur Projektarbeit). In: *Grundschulmagazin Englisch* 2 (2007), P. 6–7.

BECKER, CARMEN & ANKE DIEKMANN: "Bridging the Gap – Strategies for Primary Teachers." In: *Grundschule Englisch* 10 (2005a), P. 42–44.

BECKER, CARMEN & ANKE DIEKMANN: "Transport Dialogues." In: *Grundschule Englisch* 10 (2005b), P. 12–13.

BEHR, URSULA & ADELHEID KIEREPKA: „Der Übergang von Klasse 4 nach Klasse 5. Abschlussprofile als Anschlussprofile." In: *Grundschulmagazin Englisch* 2 (2004), P. 6–9.

BELL, STEVE: "The Children's Zoo – A Storyline Topic." In: *Fremdsprachen Frühbeginn* 2 (2000), P. 51–53.

BERGNER, GRIT: „Lesen anbahnen: Am Beispiel von ‚The Very Hungry Caterpillar'." In: *Primary English* 3, 1 (2005), P. 14–17.

BIG KREIS DER STIFTUNG LERNEN: *Empfehlungen des BIG Kreises in der Stiftung Lernen, ‚Fremdsprachenunterricht in der Grundschule'. Standards, Unterrichtsqualität, Lehrerbildung.* München: Domino Verlag 2005.

BIG KREIS DER STIFTUNG LERNEN: *Empfehlungen des BIG Kreises in der Stiftung Lernen, ‚Fremdsprachenunterricht in der Grundschule'. Standards für die Lehrerbildung.* München: Domino Verlag 2007.

BIG-KREIS: *Lernstandsermittlung, Förderung und Bewertung im Fremdsprachenunter-*

richt der Grundschule. München: Domino Verlag 2008.

BIMBERG, CHRISTIANE: "Reading for Pleasure." In: *Primary English* 1,1 (2003), P. 28–30.

BLEYHL, WERNER (Ed.): *Fremdsprachen in der Grundschule. Geschichten erzählen im Anfangsunterricht*. Hannover: Schroedel 2002.

BLEYHL, WERNER: „Empfehlungen zur Verwendung des Schriftlichen im Fremdsprachenerwerb in der Grundschule." In: BLEYHL 2002. P. 84–91.

BLONDIN, CHRISTIANE, MICHEL CANDELIER, PETER EDELENBOS, RICHARD JOHNSTONE, ANGELIKA KUBANEK & TRAUTE TAESCHNER: *Fremdsprachen für die Kinder Europas. Ergebnisse und Empfehlungen der Forschung*. Berlin: Cornelsen 1998.

BORGWARDT, ULF: „Sprachenpass und Portfolio in der Erprobung. Erfahrungen aus Mecklenburg-Vorpommern." In: *Praxis des neusprachlichen Unterrichts* 50 (2003), P. 72–81.

BÖRNER, OTFRIED: „Verwendung der Schrift im 3. und 4. Schuljahr." In: *Englisch in der Grundschule und darüber hinaus: Eine praxisnahe Orientierungshilfe*. Ed.: CHRISTOPH EDELHOFF. Frankfurt: Diesterweg 2003. P. 89–97.

BÖRNER, OTFRIED: „'Dän kamm the neit': Plädoyer für einen natürlichen Umgang mit Schrift." In: *Grundschulmagazin Englisch* 2, 5 (2004), P. 6–8.

BÖRNER, OTFRIED & WILFRIED BRUSCH: „Die Hamburger Bücherkiste für den Englischunterricht in der Grundschule: Ein Praxisbericht." In: *Englisch* 39, 4 (2004), P. 146–152.

BÖRNER, OTFRIED: „KESS – Eine flächendeckende Untersuchung mündlicher Sprachleistungen im Englischunterricht der Hamburger Grundschulen." In: SCHLÜTER 2006. P. 169–172.

BÖRNER, OTFRIED: „Lehrwerke für den Englischunterricht in der Grundschule." In: *Grundschule* 1 (2007), P. 50 et seq.

BÖRNER, OTFRIED: „Fremdsprachenlernen in der Grundschule: Die Hamburger KESS-Studie." In: *Englisch in der Primarstufe – Chancen und Herausforderungen. Evaluationen und Erfahrungen aus der Praxis*. Eds.: GABRIELE ENGEL, BERND GROOT-WILKEN & EIKE THÜRMANN. Berlin: Cornelsen 2008 (in press).

BOS, WILFRIED & MARCUS PIETSCH: „Erste Kurzergebnisse aus KESS 4." 2004. Avail.: http://www.erzwiss.uni-hamburg.de/kess/kurzbericht.pdf (20.03.2008).

BOS, WILFRIED & MARCUS PIETSCH (Eds.): *KESS 4. Kompetenzen und Einstellungen von Schülerinnen und Schülern Jahrgangsstufe 4*. Hamburg: Behörde für Bildung und Sport 2005.

BÖTTGER, HEINER: „Differenzierung und Heterogenität. Englischlernen – ein höchst individueller Prozess." In: *Primary English, Fachbeilage des Grundschulmagazin Englisch* 5 (2006a), P. 3–5.

BÖTTGER, HEINER: „Möglichkeiten der Berücksichtigung der Individualität. Everyone's different." In: *Grundschulmagazin Englisch* 5 (2006b), P. 6–8.

BREDELLA, LOTHAR: „Bildung als Interaktion zwischen literarischen Texten und Leser/innen. Zur Begründung der rezeptionsästhetischen Literaturdidaktik." In: HALLET & NÜNNING 2007. P. 49–68.

BREDELLA, LOTHAR & EVA BURWITZ-MELZER: *Rezeptionsästhetische Literaturdidaktik mit Beispielen aus dem Fremdsprachenunterricht Englisch*. Tübingen: Narr 2004.

BREEN, MICHAEL P.: "Authenticity in the Language Classroom." In: *Applied Linguistics* 6, 1 (1985), P. 60–70.

BREEN, MICHAEL P.: "The Social Context for Language Learning: A Neglected Situation?" In: *Studies in Second Language Acquisition* 7 (1985), P. 135–158.

BREEN, MICHAEL P.: "Learner Contributions to Task Design." In: CANDLIN & MURPHY 1987. P. 23–46.

Brewster, Jean & Gail Ellis: *The Primary English Teacher's Guide.* 2nd edition. Harlow: Pearson 2002.

Brumfit, Christopher, Jayne Moon & Ray Tongue (Eds.): *Teaching English to Children.* London: Harper Collins 1991.

Brusch, Wilfried: *Text und Gespräch in der fremdsprachlichen Erziehung.* Hamburg: ELT 1986.

Brusch, Wilfried: „Englisch vom ersten Schultag an." In: *Grundschule* 32, 6 (2000a), P. 38–42.

Brusch, Wilfried: „Englisch: die vierte Kulturtechnik?" In: *Grundschule* 32, 6 (2000b), P. 34.

Burmeister, Petra: „Immersion und Sprachunterricht im Vergleich." In: Pienemann et al 2006. P. 197–216.

Burns, Anne: "Action Research." In: *Handbook of Research in Second Language Teaching and Learning.* Ed.: Eli Hinkel. Mahwah & London: Lawrence Erlbaum 2005. P. 241–256.

Burwitz-Melzer, Eva: *Literatur (nicht nur) für Kinder. Studienbrief im Zusatzstudium ‚Englisch an Grund- und Hauptschulen'.* Koblenz: Universität Koblenz-Landau 2000.

Burwitz-Melzer, Eva: „Literarische Texte für junge Fremdsprachenlernende." In: Hallet & Nünning 2007. P. 218–237.

Burwitz-Melzer, Eva & Michael K. Legutke: „Die Übergangsproblematik." In: *Der Fremdsprachliche Unterricht Englisch* 38, 69 (3) (2004), P. 2–8.

Burwitz-Melzer, Eva & Jürgen Quetz: *Lehrmaterialanalyse und die Erstellung eigenen Materials für den Fremdsprachenunterricht in der Grundschule. Studienbrief Fachdidaktik.* Koblenz: Universität Koblenz-Landau 2000.

Butzkamm, Wolfgang: „Wenn schon, denn schon! Zum Gebrauch der Muttersprache im Fremdsprachenunterricht." In: *Primary English, Fachbeilage des Grundschulmagazin Englisch* 3 (2005), P. 17–19.

Butzkamm, Wolfgang & Gisela Schmid-Schönbein: „Funktionale Fremdsprachigkeit." In: *Grundschulmagazin Englisch* 5 (2008) (in press).

Byram, Michael: *Teaching and Assessing Intercultural Communicative Competence.* Clevedon: Multilingual Matters 1997.

Cameron, Lynne: *Teaching Languages to Young Learners.* Cambridge: Cambridge UP 2001.

Candlin, Christopher N.: "Communicative Language Teaching revisited." In: *Kommunikativer Fremdsprachenunterricht: Rückblick nach vorn.* Eds.: Michael K. Legutke & Marita Schocker-von Ditfurth. Tübingen: Narr 2003. P. 41–58.

Candlin, Christopher N. & Dermot Murphy (Eds.): *Language Learning Tasks.* Englewood Cliffs, NJ: Prentice-Hall International 1987 (= Lancaster Practical Papers in English Language Education, Vol. 7).

Carter, Ronald, Rebecca Hughes & Michael McCarthy: "Telling tails (note: this is no misprint!): grammar, the spoken language and materials development." In: *Materials Development in Language Teaching.* Ed.: Brian Tomlinson. Cambridge: Cambridge UP 1998. P. 67–86.

Christ, Herbert: „Erwerb von Fremdsprachen im Vorschul- und Primarschulalter." In: *Handbuch Fremdsprachenunterricht.* Eds.: Karl-Richard Bausch, Herbert Christ & Hans-Jürgen Krumm. Tübingen/Basel: Francke 2003. P. 449–454.

Christ, Herbert: „Beobachtungen bei der Arbeit mit dem ‚Europäischen Portfolio der Sprachen' in der Grundschule." In: *Aufgabenorientierung im Fremdsprachenunterricht. Task-based Language Learning and Teaching. Festschrift für Michael K. Legutke.* Eds.: Andreas Müller-Hartmann & Marita Schocker-von Ditfurth. Tübingen: Narr 2004. P. 347–358.

CLAUS, ANETTE: „The Teddy Bear Project. Ein Austauschprojekt mit Neuseeland." In: *Primary English* 4 (2003), P. 20–21.

CLAUS, ANETTE & GÜNTER GERNGROSS: „Lesen sollen die Kinder auch noch lernen?" In: *FF – Fremdsprachen Frühbeginn* 2 (2003), P. 27–30.

CLAUS, ANETTE, MAIKE GRAU, MICHAEL K. LEGUTKE, & NATHALIE RAU: *Pädagogische Leistungskultur: Englisch als erste Fremdsprache.* Frankfurt: Grundschulverband 2008. (= *Beiträge zur Reform der Grundschule*, Band 124, Heft 2).

COLLIE, JOANNE & STEPHEN SLATER: *Literature in the Language Classroom – A Resource Book of Ideas and Activities.* Cambridge: Cambridge UP 1987.

COMMISSION OF THE EUROPEAN COMMUNITIES: "Promoting Language Learning and Linguistic Diversity: An Action Plan 2004-2006." 2003. Avail.: http://ec.europa.eu/education/doc/official/keydoc/actlang/act_lang_en.pdf (05.08.2008).

COUNCIL OF EUROPE: *European Language Portfolio. Proposals for Development.* Strassbourg: CoE 1997.

COUNCIL OF EUROPE: *European Language Portfolio (ELP) – Principles and Guidelines.* 2000. Avail.: http://www.coe.int/t/dg4/portfolio/default.asp?l=e&m=/main_pages/welcome.html (27.06.2008).

COUNCIL OF EUROPE: *Common European Framework of Reference for Languages. Learning, Teaching, Assessment.* Cambridge: Cambridge UP 2001.

COUNCIL OF EUROPE: *Gemeinsamer Europäischer Referenzrahmen für Sprachen.* München: Langenscheidt 2001.

CUMMINS, JIM: "Immersion Education for the Millennium: What We Have Learned from 30 Years of Research on Second Language Immersion." 1999. Avail.: http://www.iteachlearn.com/cummins/immersion2000.html (27.06.2008).

CURTAIN, HELENA & CAROL ANN B. PESOLA: *Languages and Children. Making the Match. Foreign Language Instruction for an Early Start.* Grades K-8. 2nd edition. London: Longman 1994 [1988].

DE LEEUW, HOWARD: *English as a Foreign Language in the German Elementary School – What Do the Children Have to Say?* Tübingen: Narr 1997.

DE LEEUW, HOWARD & MICHAEL K. LEGUTKE: „Unser Baumhaus. Ein Lehrwerk entsteht." In: *Sprachenlernen. Primarschule. Unterrichtsanalyse.* Ed.: MICHAEL K. LEGUTKE. München: Goethe-Institut 1997. P. 23–52.

DIEHR, BÄRBEL: „TAPS – Testing and Assessment in Primary Schools. Ein Konzept zur Leistungsbewertung im Englischunterricht der Grundschule." In: *Neusprachliche Mitteilungen* 58, 1–2 (2005), P. 25–33.

DIEHR, BÄRBEL & STEFANIE FRISCH: „Diagnostische Kompetenz. Lernfreude wecken – Sprechleistung beurteilen – Qualität verbessern." In: *Primary English, Fachbeilage des Grundschulmagazin Englisch* 6 (2006), P. 16–18.

DIEHR, BÄRBEL & JUTTA RYMARCZYK: „Zur Basis von Lese- und Schreibversuchen in Klasse 1 und 2. ‚Ich weiß es, weil ich es so spreche'." In: *Grundschulmagazin Englisch* 1 (2008), P. 6–8.

DIEKMANN, ANKE: „I forgot my Frühstück: Reale Kommunikationssituationen schaffen." In: *Grundschulmagazin Englisch 2,* 6 (2004), P. 13–14.

DINES, PETER: „Themenorientierter Fremdsprachenunterricht in der Grundschule." In: BLEYHL 2000. P. 72–80.

DÖRNYEI, ZOLTAN: *Teaching and Researching Motivation.* Harlow: Longman 2001.

DÖRNYEI, ZOLTAN: *Research Methods in Applied Linguistics.* Oxford: Oxford UP 2007.

DOYÉ, PETER: *The Intercultural Dimension. Foreign Language Education in the Primary School.* Berlin: Cornelsen 1999.

DOYÉ, PETER: „Exemplarischer Fremdsprachenunterricht." In: *Kernfragen des*

Fremdsprachenunterrichts an der Grundschule. Ed.: Peter Doyé. Braunschweig: Westermann 2005. P. 30–39.

Doyé, Peter & Dieter Lüttge: *Untersuchungen zum Englischunterricht in der Grundschule.* Braunschweig: Westermann 1977.

Drese, Karin: „Klassenkorrespondenz im Frühenglischunterricht... geht das? Und wie!" In: *Der Fremdsprachliche Unterricht Englisch* 34, 45 (2000), P. 14–17.

Drese, Karin: „Englisch ab Klasse 1 – Knock, Knock, Knock, Here Comes the Postman." In: *Englisch ab Klasse 1.* Eds.: Michael K. Legutke & Wiltrud Lortz. Berlin: Cornelsen 2002. P. 77–86.

Drese, Karin: „Mündliche Leistung einschätzen: Ein innovativer Weg im frühen Englischunterricht." In: *Primary English 5* (2006), P. 9–11.

Drese, Karin: „Englischunterricht in der Grundschule. Produktive mündliche Leistung im Fokus." In: *Fremdsprachen in der Grundschule: Auf dem Weg zu einer neuen Lern- und Leistungskultur.* Eds.: Maike Grau & Michael K. Legutke. Frankfurt: Grundschulverband 2008, P. 114–115.

Duda, Marion: „Magicland. Eintritt in eine Fantasiewelt." In: *Primary English. Fachbeilage des Grundschulmagazin Englisch* 1 (2006), P. 9–10.

Dudek, Jelena: „Von der Imitation zur bewussten Verwendung von Sprachmitteln: Unterrichtseinheit zum Modalverb can." In: Schlüter 2006. P. 82–87.

Eckerth, Johannes: "Task-based Language Learning and Teaching: Old Wine in New Bottles?" In: *Research on Task-based Language Learning and Teaching. Theoretical, Methodological and Pedagogical Perspectives.* Eds.: Johannes Eckerth & Sabine Siekmann. New York: Lang 2008. P. 13–16.

Edelenbos, Peter & Angelika Kubanek-German: „Fremdsprachenfrühbeginn: einzigartige Lernchancen nutzen." (Zu den Ergebnissen der Studie EAC 89/04 für die Europäische Kommission). In: *Frühes Deutsch* 10 (2007), P. 26–38.

Edelenbos, Peter & Marja P. Vinjé: "The Assessment of a Foreign Language at the End of Primary (Elementary) Education." In: *Language Testing* 17, 2 (2000), P. 144–162.

Edelenbos, Peter, Richard Johnstone & Angelika Kubanek: "The Main Pedagogical Principles Underlying the Teaching of Languages to Very Young Learners. Languages for the Children of Europe. Published Research, Good Practice and Main Principles." In: *Final Report of the EAC 89/04, Lot 1 study (October 2006).* Brüssel: European Commission 2006. Avail.: http://ec.europa.eu/education/policies/lang/key/studies_en.html (19.03.2008).

Egan, Kiran: *Teaching as Story Telling.* Chicago: University of Chicago Press 1986.

Egan, Kiran: *Primary Understanding.* New York: Routledge 1988.

Ellermann, Carmen: „Interkulturelles Lernen: ‚Travel-Buddy-Projekt'." In: *Praxis Fremdsprachenunterricht 5* (2007), P. 13–19.

Ellermann, Carmen: „Half Way Around the World in 80 Clicks – Weblogging mit einer Partnerklasse in ‚Down Under'." In: *Der Fremdsprachliche Unterricht Englisch* 6 (2008), P. 14–19.

Ellis, Gail & Keith Morrow (Eds.): *Year of the Young Learner.* Special Edition. Oxford: Oxford UP 2004.

Ellis, Rod: *The Study of Second Language Acquisition.* Oxford: Oxford UP 1994.

Ellis, Rod: *Task-based Language Learning and Teaching.* Oxford: Oxford UP 2003.

Enever, Janet: "Europeanisation or Globalisation in Early Start EFL Trends Across Europe?" In: *The Globalisation of English and the English Language Classroom.* Eds.: Claus Gnutzmann & Frauke Intemann. Tübingen: Narr 2005, P. 177–191.

Esser-Mirbach, Dorothee: „*Colour Land.* Integration authentischer Bilderbücher."

In: *Primary English. Fachbeilage des Grundschulmagazin Englisch* 1 (2006), P. 12–13.

Esser, Ferdinand: „Authentische Texte von Anfang an." In: *Primary English* 3 (2004), P. 8–11.

European Commission: "A Rewarding Challenge. How the Multiplicity of Languages Could Strengthen Europe." (Proposals from the Group of Intellectuals for Intercultural Dialogue Set Up at the Initiative of the European Commission, Final Report.). 2008. Avail.: http://ec.europa.eu/education/policies/lang/doc/maalouf/report_en.pdf (19.03.2008).

Felberbauer, Maria: „Der Englischunterricht in der Grundschule. Ein Beitrag zum interkulturellen Lernen." In: *Der Fremdsprachliche Unterricht Englisch* 25, 1 (1991), P. 10–14.

Finkenstaedt, Thomas & Konrad Schröder: „Sprachen im Europa von Morgen." In: *Lehrplan für die Gesamtschule. Sekundarstufe I. Englisch.* Ed.: Freie und Hansestadt Hamburg, Behörde für Schule, Jugend und Berufsbildung, Amt für Schule. Hamburg: 1992.

Franceschini, Rita: *Effizienz des Frühunterrichts: begleitende Forschung im Rahmen der Fremdsprachenreformen. Schlussbericht über das erste Förderjahr 1.1.2001–28.2.2002.* Saarbrücken: Universität des Saarlandes 2002. Avail.: http://www.phil.unisb.de/FR/romanistik/linguistik/lf/Dokumente/schlussbericht_version_internet.pdf. (10.02.2008).

Freeman, Donald & Karen E. Johnson: "Reconceptualizing the Knowledge-Base of Language Teacher Education." In: *TESOL Quarterly* 32, 3 (1998), P. 397–417.

Freudenstein, Reinhold: „Funktion von Unterrichtsmitteln und Medien: Überblick." In: *Handbuch Fremdsprachenunterricht.* Eds.: Karl-Richard Bausch, Herbert Christ & Hans-Jürgen Krumm. 3rd edition. Tübingen: Francke 2003, P. 288–291.

Fröhlich-Ward, Leonora & Gisela Schmid-Schönbein: *English for Mopsy and Me. Englisch in Kindergarten und Grundschule.* 2nd edition. Lichtenau: AOL-Verlag 1999.

Garvie, Edie: "An Integrative Approach with Young Learners." In: Brumfit, Moon & Tongue 1991, P. 115–126.

Geisler, Peter: „*Keystones.* Ein Erfahrungsbericht." In: *Primary English, Fachbeilage des Grundschulmagazin Englisch* 4 (2006), P. 10–11.

Genesee, Fred: *Learning Through Two Languages: Studies of Immersion and Bilingual Education.* Cambridge MA: Newbury House Publ. 1987.

Genesee, Fred & John Upshur: *Classroom-based Evaluation in Second Language Education.* Cambridge: Cambridge UP 1996.

Gerngross, Günter: „'The Little Mouse, the Red Ripe Strawberry, and the Big Hungry Bear'. Professionelles Lehrerverhalten." In: *Grundschulunterricht* 4 (2001), P. 6–10.

Gerngross, Günter: „Die Fertigkeit des Sprechens im Englischunterricht der Grundschule." In: *Primary English* 1,1 (2003), P. 12–15.

Gerngross, Günter: „Action Stories. Verstehen mit allen Sinnen und langfristiges Behalten." In: *Primary English* 1 (2004a), P. 4–6.

Gerngross, Günter: „Bedürfnisse der Fortbildung. Eine explorative Studie." In: *Primary English* 1 (2004b), P. 37–39.

Gerngross, Günter & Herbert Puchta: *Do and Understand.* Harlow: Addison Wesley Longman 1996.

Gerngross, Günter & Marita Schocker-v. Ditfurth: „Qualitätskriterien guter Lehrwerke: Eine Orientierungshilfe für die Auswahl." In: *Primary English, Fachbeilage des Grundschulmagazin Englisch* 1 (2006), P. 3–5.

GROEBEN, ANNEMARIE V. D.: „Verstehen lernen. Diagnostik als didaktische Herausforderung." In: *Pädagogik* 4 (2003), P. 6–9.

GROOT-WILKEN, BERND, GABY ENGEL & EIKE THÜRMANN: „Listening and Reading Comprehension. Erste Ergebnisse einer Studie zu Englisch ab Klasse 3 an nordrhein-westfälischen Grundschulen." In: *Forum Schule* 1 (2007). Avail.: www.forum-schule.de (14.04.2008).

GROOT-WILKEN, BERND & EIKE THÜRMANN: „Learn to speak English. Eine Studie zeigt, dass Kinder im Englischunterricht der Grundschule mehr sprechen sollten." In: *Forum Schule* 2 (2007), P. 32–33. Avail.: www.forum-schule.de (14.04.2008).

GROSS, CHRISTIAN: „Welche, wann und wie? Korrektur von Fehlern." In: *Grundschulmagazin Englisch* 3 (2007), P. 9–11.

GRUNDSCHULMAGAZIN ENGLISCH: *Themenheft: Arbeiten mit Lehrwerken* 4, 1 (2006). München: Oldenbourg.

GUILLOTEAUX, MARIE & ZLOTÁN DÖRNYEI: "Motivating Language Learners: A Classroom-Oriented Investigation of the Effects of Motivational Strategies on Student Motivation." In: *TESOL Quarterly* 42, 1 (2008), P. 55–77.

HÄGELE, GUDRUN: „Erste Begegnung mit englischer Schrift. 'Let's Read and Write!'" In: *Grundschulmagazin Englisch* 1 (2008), P. 9–12.

HAHN, SYLVIA & JULIA BÄCHLE: „Animal Olympics. Ein Storyline-Projekt." In: *Primary English* 4 (2003), P. 10–13.

HALLET, WOLFGANG: *Fremdsprachenunterricht als Spiel der Texte und Kulturen – Intertextualität als Paradigma einer kulturwissenschaftlichen Didaktik.* Trier: Wissenschaftlicher Verlag 2002 (= Studies in English Literary and Cultural History, Band 6).

HALLET, WOLFGANG: *Didaktische Kompetenzen – Lehr- und Lernprozesse erfolgreich gestalten.* Stuttgart: Klett 2006.

HALLET, WOLFGANG: „Literatur und Kultur im Unterricht. Ein kulturwissenschaftlicher didaktischer Ansatz." In: HALLET & NÜNNING 2007, P. 31–48.

HALLET, WOLFGANG: „Diskursfähigkeit heute. Der Diskursbegriff in Piephos Theorie der kommunikativen Kompetenz und seine zeitgemäße Weiterentwicklung für die Fremdsprachendidaktik." In: *Kommunikative Kompetenz als fremdsprachendidaktische Vision.* Ed.: MICHAEL K. LEGUTKE. Tübingen: Narr 2008, P. 76–96.

HALLET, WOLFGANG & ANDREAS MÜLLER-HARTMANN: „For better or for worse? Bildungsstandards Englisch im Überblick." In: *Der Fremdsprachliche Unterricht Englisch* 40, 81 (2006), P. 2–11.

HALLET, WOLFGANG & ANSGAR NÜNNING (Eds.): *Neue Ansätze und Konzepte der Literatur- und Kulturdidaktik.* Trier: Wissenschaftlicher Verlag 2007 (= Handbücher zur Literatur- und Kulturdidaktik).

HALLIWELL, SUSAN: *Teaching English in the Primary Classroom.* Harlow: Pearson 1992.

HARRIS, MICHAEL & PAUL MCCANN: *Assessment.* Oxford: Heinemann 1994.

HASSHEIDER, REINHARD & HEIDRUN SCHEFFLER: „Handpuppen beim Fremdsprachenlernen in der Grundschule." In: *Englisch* 30, 2 (1995), P. 59–62.

HATCH, EVELYN & CHERY BROWN: *Vocabulary, Semantics, and Language Education.* Cambridge: Cambridge UP 1995.

HAUDECK, HELGA: „Die erste Stunde." In: *Fremdsprachen in der Grundschule.* Ed.: WERNER BLEYHL. Hannover: Schroedel 2000. P. 69–72.

HAUDECK, HELGA: „Handpuppen im fremdsprachlichen Anfangsunterricht – mehr als nur Spielerei." In: *Fremdsprachenunterricht* 45, 54 (4) 2001, P. 258–262.

HELLWIG, KARLHEINZ: *Fremdsprachen an Grundschulen als Spielen und Lernen.* Ismaning: Hueber 1995.

HESSISCHES SOZIALMINISTERIUM/HESSISCHES KULTUSMINISTERIUM (Eds.): *Bildungs- und Erziehungsplan für Kinder von 0–10*

Jahren in Hessen. Bildung von Anfang an. Wiesbaden: HKM 2007. Avail.: http://www.kultusministerium.hessen.de/irj/HKM_Internet?uid=422503e0-cf26-2901-be59-2697ccf4e69f (05.06.2008).

HOFFER, MARTINA: „Freiarbeit im Englischunterricht. Wie allen Kindern gerecht werden?“ In: *Grundschulmagazin Englisch* 6 (2007), P. 6–8.

HOFFMANN, INGRID-BARBARA: „'Now Listen Carefully!'. Vom Hören, Zuhören und Verstehen.“ In: *Primary English* 1 (2005), P. 7–9.

HOLDERNESS, JACKIE: "Activity-based Teaching: Approaches to Topic-centred Work.“ In: BRUMFIT, MOON & TONGUE 1991. P. 18–32.

HU, ADELHEID: *Schulischer Fremdsprachenerwerb und migrationsbedingte Mehrsprachigkeit.* Tübingen: Narr 2003.

HÜTTNER, DANIELA: „Early Bird. Lernen mit Themenpaketen.“ In: *Primary English, Fachbeilage des Grundschulmagazin Englisch* 1 (2006), P. 8–9.

HUTZ, MATTHIAS & ANNIKA KOLB: „*Gummybears and *Handshoes. Zur Entstehung von Fehlern.” In: *Grundschulmagazin Englisch – The Primary English Magazine* 3 (2007), P. 6–8.

JACOBS, EDITH: „Englisch ab Klasse 1 – Tor zu einer anderen Welt.“ In: *Englisch ab Klasse 1.* Eds.: MICHAEL K. LEGUTKE & WILTRUD LORTZ. Berlin: Cornelsen 2002. P. 36–76.

JOHNSON, RICHARD & MERRILL SWAIN: *Immersion education: International Perspectives.* Cambridge: Cambridge UP 1997.

KARBE, URSULA: „Keine Angst vor Schrift und Schreiben im Englischunterricht!“ In: *Grundschulunterricht. Sonderheft Fremdsprachen* 48 (2001), P. 31–34.

KERN, RICHARD: "Perspectives on Technology in Learning and Teaching Languages." In: *TESOL Quarterly* 40 (2006), P. 183–210.

KESSLER, JÖRG-ULRICH: „Frühbeginn und Lernersprache: Englischerwerb in der Primarstufe.“ In: SCHLÜTER 2006. P. 101–108.

KIEREPKA, ADELHEID: „Eine Analyse der Lehrer-Schüler-Interaktion im Englisch-unterricht der Klassen 1–4. Ergebnisse aus einem Schulversuch.“ In: *Frühes Fremdsprachenlernen im Blickpunkt: Status quo und Perspektiven.* Eds.: ADELHEID KIEREPKA ET AL. Tübingen: Narr 2004. P. 163–172.

KIEWEG, WERNER: „Der Übergang. Zäsur oder Kontinuität? Vorschläge zur Leistungsstandserhebung.“ In: *Der Fremdsprachliche Unterricht Englisch* 38, 69 (3) (2004), P. 34–41.

KIEWEG, WERNER: „Fördern und fordern – Überlegungen zum Englischunterricht der Grundschule.“ In: *Englisch* 40, 2 (2005), P. 19–22.

KITZ, KATHARINA & ELFRIEDE GÖB-ENDRES: „*Sally.* Ein motivierendes Lehrwerk für den Englischunterricht.“ In: *Primary English, Fachbeilage des Grundschulmagazin Englisch 1* (2006), P. 15–16.

KLIPPEL, FRIEDERIKE: *Englisch in der Grundschule. Handbuch für einen kindgemäßen Fremdsprachenunterricht. Übungen, Spiele, Lieder für die Klassen 1 bis 4.* Berlin: Cornelsen Scriptor 2000.

KLIPPEL, FRIEDERIKE: "Teaching in English – Teacher Language in Primary School." In: *Früher oder Später? Englisch in der Grundschule und Bilingualer Sachfachunterricht.* Eds.: LIESEL HERMES & FRIEDERIKE KLIPPEL. München: Langenscheidt 2003. P. 53–68.

KOCHER, DORIS: *Das Klassenzimmer als Lernwerkstatt. Medien und Kommunikation im Englischunterricht nach der Storyline-Methode.* Hamburg: Kovac 1999.

KOLB, ANNIKA: *Portfolioarbeit. Wie Grundschulkinder ihr Sprachenlernen reflektieren.* Tübingen: Narr 2007.

KRAMSCH, CLAIRE: "Literary Texts in the Classroom: A discourse." In: *The Modern Language Journal* 69, 4 (1985), P. 356–366.

KRAMSCH, CLAIRE: *Context and Culture in Language Teaching.* Oxford: Oxford UP 1993.

KRAMSCH, CLAIRE: "The Privilege of the Intercultural Speaker." In: *Language Learning in Intercultural Perspective. Approaches through Drama and Ethnography.* Eds.: MICHAEL BYRAM & MICHAEL FLEMING. Cambridge: Cambridge UP 1998. P. 16–31.

KRUMM, HANS-JÜRGEN & EVA-MARIA JENKINS: *Kinder und ihre Sprachen – lebendige Mehrsprachigkeit.* Wien: Eviva 2001.

KUBANEK-GERMAN, ANGELIKA: „Geschichten und narrative Prinzipien. Überlegungen am Beispiel des Frühen Fremdsprachenlernens." In: *Der Fremdsprachliche Unterricht Englisch* 26, 2 (1992), P. 11–12.

KUBANEK-GERMAN, ANGELIKA: *Kindgemäßer Fremdsprachenunterricht. Zur Entwicklung eines Leitbegriffs für beginnende fremdsprachliche Lehre.* Eichstätt: Katholische Universität Eichstätt 1996.

KUBANEK-GERMAN, ANGELIKA: *Kindgemäßer Fremdsprachenunterricht. Didaktik der Gegenwart.* Band 2. Münster, New York: Waxmann 2003.

KUBANEK-GERMAN, ANGELIKA & PETER EDELENBOS: "Teacher Assessment: the Concept of 'Diagnostic Competence'." In: *Language Testing* 21, 3 (2004), P. 259–283.

KUBANEK-GERMAN, ANGELIKA & PETER EDELENBOS: "Diagnostic Competence as a Key Qualification of the Foreign Language Teacher in the 21st Century." In: *Englisch in der Erwachsenenbildung des 21. Jahrhunderts.* Ed.: RÜDIGER AHRENS. Heidelberg: Winter 2005. P. 91–103.

KUHN, TATJANA: *Grammatik im Englischunterricht der Primarstufe: Theoretische Grundlagen und praktische Unterrichtsvorschläge.* Heidelberg: Winter 2006.

KULTUSMINISTERIUM DES LANDES NORDRHEIN WESTFALEN: *Begegnung mit Sprachen in der Grundschule. Erlass vom 13.2.92.* Düsseldorf 1992.

KULTUSMINISTERKONFERENZ (KMK): *Bericht: „Fremdsprachen in der Grundschule – Sachstand und Konzeptionen." Beschluss der Kultusministerkonferenz vom 01.03.2002.* Avail.: www.kmk.org (23.06.2008).

KUMARAVIDELU, B.: „Learner Perception of Learning Tasks". In: *Tasks in Action: Task-based Language Education from a Classroom-based Perspective.* Eds.: KRIS VAN DEN BRANDEN, KOEN VAN GORP & MACHTELD VERHELST. Cambridge: Cambridge Scholars Publishing 2007. P. 22.

KURTZ, JÜRGEN: „Mini-Dialoge entwickeln!" In: *Primary English* 2, 3 (2004), P. 21–23.

KURTZ, JÜRGEN: „Schülerbeteiligung als Herausforderung. Sprechhandlungsfähigkeit entwickeln." In: *Grundschulmagazin Englisch* 3 (2008), P. 6–8.

LADO, ROBERT: *Language Teaching. A Scientific Approach.* New York: McGraw-Hill 1964.

LEGUTKE, MICHAEL K.: „Fremdsprachen in der Grundschule: Brennpunkt Weiterführung." In: *Kognitive Aspekte des Lehrens und Lernens von Fremdsprachen.* Ed.: CLAUDIA RIEMER. Tübingen: Narr 2000. P. 38–54.

LEGUTKE, MICHAEL K.: „Das Junior-Portfolio als didaktische Herausforderung: Anmerkungen zur Selbst- und Fremdbewertung im Fremdsprachenunterricht der Grundschule." In: *... in Sachen Deutsch als Fremdsprache. Festschrift für Hans-Jürgen Krumm zum 60. Geburtstag.* Eds.: HANS BARKOWSKI & R. FAISTAUER. Hohengehren: Schneider-Verlag 2002a. P. 104–120.

LEGUTKE, MICHAEL K.: „Stufenprofile und Lernstände am Ende der Klasse 4: Was haben die Kinder im Englischunterricht gelernt?" In: LEGUTKE & LORTZ 2002b. P. 92–106.

LEGUTKE, MICHAEL K.: „Englisch in der Grundschule – und dann? Anmerkungen zur Didaktik der Mehrsprachigkeit." In: *Mehrsprachigkeitsdidaktik, gestern, heute und morgen. Festschrift für Franz-Joseph Meißner zum 60. Geburtstag.* Eds.:

HELENE MARTINEZ & MARKUS REINFRIED. Tübingen: Narr 2006. P. 293–304.

LEGUTKE, MICHAEL K.: „Textproduktion und die Rolle von Lernertexten im Fremdsprachenunterricht." In: *Textkompetenzen.* Eds.: KARL-RICHARD BAUSCH et al. Tübingen: Narr 2007. P. 131–138.

LEGUTKE, MICHAEL K.: „Alte und neue Medien im fremdsprachlichen Klassenzimmer: discourse – szenario – task." In: *Aufgabenorientiertes Lernen und Lehren mit Medien: Ansätze, Erfahrungen, Perspektiven.* Eds.: ANDREAS MÜLLER-HARTMANN & MARITA SCHOCKER-VON DITFURTH. Frankfurt: Lang 2008. P. 65–84.

LEGUTKE, MICHAEL K. & WILTRUD LORTZ (Eds.): *Englisch ab Klasse 1. Das hessische Merry-go-round-Projekt. Analysen und Berichte.* Berlin: Cornelsen 2002a.

LEGUTKE, MICHAEL K. & WILTRUD LORTZ (Eds.): *Mein Sprachenportfolio.* Frankfurt: Diesterweg 2002b. Avail: http://www.diesterweg.de/suche/reihenansicht.xtp?id=SPRACHPORT (17.06.2008).

LEGUTKE, MICHAEL K. & MARITA SCHOCKER-V. DITFURTH: "School-Based Experience." In: *Cambridge Guide to Second Language Education.* Eds.: ANN BURNS & JACK RICHARDS. Cambridge: Cambridge UP 2008 (in press).

LEGUTKE, MICHAEL K. & HOWARD THOMAS: *Process and Experience in the Language Classroom.* Harlow: Longman 1991, 1999.

LEIDNER, MICHAEL: *Englisch im Kindergarten. Leitfaden für Erzieherinnen.* München: Ernst Reinhardt 2007.

LEWIS, GORDON: "An Internet Project for Young Learners of English." In: *Primary English* 4 (2003), P. 31–32.

LEWIS, MICHAEL: *The Lexical Approach. The State of ELT and a Way Forward.* Hove: Language Teaching Publications 1993.

LIEBENHOFF, KRISTINA: "The Very Hungry Caterpillar. Ein Theaterstück." In: *Primary English* 3 (2004), P. 12–18.

LIGHTBOWN, PATSY & NINA SPADA: *How Languages are Learned.* Oxford: Oxford UP 1999.

LIPPELT, BIRGIT, URSULA WILLGEROTH & EDELTRAUT WINDOLPH: „Portfolio in der Grundschule in Niedersachsen." In: *Fremdsprachenunterricht* 46, 55 (2002), P. 272–277.

LONG, MICHAEL H.: "Input and Second Language Acquisition Theory." In: *Input and Second Language Acquisition.* Eds.: SUSAN M. GASS & CAROLYN G. MADDEN. ROWLEY, MA: Newbury House 1985. P. 377–393.

LUTZ, HARTMUT: *„Indianer" und „Native Americans". Zur sozial- und literaturhistorischen Vermittlung eines Stereotyps.* Hildesheim: Georg Olms Verlag 1985.

MARSCHOLLEK, ANDREAS: *Kognitive und affektive Flexibilität durch fremde Sprachen – Eine empirische Untersuchung in der Primarstufe.* Münster: Lit 2002.

MARSCHOLLEK, ANDREAS: „Persönlichkeitsentwicklung im Fremdsprachenunterricht der Grundschule." In: *Primary English* 4 (2003), P. 4–6.

MARTIN, ISABEL: "Internet guide." *Primary English* 3 (2003), P. 31–32.

MAYER, NIKOLA: „Entdeckendes Lernen im Fremdsprachenunterricht der Grundschule." In: DOYÉ 2005. P. 54–66.

MAYER, NIKOLA: *„Discovery.* Entdeckendes Lernen." In: *Primary English. Fachbeilage des Grundschulmagazin Englisch* 1 (2006), P. 11–12.

MCDERMOTT, CHRIS: „Dealing with Mother-Tongue Interference. Next-door Neighbors." *Grundschulmagazin Englisch* 3 (2007), P. 12–13.

MCMORROW, MARTIN: Message sent in *Yahoo Young Learners Discussion Group* (on 15th of January 2008) on Critical Age Hypothesis (2008).

MEISSNER, FRANZ-JOSEPH & MICHAEL K. LEGUTKE: „Mehrsprachigkeit – ein realistisches Lernziel?" In: *Fremdsprachen Lehren und Lernen* 26 (2007), P. 234–235.

MICHAELS, WENDY & MAUREEN WALSH: *Up and Away: Using Picture Books.* Melbourne: Oxford Australia 1991.

MINDT, DIETER & NORBERT SCHLÜTER: *Englisch in den Klassen 3 und 4.* Berlin: Cornelsen 2003.

MINDT, DIETER & NORBERT SCHLÜTER: *Ergebnisorientierter Englischunterricht. Für die Klassen 3 und 4.* Berlin: Cornelsen 2007.

MINISTERIUM FÜR KULTUS, JUGEND UND SPORT BADEN-WÜRTTEMBERG: *Bildungsplan 2004 Grundschule.* Stuttgart 2004.

MÖGLICH, SONJA: „Von der Imitation zur bewussten Verwendung von Sprachmitteln: Unterrichtseinheit zum Wortschatzthema weather." In: SCHLÜTER 2006, P. 82–87.

MÖLLER, OLAF: *Große Handpuppen ins Spiel bringen. Technik, Tipps und Tricks für den kreativen Einsatz in Kindergarten, Schule, Familie und Therapie.* Münster: Ökotopia-Verlag. 2007.

MÜLLER-HARTMANN, ANDREAS: „E-Mail Kontakte. Wie findet man passende Partnerklassen?" In: *Primary English* 1, 4 (2003), P. 9–30.

MÜLLER-HARTMANN, ANDREAS & MAIKE GRAU: „Nur Tourist sein oder den Dialog wagen. Interkulturelles Lernen in der Begegnung." In: *Der Fremdsprachliche Unterricht Englisch* 38, 70 (2004), P. 2–9.

MÜLLER-HARTMANN, ANDREAS & MARITA SCHOCKER-V. DITFURTH: *Introduction to English Language Teaching.* Stuttgart: Klett 2004.

NATION, I.S.P.: *Learning Vocabulary in Another Language.* Cambridge: Cambridge UP 2001.

NATTINGER, JAMES: "Some Current Trends in Vocabulary Teaching." In: *Vocabulary and Language Teaching.* Eds.: RONALD CARTER & MICHAEL MCCARTHY. London: Longman 1988. P. 62–82

NEUNER, GERHARD: „Lehrwerke." In: *Handbuch Fremdsprachenunterricht.* Eds.: KARL-RICHARD BAUSCH, HERBERT CHRIST & HANS-JÜRGEN KRUMM. Tübingen und Basel: Francke 2003. P. 399–402.

NISSEN, RUDOLF: „Phasen und Formen des textverarbeitenden Lerngesprächs im Englischunterricht." In: *Neusprachliche Mitteilungen aus Wissenschaft und Praxis* 35 (1982), P. 114–125.

NÜNNING, ANSGAR & CAROLA SURKAMP: *Englische Literatur unterrichten. Grundlagen und Methoden.* Seelze-Felber: Kallmeyer Verlag 2006.

NUNAN, DAVID: *Second Language Teaching and Learning.* Massachusetts: Heinle & Heinle 1999.

NUNAN, DAVID: "Seven Hypotheses About Language Teaching and Learning." In: *TESOL Matters* 10, 2 (2000), P. 1&8.

NUNAN, DAVID: *Designing Tasks for the Communicative Classroom.* Cambridge: Cambridge UP 2001.

NUNAN, DAVID: *Task-Based Language Teaching.* Cambridge: Cambridge UP 2004.

OECHSLE, SERENA & KATHRIN GLATZ: „From Seed to Plant. Ein zweisprachiges Projekt." In: *Primary English* 6 (2005), P. 8–10.

O'MALLEY, MICHAEL & LORRAINE VALDEZ PIERCE: *Authentic Assessment for English Language Learners.* New York: Addison-Wesley 1996.

O'SULLIVAN, EMER & DIETMAR RÖSLER: "Picture Books in Teacher Training: Creative Writing and Intercultural Learning with Das Land der Ecken und Die Englandreise." In: *Niemals zu früh und selten zu spät: Fremdsprachenunterricht in Schule und Erwachsenenbildung. Festschrift für Jürgen Quetz.* Eds.: EVA BURWITZ-MELZER & GERT SOLMECKE. Berlin: Cornelsen 2005. P. 161–169.

OTHMER, FRANZISKA: „Realbegegnung als Projekt: Meeting the British." In: *Grundschulmagazin Englisch* 2 (2007), P. 8–12.

OVERLACK, IRENE: „Under the Big Top. Eine Unterrichtsreihe zum Thema Zirkus."

In: *Primary English* 1 (2004), P. 16–20.

Peltzer-Karpf, Annemarie: „Frühkindliche Erziehung zur Zweisprachigkeit.“ In: *Handbuch Fremdsprachenunterricht.* Eds.: Karl-Richard Bausch, Herbert Christ & Hans-Jürgen Krumm. Tübingen: Francke 2003. P. 445–448.

Pelz, Manfred & André Weckmann: „Grenzüberschreitende Spracharbeit zwischen Baden und Elsass im Rahmen des Europaprogramms ‚Lerne die Sprache des Nachbarn'.“ In: *Die Neueren Sprachen* 88 (1989), P. 370–395.

Philip, Jenefer, Rhonda Oliver & Alison Mackey: “The Impact of Planning Time on Children's Task-based Interactions.” In: *System* 34 (2006), P. 547–565.

Phillips, Sarah: *Drama with Children. Resource Books for Teachers.* Oxford: Oxford UP 1999.

Pielen, Angelika: „*Ikuru.* Englisch lernen ab Klasse 1.“ In: *Primary English, Fachbeilage des Grundschulmagazin Englisch* 1 (2006), P. 17.

Pienemann, Manfred: *Language Processing and Second Language Development: Processability Theory.* Amsterdam: John Benjamins 1999.

Pienemann, Manfred: „Spracherwerb in der Schule: Was in den Köpfen der Kinder vorgeht.“ In: Pienemann, Kessler & Roos 2006. P. 33–63.

Pienemann, Manfred, Jörg-Ulrich Kessler & Eckhard Roos (Eds.): *Englischerwerb in der Grundschule: Ein Studien- und Arbeitsbuch.* Paderborn: Schöningh 2006.

Piepho, Hans-Eberhard: „Kulturelle Aufmerksamkeit im Englischunterricht der Grundschule.“ In: *Grundschulunterricht* 12 (1998), P. 36–38.

Piepho, Hans-Eberhard: „Pitfalls in Teaching English with Beginners. 10 didaktische Stolpersteine.“ In: *Grundschulunterricht* 7–8 (2000), P. 2–4.

Piepho, Hans-Eberhard: “Bridge the Gaps instead of Gaping at them.” In: *Grundschulunterricht, Sonderheft Fremdsprachen* 48 (2001), P. 11–13.

Piepho, Hans-Eberhard: „Von der Übungs- und Aufgabentypologie zur Szenariendidaktik – es hat sich etwas entwickelt.“ In: *Kommunikativer Fremdsprachenunterricht: Rückblick nach vorn.* Eds.: Michael K. Legutke & Marita Schocker-v. Ditfurth. Tübingen: Narr 2003.

Piepho, Hans-Eberhard: *Narrative Dimensionen im Fremdsprachenunterricht.* Braunschweig: Schroedel 2007.

Pinter, Annamaria: “Investigations into Task-related Strategy Use with Young Learners of English.” In: *Young Learners of English: Some Research Perspectives.* Ed.: Shelagh Rixon. Harlow: Pearson Education Limited 1999. P. 1–17.

Pinter, Annamaria: *Teaching Young Language Learners.* Oxford: Oxford UP 2006a.

Pinter, Annamaria: “Verbal Evidence of Task Related Strategies. Child Versus Adult Interactions.” In: *System* 34 (2006b), P. 615–630.

Pinter, Annamaria: “Some Benefits of Peer-Peer Interaction: 10-year-old Children Practising with a Communication Task.” In: *Language Teaching Research* 11, 2 (2007), P. 189–207.

Prabhu, N.S.: *Second Language Pedagogy.* Oxford: Oxford UP 1987.

Prabhu, N.S.: “There Is No Best Method-Why?”. In: *TESOL Quarterly*, 24, 2. (Summer, 1990), pp. 161–176.

Prochazka, Anton: “Cross-curricular Language Teaching is like a ‘Starry Night'”. In: Schlüter 2006. P. 133–143.

Prowse, Phillip: “How Writers Write: Testimony from Authors.” In: *Materials Development in Language Teaching.* Ed.: Brian Tomlinson. Cambridge: Cambridge UP 1998. P. 130–145.

Rau, Nathalie & Michael K. Legutke: „Sprachliches Können dokumentieren und präsentieren. Anmerkungen zur Arbeit mit dem Dossier (der ‚Schatztruhe') des Juniorportfolios." In: *Fremdsprachen in der Grundschule: Auf dem Weg zu einer neuen Lern- und Leistungskultur.* Eds.: Maike Grau & Michael K. Legutke. Frankfurt: Grundschulverband 2008. P. 211–229.

Rea-Dickins, Pauline: "Classroom Assessment." In: *Teaching and Learning in the Language Classroom.* Ed.: Tricia Hedge. Oxford: Oxford UP 2000. P. 375–401.

Reilly, Vanessa & Sheila M. Ward: *Very Young Learners.* Oxford: Oxford UP 1997.

Reilly, Vanessa & Jackie Reilly: *Writing With Children.* Oxford: Oxford UP 2005.

Richards, Jack C., John Platt & Heidi Platt: *Dictionary of Language Teaching & Applied Linguistics.* Harlow: Longman 1992.

Richards, Jack C. & Theodore S. Rodgers: *Approaches and Methods in Language Teaching.* 2nd ed. Cambridge: Cambridge UP 2001.

Ritter, Markus: „Neue Technologien: Chance für eine neue Schule und einen neuen Sprachunterricht?" In: *Kommunikation und Lernen mit alten und neuen Medien.* Eds.: Bernd Rüschhoff & Ulrich Schmitz. Frankfurt: Lang. 1996. P. 39–49.

Rogers, Carl: "The Interpersonal Relationship in the Facilitation of Learning." In: Leeper, R. [1967], quoted in: *The Carl Rogers Reader.* Eds.: Howard Kirschenbaum & Valerie-Land Henderson. London: Constable 1990 [1967].

Roos, Jana: *Spracherwerb und Sprachproduktion. Lernziele und Lernergebnisse im Englischunterricht der Grundschule.* Tübingen: Narr 2007.

Rösler, Dietmar: "Foreign Language Learning With the New Media: Between the Sanctuary of the Classroom and the Open Train of Natural Language Acquisition." In: *German as a foreign language* 1 (2006), P. 16–31. Avail.: http://www.gfl-journal.de/1-2000/roesler.html (23.06.08).

Rösler, Dietmar: *E-Learning Fremdsprachen – eine kritische Einführung.* Tübingen: Stauffenburg 2007.

Rück, Heribert: *Fremdsprachen in der Grundschule. Französisch und Englisch.* Landau: Knecht 2004.

Rüschoff, Bernd: „Authentische Materialien. Über den Begriff der Authentizität und die Einsatzmöglichkeiten authentischer Materialien." In: *Grundschulmagazin Englisch* 3 (2003), P. 6–9.

Rymarczyk, Jutta: *Kunst auf Englisch?* München: Langenscheidt-Longman 2003. (= Münchner Arbeiten zur Fremdsprachen-Forschung, Band 6).

Rymarczyk, Jutta: „Integratives Arbeiten. Zur Verknüpfung von Englisch mit anderen Unterrichtsfächern in der Primarstufe." In: *Primary English, Fachbeilage des Grundschulmagazin Englisch* 6 (2005), P. 3–6.

Rymarczyk, Jutta: *„Lulu and the Flying Babies.* Erstlesen im integrativen Englischunterricht." In: *Praxis Grundschule* 5 (2006), P. 18–21.

Rymarczyk, Jutta: „Früher oder später? Zur Einführung des Schriftbildes in der Grundschule." In: *Fortschritte im frühen Fremdsprachenlernen. Ausgewählte Tagungsbeiträge Nürnberg.* Ed.: Heiner Böttger. München: Domino Verlag 2007, P. 170–182.

Samuda, Virginia & Martin Bygate: *Tasks in Second Language Learning.* Basingstoke: Palgrave Macmillan 2008.

Sauer, Helmut: „Frühes Fremdsprachenlernen in Grundschulen – ein Irrweg?" In: *Neusprachliche Mitteilungen* 1 (2000), P. 2–7.

Sauer, Helmut: „Über Sprache reden. ‚Language awareness' im Englischunterricht." In: *Primary English, Fachbeilage des Grundschulmagazin Englisch* 2 (2006), P. 3–6.

SAVIGNON, SANDRA J.: "Communicative Language Teaching for the Twenty-First Century." In: *Teaching English as a Foreign Language*. Ed.: MARIANNE CELCE-MURCIA. 3rd edition. Boston: Heinle & Heinle 2001. P. 13–28.

SCHÄRER, ROLF: „Sprachenportfolio." In: *Handbuch Fremdsprachenunterricht*. Eds.: KARL-RICHARD BAUSCH, HERBERT CHRIST & HANS-JÜRGEN KRUMM. Tübingen: Francke 2003. P. 387–390.

SCHART, MICHAEL: "What Matters in TBLT – Task, Teacher or Team? An Action Research Perspective from a Beginning German Language Classroom." In: *Research on Task-based Language Learning and Teaching. Theoretical, Methodological and Pedagogical Perspectives*. Eds.: JOHANNES ECKERTH & SABINE SIEKMANN. New York: Lang 2008.

SCHLÜTER, NORBERT: „Sprachbestände eines ergebnisorientierten Abschlussprofils für den Englischunterricht am Ende von Klasse 4." In: *Primary English* 2 (2003), P. 4–5.

SCHLÜTER, NORBERT (Ed.): *Fortschritte im frühen Fremdsprachenlernen: Ausgewählte Tagungsbeiträge Weingarten 2004*. Berlin: Cornelsen 2006.

SCHMELTER, LARS: „Rezensionsaufsatz: Fremdsprachenunterricht in der Grundschule aus der Perspektive einiger neuerer Publikationen." In: *Zeitschrift für Fremdsprachenforschung* 18, 1 (2007), P. 85–109.

SCHMID-SCHÖNBEIN, GISELA: *Möglichkeiten und Grenzen des gesteuerten Fremdsprachenerwerbs im Vorschulalter*. München: Minerva 1978.

SCHMID-SCHÖNBEIN, GISELA: „Teacher Talk – Eine neue Serie. Praise and Encouragement." In: *Primary English* 4 (2004), P. 30–31.

SCHMID-SCHÖNBEIN, GISELA: „Fehler korrigieren – wie und wann?" In: *Primary English* 3 (2005a), P. 6–7.

SCHMID-SCHÖNBEIN, GISELA: "Teacher Talk: Elicitation – The Fine Art of Getting Learners to Use Their English." In: *Primary English* 3 (2005b), P. 24–25.

SCHMID-SCHÖNBEIN, GISELA: "Teacher Talk: Scaffolding." In: *Primary English* 3 (2005c), P. 6.

SCHMID-SCHÖNBEIN, GISELA: „Vom Hören zum Sprechen: Der Weg zu einem komplexen Lernziel." *Primary English* 4, 3 (2006a), P. 3–5.

SCHMID-SCHÖNBEIN, GISELA: „Vom Lesen zum Schreiben: Der Weg zum kommunikativen Gebrauch des Englischen." In: *Primary English* 4, 4 (2006b), P. 3–5.

SCHMID-SCHÖNBEIN, GISELA: „Schweigen – die ungenützte Chance. Argumente für mehr Einsatz der Zielsprache im Unterricht." In: *Primary English, Fachbeilage des Grundschulmagazin Englisch* 3 (2006c), P. 6–7.

SCHMID-SCHÖNBEIN, GISELA: „Kontakt zum Elternhaus. Erwünscht und notwendig." In: *Grundschulmagazin Englisch* 1 (2007), P. 6–8.

SCHMITT, NORBERT: *Vocabulary in Language Teaching*. Cambridge: Cambridge UP 2000.

SCHOCKER-V. DITFURTH, MARITA: „Fremdsprachenlehrerausbildung für die Primarstufe: Erfahrungen mit praxisbezogenen und teilnehmerorientierten Didaktikseminaren." In: *Früher oder später? Englisch in der Grundschule und Bilingualer Sachfachunterricht*. Eds.: LIESEL HERMES & FRIEDERIKE KLIPPEL. München: Langenscheidt 2003a. P. 87–100.

SCHOCKER-V. DITFURTH, MARITA: „Fern/Kontakt-Studiengang: Didaktik des frühen Fremdsprachenlernens." In: *Primary English* 1 (2003b), P. 22.

SCHOCKER-V. DITFURTH, MARITA: „Gemeinsamer Europäischer Referenzrahmen für Sprachen für die Primarstufe?" In: *Primary English* 3 (2004a), P. 37–38.

SCHOCKER-V. DITFURTH, MARITA: „‚Wie lernen Kinder Sprachen?' Prinzipien aufgabenorientierten Lernens." In: *Primary English* 3 (2004b), P. 24–26.

SCHOLZ, KERSTIN: „*Ginger*. Von der Reiselust gepackt." In: *Primary English, Fachbeilage des Grundschulmagazin Englisch* 1 (2006), P. 13–14.

SCHÖN, DONALD A.: *The Reflective Practitioner: How Professionals Think in Action.* New York: Basic Book 1983.

SCHOTTE-GREBENSTEIN, EVELIN: *Vermittelter Fremdsprachenerwerb im Elementarbereich: Englisch als erste Fremdsprache im Kindergarten.* Würzburg: Ergon 2006.

SCOTTISH EXECUTIVE (2005): *Citizens of a Multilingual World. Rationale. Why are Languages Important?* Avail.: http://www.scotland.gov.uk/library3/education/rati-00.asp (23.06.2008).

SCRIVENER, JIM: *Learning Teaching.* Oxford: Heinemann 1994.

SEKRETARIAT DER STÄNDIGEN KONFERENZ DER KULTUSMINISTER DER LÄNDER IN DER BUNDESREPUBLIK DEUTSCHLAND: *Fremdsprachen in der Grundschule – Sachstand und Konzeptionen 2004. Beschluss der Kultusministerkonferenz vom 10.02.2005.* Bonn: Sekretariat der Ständigen Konferenz der Kultusminister der Länder in der Bundesrepublik Deutschland 2005. Avail.: www.kmk.org/doc/beschl/fremdsprachen_in_der_grundschule.pdf (23.06.2008).

SELINKER, LARRY: "Interlanguage." In: *International Review of Applied Linguistics, IRAL* 10 (1972), P. 209–231. [Re-printed in: *Error Analysis. Perspectives on Second Language Acquisition.* Eds.: JACK C. RICHARDS. London: Longman, (1972), P. 31–54.]

SINGLETON, DAVID & LISA RYAN: *Language Acquisition: The Age Factor.* Clevedon: Multilingual Matters 1989.

SLATTERY, MARY & JANE WILLIS: *English for Primary Teachers: A Handbook of Activities and Classroom Language.* Oxford: Oxford UP 2001.

STEINBACH, GUDRUN: "Words are like flowers..." In: *Der Fremdsprachliche Unterricht Englisch* 1 (1995), P. 12–16.

STEVICK, EARL W.: *Memory, Meaning & Method. A View of Language Teaching.* Boston (MA): Heinle & Heinle 1996.

STOFFEL, ANDREA: „Englisch für die Hosentasche. Begegnung mit dem Schriftbild – vom Pocket Dictionary zur Pocket Story." In: *Primary English* 1 (2004), P. 13–15.

SWAIN, MERRILL: "Communicative Competence: Some Roles of Comprehensive Input and Comprehensible Output in its Development." In: *Input and Second Language Acquisition.* Eds.: SUSAN M. GASS & CAROLYN G. MADDEN. Rowley, MA.: Newbury House 1985.

TEUBNER, KRISTINE: „Bewusstmachende Verfahren: Fortschritt oder Behinderung?" In: SCHLÜTER 2006, P. 62–67.

THIELEN, HILDEGARD: „Bumblebee. Interkulturelles Lernen als Hauptanliegen." In: *Primary English, Fachbeilage des Grundschulmagazin Englisch* 4 (2006), P. 11–12.

TOMLINSON, BRIAN (Ed.): *Materials Development in Language Teaching.* Cambridge: Cambridge UP 1998.

TYDECKS, STEFFI: „Selbstbestimmtes Lernen fördern. Off to Australia!" In: *Grundschulmagazin Englisch* 6 (2007), P. 9–12.

VALE, DAVID & ANNE VEUNTEUN: *Teaching Children English. A Training Course for Teachers of English to Children.* Cambridge: Cambridge UP 1995.

VAN DEN BRANDEN, KRIS (Ed.): *Task-Based Language Education. From Theory to Practice.* Cambridge: Cambridge UP 2006.

VOLLMER, HELMUT: „Bildungsstandards von oben, Bildungsstandards von unten." In: *Der Fremdsprachliche Unterricht Englisch* 40, 81 (2006), P. 12–17.

VYGOTSKY, LEV S.: *Mind in Society. The Development of Higher Psychological Processes.* Cambridge, MA: Harvard 1978.

VYGOTSKY, LEV S.: *Thought and Language.* Cambridge, MA: MIT Press 1986.

WASCHK, KATJA: „Medieneinsatz im Fremdsprachenunterricht der Grundschule." In:

Kernfragen des Fremdsprachenunterrichts an der Grundschule. Ed.: PETER DOYÉ. Braunschweig: Westermann 2001. P. 94–109.

WASCHK, KATJA: „Stationenlauf zum Thema Fruit. Eine ganzheitliche Erfahrung." In: *Primary English* 4 (2004), P. 8–11.

WASZAK, MARION: „The animals' eyes. Fächerübergreifendes Unterrichten." In: *Grundschulmagazin Englisch* 6 (2005), P. 7–10.

WERLEN, ERIKA, CHRISTIANE BLEUTGE & STEFANIE MANZ: „Grundlagen für eine Didaktik des frühen Fremdsprachenunterrichts – Zwischenergebnisse der Wissenschaftlichen Begleitung der Pilotphase Fremdsprache in der Grundschule in Baden-Württemberg." In: SCHLÜTER 2006, P. 42–60.

WESTWOOD, PETER & WENDY ARNOLD: "Meeting Individual Needs with Young Learners." In: *ELT Journal* 58, 4 (2004), P. 375–378.

WIGGEMANN, DOROTHEE: „Erste kreative Schreibversuche. ‚A ... in Our Classroom!'" In: *Grundschulmagazin Englisch* 4 (2006), P. 6–8.

WILLIS, JANE: *A Framework for Task-based Learning.* Harlow: Longman 1996.

WINTER, FELIX: *Leistungsbewertung. Eine neue Lernkultur braucht einen anderen Umgang mit den Schülerleistungen.* Baltmannsweiler: Schneider Verlag Hohengehren 2004.

WODE, HENNING: „Bilingualer Unterricht – wie geht's weiter?" In: *I beg to differ. Beiträge zum sperrigen interkulturellen Nachdenken über eine Welt in Frieden. Festschrift für Hans Hunfeld.* Eds.: HANS-EBERHARD PIEPHO & ANGELIKA KUBANEK-GERMAN. München: Iudicium 1998. P. 215–231.

WODE, HENNING: „Fremdsprachen im Kindergarten: Ein Modell in der Erprobung (Teil 1)." In: *Fremdsprachen-frühbeginn* 1 (2002a), P. 18–21.

WODE, HENNING: „Fremdsprachen im Kindergarten: Ein Modell in der Erprobung (Teil 2)." In: *Fremdsprachenfrühbeginn* 2 (2002b), P. 25–28.

WODE, HENNING: „Fremdsprachenvermittlung in KITA, Grundschule und Sekundarbereich: Ein integrierter Ansatz." In: *Bilingualität und Mehrsprachigkeit.* Ed.: CLAUDIA FINKBEINER. Hannover: Schroedel 2002c. P. 33–42. Avail.: http://www.anglistik.uni-kiel.de/Chairs/Linguist/docs/ger/texte/FremdsprKita.pdf (23.06.2008).

WODE, HENNING: „Mehrsprachigkeit durch immersive KITAs. Eine überzeugende Methode zum nachhaltigen Fremdsprachenerwerb." Avail.: www.fmks-online.de/_wd_showdoc.php?pic=218 (23.06.2008).

WODE, HENNING et al: „Verbundmöglichkeiten von Kindergarten, Grundschule und Sekundarstufe im Hinblick auf den Einsatz von bilingualem Unterricht." In: *Zeitschrift für interkulturellen Fremdsprachenunterricht* 4, 2 (1999). Avail.: http://www.spz.tu-darmstadt.de/projekt_ejournal/jg-04-2/beitrag/wode2.htm (27.06.2008).

ZAADE, SARA: „Lernen mit fremdsprachlichen Büchern. A Book Corner in the English Classroom." In: *Primary English* 3 (2003), P. 14–15.

ZANGL, RENATE & ANNEMARIE PELTZER-KARPF: *Die Diagnose des frühen Fremdsprachenerwerbs.* Tübingen: Narr 1998.

ZEIDLER, BETTINA: „An E-learning Project. Verständigung von Anfang an." In: *Grundschulmagazin Englisch* 1, (2007), P. 35–37.

ZYDATIß, WOLFGANG: *Bilingualer Unterricht in der Grundschule. Entwurf eines Spracherwerbskonzepts für zweisprachige Immersionsprogramme.* Ismaning: Hueber 2000.

2 Texts and resources

1 Standards and curricular guidelines

BIG-Kreis: *Standards, Unterrichtsqualität, Lehrerbildung – Empfehlungen des BIG-Kreises* (2. Auflage 2005). Avail.: http://www.praktisches-lernen.de/btk/pdf/big_veroeffentlichung_2005_Auflage2_von_2004.pdf (04.06.2008).

BIG-Kreis: *Standards für die Lehrerbildung – Empfehlungen des BIG-Kreises* (2007). Avail.: http://www.praktisches-lernen.de/btk/pdf/big_standards_01_2007.pdf (04.06.2008).

BIG-Kreis: *Lernstandsermittlung, Förderung und Bewertung im Fremdsprachenunterricht der Grundschule* (2008). Avail.: http://www.praktisches-lernen.de/btk/pdf/BIG_01_2008_Internet.pdf (4.6.2008).

BLK-Verbundprojekt Sprachen Lehren und Lernen Als Kontinuum: *Fremdsprachen lehren und lernen in Grundschule und weiterführender Schule. Ein Handbuch zum Übergang für Schulpraxis, Lehrerbildung und Schulverwaltung.* München, Wiesbaden, Halle, Bad Berka: 2006a.

BLK-Verbundprojekt Sprachen Lehren und Lernen Als Kontinuum: *Coming Together. Videogestützte Lehrerfortbildung zum Übergang im Englischunterricht von der Grundschule in die weiterführenden Schulen.* Bad Berka: Thüringer Institut für Lehrerfortbildung, Lehrplanentwicklung und Medien (ThILLM) 2006b.

Hessisches Sozialministerium & Hessisches Kultusministerium: *Bildung von Anfang an. Bildungs- und Erziehungsplan für Kinder von 0 bis 10 Jahren in Hessen* (2007). Avail.: http://www.kultusministerium.hessen.de/irj/HKM_Internet?uid=422503e0-cf26-2901-be59-2697ccf4e69f (4.6.2008).

2 Course books & classroom materials

Bausteine Magic. Pupil's Book 3 + 4, Kommentare, Kopiervorlagen. Piepho, Hans-Eberhard (Ed.). Frankfurt: Diesterweg 2004.

Busy Moments 1. Workbook. Agostinelli, Marisa et al. Monte San Vito: Raffaello 1997.

Conrad and Company 2. Ballinger, Davis et al. Harlow: Longman 1993.

Discovery 3 + 4. Pupil's Book 3 + 4, Activity Book 3 + 4, Teacher's Guide 3 + 4. Behrendt, Melanie, Barbara Christmann & Nikola Mayer. Braunschweig: Westermann 2005.

Ginger 1 + 2. Pupil's Book, Writing Book, Handreichungen für den Unterricht, Teacher's guide, Activity Book, Kartenspiel. Hollbrügge, Birgit & Ulrike Kraaz. Berlin: Volk und Wissen und Cornelsen 2003.

Ginger and Friends. Pupil's Book. Bayern. 4. Hollbrügge, Birgit & Ulrike Kraaz. Berlin: Cornelsen 2004.

Ikuru. Activity Book 4. Candy, Debbie, Cary Castle & Richard Martin. Berlin: Cornelsen 2004.

Magicland 1 + 2. Class Book 1 + 2, Activity Book 1 + 2, Lehrerhandreichungen, CD. Hancock Penny, Susannah Reed & Marita Schocker-v. Ditfurth. München: Langenscheidt 2003.

Magicland Class Book 2. Hancock, Penny; Susannah Reed & Marita Schocker-v. Ditfurth: München: Langenscheidt 2004.

Playway 3 – Cartoon Stories and Mr Matt. Sketches. Gerngross, Günter & Herbert Puchta: Innsbruck & Stuttgart: Helbling & Klett 2007.

Playway 3, Pupil's Book, Activity Book, Teacher's Book, CD-Rom. Gerngross, Günter & Herbert Puchta, P. 21 (Read and match) & P. 25 (Listen and point). Innsbruck: Helbling & Klett 2007.

Playway to English 2 – Video, Pupil's Book, Story Cards, Picture Cards, Teacher's Book. GERNGROSS, GÜNTER & HERBERT PUCHTA. Innsbruck und Leipzig: Helbling und Klett 1998.

Playway to English 3 – Rainbow Edition – Pupil's Book, Activity Book, Teacher's Guide, CD. GERNGROSS, GÜNTER & HERBERT PUCHTA. Innsbruck und Leipzig: Helbling und Klett 2001.

Playway to English 4 – Pupil's Book, Activity Book, CD. GERNGROSS, GÜNTER & HERBERT PUCHTA. Innsbruck und Leipzig: Helbling und Klett. 2002.

Sally. Schülerbuch 4. BREDENBÖCKER, MARTINA et al. München: Oldenbourg 2006.

Sunshine 1 + 2. Activity Book, Pupil's Book 1 + 2, Handreichungen für den Unterricht, Audio-CD. PRIESACK, TIM, PETER WILSON & VAL WILSON. Milan: Mondadori. 2001 [example: It's a yellow kite, P. 26].

Supermouse. BAUMANN, GUDRUN; PROCHAZKA, ANTON; PROKOP, SANDRA & LORETTA WEIßKOPF. Isaming: Hueber 2005.

Tell it Again!.The New Storytelling Handbook for Primary Teachers. ELLIS, GAIL & & JEAN BREWSTER. Harlow: Penguin 2002.

3 Fairy tales & picture books

BECK, IAN: *The Three Little Pigs*. Oxford: Oxford UP 2002.

CARLE, ERIC: *The Very Hungry Caterpillar.* London: Puffin Books 1974.

DAHL, ROALD & QUENTIN BLAKE: *The Magic Finger.* In: JANET SCHULMAN (Ed.): *You Read to Me & I'll Read to You. 20th Century Stories to Share*. New York: Random House 2001. P. 10–25.

Fairy Tales by the Grimm Brothers. Avail.: http://www.fln.vcu.edu/grimm/grimm_menu.html (19.06.2008).

Fairy Tales Theme – Preschool Activities and Crafts. Avail.: http://www.first-school.ws/theme/fairytales.htm (19.06.2008).

FALCONER, IAN: *Olivia*. London: Simon & Schuster 2000.

ROSEN, MICHAEL & HELEN OXENBURY: *We're Going on a Bear Hunt*. New York, New York: Little Simon 1997.

SENDAK, MAURICE: *Where the Wild Things Are*. New York: HarperCollins 1988.

SIMMONDS, POSY: *Lulu and the Flying Babies*. London: Puffin Books 1991.

4 Debate on early start – daily newspapers & magazines

EISSELE, INGRID: „Neues Bildungsgutachten: Pflichtkindergarten für Zweijährige." 2008. Avail.: www.stern.de/politik/panorama/613268.html (04.06.2008).

JACOBS, CLAUDIA: „21 Irrtümer übers Lernen." In: *Focus-Schule* 2 (2008), P. 10–20.

KÄRST, THOMAS: „Grundschüler als Sprachgenies: ‚Eine Stunde am Tag bringt nichts.'" In: *Spiegel Online*. 2006 Avail.: www.spiegel.de/unispiegel/studium/0,1518,391355,00.html (04.06.2008).

KUSIDLO, SILVIA (2004): „Sprachen im Kindergarten – Schon Knirpse sollen Englisch lernen." *Spiegel Online*. Avail.: www.spiegel.de/schulspiegel/0,1518,323435,00.html (04.06.2008).

Mer/dpa/AP/AFP: „Bildungs-Standort D: Fremde Sprache, schwere Sprache." In: *Spiegel Online*. 2008 Avail.: www.spiegel.de/unispiegel/studium/0,1518,539886,00.html (04.06.2008).

OPPERMANN, SILKE: „Englisch schon im Kindergarten?" In: *Deutsche Welle*. 2007. Avail.: www.dw-world.de/dw/article/0,2144,3012894,00.html (04.06.2008).

RADÜ, JENS: „Knirpse und Fremdsprachen: ‚Dem Gehirn ist das Wurscht.'" In: *Spiegel Online*. 2005. Avail.: www.spiegel.de/schulspiegel/0,1518,375731,00.html (04.06.2008).

SCHULTZ, TANJEV: „Englisch mit der Muttermilch." In: *Süddeutsche Zeitung.* 2008 Avail.: www.sueddeutsche.de/jobkarriere/berufstudium/artikel/501/162054/ (04.06.2008).

5 Early start & immersion

Altenholz – Eine bilinguale Kindertagesstätte. Avail.: http://www.awokita-altenholz.de/ (04.06.2008).

Association Canadienne des Professeurs d'Immersion. Avail.: http://www.acpi.ca/ (04.06.2008).

BACKE, KARIN-UTA: *Birdie Bird. EARLY IS EASY - Spielend Englisch lernen im Kindergartenalter mit Birdie Bird.* Avail.: http://birdie-bird-school.com/kinder.htm (04.06.2008).

FMKS – Verein für Frühe Mehrsprachigkeit an Kindertageseinrichtungen und Schulen e.V. Avail.: http://www.fmks-online.de/ (4.6.2008).

Immersion in Kanada und Geschichte des Immersionsunterrichts. Avail.: http://www.sprachenunterricht.ch/kanada.php (04.06.2008).

WODE, HENNING: *Englisch lernen durch „Eintauchen" – Früher Fremdsprachenerwerb in Kindergarten und Grundschule.* 2004. Avail.: http://www.familienhandbuch.de/cmain/f_Aktuelles/a_Schule/s_789.html (04.06.2008).

6 Professional Journals

Grundschule Englisch. Seelze: Kallmeyer. Avail.: http://www.grundschule-englisch.de/(23.10.08).

Primary English + Grundschulmagazin Englisch. München & Berlin: Oldenbourg & Cornelsen Avail.: http://www.grundschulmagazin-englisch.de (23.10.08)

Take off! Zeitschrift für frühes Englischlernen. Braunschweig: Westermann Verlag. Avail.: http://www.takeoff-westermann.de/ (19.06.2008).

7 Websites for Teachers

http://www.bbc.co.uk/cbeebies/ (19.06.2008).

http://www.englishbox.de (30.06.2008).

http://www.learningpage.com/ (20.06.2008).

http://www.learn-line.nrw.de/start.html. Bildungsserver Nordrhein-Westfalen (Online resources for teaching English in Primary School) (30.06.2008).

http://www.oup.com/elt/englishfile/elementary (20.06.2008).

http://www.songs4teachers.com/ (20.06.2008).

http://www.teachingenglish.org.uk/try/resources/teaching-children (20.06.2008).

http://www.the-voyage.com/d/kids/ressourcen/ or http://www.ukgermanconnection.org/cms/?location_id=3/kids/ressourcen/ „The Voyage" (The British German Connection) (30.06.2008).

For further useful links confer also to MARTIN 2003.